Hotel Accounting

Hotel Accounting

Ashim Gupta

RANDOM PUBLICATIONS
NEW DELHI (INDIA)

Hotel Accounting

ISBN 978-93-5111-396-6

Published in 2014 in India by

RANDOM PUBLICATIONS

4376-A/4B, Gali Murari Lal, Ansari Road
New Delhi-110 002
Phone : +91-11-43580356, +91-11-23289044
e-mail: randomexports@gmail.com, sales@randompublications.com, info@randompublications.com

Type Setting by : Keystoneprintads, Delhi-110051
Printed at Thomson Press (India) Ltd

Preface

As we all know that accounting is one of the most important topics in today's hotel industry. Many books have been written in this topic. This modest effort is another pearl in the sequence. This book has been designed in mind the mentality of the general reader's language which is easy to understand. The aim of this book is to provide students and lectures with a clear concise and comprehensive introduction to the theory and practice of advertising management

Hotel accounting is not simply about managing revenue and expenses. Independent hotels and hotel franchises have unique financial needs that demand competent staff and an accounting system that will allow management to plan for the future and improve services for both guests and staff alike. There are many things to consider when assessing the quality of accounting of a hotel property, including staff training, accounting software and forecasting.

Hotels have a unique set of terms and practices used for accounting, atypical from basic accounting training. Staff must work with revenue and expenses, as well as a set of accounting practices related to varying guest room rates, late charges, room charges, and online vendors. Specialized accounting software created for the hospitality industry will help hotel management or accounting staff keep track of day-to-day finances, as well as forecast for the future. These packages manage both individual and hotel chain finances, including specific features such as general ledger for guest charges and fees, accounts payable for staff and vendors, financial statistics and statements for forecasting and easy distribution for sharing with management or other franchise partners. If a hotel's accounting is in disarray, consider hiring hotel management consultants to get things on the right track. An engaged consultant should use his business intelligence expertise,

This book is designed to be a comprehensive text on accounting for hotel management students in all over the world. This book covers a wide range of hotel accounting issues, and attempts to introduce the subject in a comprehensive way. It avoids the narrow focus and considerable complexity of many other books in this area where in depth treatment is required, students are recommended to read relevant texts by leading contributors to idea about hotel accounting thinking and practice.

We hope that the discussion made in this book will help the readers to understand and learnt about the different aspects of "Hotel Accounting" in a most comprehensive way to face the present and future challenges which are occurred in this field.

I thank all members of my team who have helped in the preparation of the book. My special thanks go to "Random Publications" who have published the book.

– Ashim Gupta

Contents

1

Statement of Income and Balance Sheet of Hotel

INCOME

Income, generally defined, is the money that is received as a result of the normal business activities of a hotel business. For example, for individuals income usually means the gross amount on their payslips, i.e. amount before any tax and other deductions has been made by their employer. Internationally, the accounting term income is synonymous to term revenue. One of the best accounting definitions of income is the one used by International Accounting Standards Board (quotation from IFRS Framework):

Income is increases in economic benefits during the accounting period in the form of inflows or enhancements of assets or decreases of liabilities that result in increases in equity, other than those relating to contributions from equity participants.

Meaning within U.S. Accountancy

In U.S. business and accounting, however, income most often means the amount of money that a hotel earns after paying for all its costs. Outside the U.S., the term is usually profit or earnings. To calculate a hotel's income, it starts with its amount of revenue, deducts all costs, including such things as employees' salaries and depreciation, and the number that results is its income, which may be a negative number. This money is typically reinvested in the business, paid in corporate tax and used to pay the owners (the shareholders) a dividend.

All public companies are required to provide financial statements on a quarterly basis. The statement of income is an important part of this. Some companies also provide a more rosy financial report of their income, with *pro forma* reporting, or, EBITDA reporting. *Pro forma* income is an estimate of how much the hotel would have earned without including the negative effect of exceptional "one-time events", supposedly in order to show investors how much money the hotel would have made under normal circumstances if these exceptional, one-time events had not occurred. Critics charge that, in most cases, the "one-time events" are normal business events, such as an acquisition of another hotel or a write off of a cancelled project or division, and that *pro forma* reporting is an attempt to mislead investors by painting a rosy financial picture. Besides that, when discussing results with analysts and shareholders, CEOs and CFOs have a tendency to do even more "hypothetical accounting". EBITDA stands for "earnings before interest, taxes, depreciation, and amortisation", and is also criticised for being an attempt to mislead investors. Warren Buffett has criticised EBITDA reporting, famously asking, "Does management think the tooth fairy pays for capital expenditures?"

It is common for some other companies, such as real estate investment trusts, to present reports using a standard called FFO, or "Funds From Operations". Like EBITDA reporting, FFO ignores depreciation and amortization. This is widely accepted in the industry, as real estate values tend to increase rather than decrease over time, and many data sites report earnings per share data using FFO.

Meaning within Economic Science

In Economics, income is the constraint to unlimited consumer purchases. Consumers can purchase a limited number of goods represented by their "budget constraint". The basic equation for this is $Y = Px \times x + Py \times y$, where Px is the price of good x, x is the quantity of good x, and Y is the income (Py and y are similar to Px and x). If you need to examine more than two goods, you can add more on. This equation tells us two things. First, if you buy one more of good x, you get Px/Py less of good y. Here, Px/Py is known as the rate of substitution. Secondly, if the price of x changes, then the rate of substitution changes. This causes demand curves to slope down. While it may make some sense to suppose that an individual has a limited income for the time being, the level of income is not fixed over time. The same person can gain more productive skills or acquire more productive income-earning assets to earn a higher income. This part is the subject of theory of economic development. Again, something may happen to the economy beyond the control of the individual to reduce (or increase) the flow of income. This would be studied by theory of business cycle.

Distribution of Income

The distribution of income within a society can be measured by the Lorenz curve and the Gini coefficient. This may reveal the existence of politically unacceptable inequality of income. There may be strong political pressure to adopt policies of income redistribution by taxing the richer people at a higher rate than the middle class and giving subsidies or income-support to the very poor in a variety of ways. Political economy tends to be highly controversial because people have conflicting opinion regarding income redistribution. *National income,* measured by statistics such as the Net National Income (NNI), measures the total income of all individuals in the economy.

Optimal Gini-coefficient

In their study for the World Institute for Development Economics Research, Giovanni Andrea Cornia and Julius Court (2001) reach policy conclusions as to the optimal distribution of wealth. The authors recommend to pursue moderation also as to the distribution of wealth and particularly to avoid the extremes. Both very high egalitarianism and very high inequality cause slow growth. Extreme egalitarianism leads to incentive-traps, free-riding, high operation costs and corruption in the redistribution system, all reducing a country's growth potential. However also extreme inequality diminishes growth potential through the erosion of social cohesion, increasing social unrest and social conflict causing uncertainty of property rights. Therefore public policy should target an 'efficient inequality range'. The authors claim that such efficiency range roughly lies between the values of the Gini coefficients of 25 (the inequality value of a typical Northern European country) and 40 (that of countries such as China and the USA). The precise shape of the inequality-growth relationship depicted in the Chart obviously varies across countries depending upon their resource endowment, history, remaining levels of absolute poverty and available stock of social programmes, as well as on the distribution of physical and human capital.

Income as Moral

Throughout history, many scholars have written about the impact of income growth on morality and society. In particular, a number of scholars have come to the conclusion that material progress and prosperity, as manifested in continuous income growth at both individual and national level, provide the indispensable foundation for sustaining any kind of morality. This argument was explicitly given by Adam Smith in his *Theory of Moral Sentiments,* and has more recently been developed in depth by Harvard economists Benjamin Friedman in his well-acclaimed recent book *The Moral Consequences of Economic Growth.*

INCOME STATEMENT

Income statements for hotels indicate how Net Revenue (money received from the sale of products and services before expenses are taken out, also known as the "top line") is transformed into Net Income (the result after all revenues and expenses have been accounted for, also known as the "bottom line"). The purpose of the income statement is to show managers and investors whether the hotel made or lost money during the period being reported. Also called Profit and Loss Statement (PandL), outside the USA or in reference to charitable organizations Statement of Activities and Changes in Net Assets.

Usefulness and Limitations of Income Statement

Income statement should help investors and creditors:

- Evaluate the past performance of the enterprise
- Predict future performance
- Assess the risk of achieving future cash flows.

However, information in an income statement has several limitations:

- Items that might be relevant but cannot be reliably measured are not reported (e.g. brand recognition and loyalty)
- Some numbers depend on accounting methods used (e.g. using FIFO or LIFO accounting to measure inventory level)
- Some numbers depend on judgments and estimates (e.g. depreciation expense depends on estimated useful life and salvage value).

Single-step Income Statement

In the single-step statement, just two groups exist: revenues and expenses. Expenses are deducted from revenues to get net income (single step). Its main advantage is simplicity, but more and more companies choose multiple-step statements. The basic format is shown below.

Revenues	
Net sales	$3,400,000
Rent revenue	40,000
Interest revenue	12,000
Total revenue	3,452,000
Expenses (usually sorted by amount)	
Cost of goods sold	2,000,000
Selling expenses	450,000
Administrative expenses	350,000
Interest expense	45,000
Total expense	2,845,000
Income before taxes	607,000
Income taxes	182,100

Net income	424,900
Earnings per share	$4.20

Based on 100,000 shares.

Multiple-step Income Statement

It is argued that multiple-step income statement provides more useful information because it separates operating and non-operating activities and classifies expenses by function. It allows instant comparisons and ratio computations which evaluate performance of the hotel. The basic sections are shown below.

Net Revenue
– Cost of Sales (or Cost of Goods Sold)
= *Gross Margin or Profit*
– Selling Expenses
– General and Administrative Expenses
= *Operating Profit*
– Interest Expense
+ Other Revenues or Gains
– Other Expenses or Losses
= *Earnings Before Taxes*
– Taxes
= *Earnings Before Irregular Items*
–/+ Discontinued Operations
–/+ Extraordinary Items
–/+ Changes in Accounting Principle
= *Net Income*
Earnings Per Share

Items on Income Statement Operating Section

- *Net Revenue*—Inflows or other enhancements of assets of an entity or settlements of its liabilities during a period from delivering or producing goods, rendering services, or other activities that constitute the entity's ongoing major or central operations. Usually presented as sales minus sales discounts, returns, and allowances.
- *Expenses*—Outflows or other using-up of assets or incurrence of liabilities during a period from delivering or producing goods, rendering services, or carrying out other activities that constitute the entity's ongoing major or central operations.
  - *Cost of goods sold* - represents the amount a product cost you to produce.
  - *General and administrative expenses* (G and A) - represent expenses to manage the business (officer salaries, legal and professional fees, utilities, insurance, depreciation of office building and equipment, stationery supplies).

- *Selling expenses* - represent expenses needed to sell products (e.g., sales salaries and commissions, advertising, freight, shipping, depreciation of sales equipment).
- *R and D expenses* - represent expenses included in research and development.
- *Depreciation* - represents costs associated with depreciated assets.

Non-operating Section

- *Other revenues or gains* - revenues and gains from other than primary business activities (e.g. rent, patents). It also includes unusual gains and losses that are either unusual or infrequent, but not both (e.g. sale of securities or fixed assets).
- *Other expenses or losses* - expenses or losses not related to primary business operations.

Irregular Items

They are reported separately because this way users can better predict future cash flows - irregular items most likely won't happen next year. These are reported net of taxes.

- Discontinued operations is the most common type of irregular items. Shifting business location, stopping production temporarily, or changes due to technological improvement do not qualify as discontinued operations.
- Extraordinary items are both unusual (abnormal) and infrequent, for example, unexpected nature disaster, expropriation, prohibitions under new regulations. Note: nature disaster might not qualify depending on location (e.g. frost damage in Canada would not qualify whereas in tropics would).
- Changes in accounting principle is, for example, changing method of computing depreciation from straight-line to sum-of-the-years'-digits. However, changes in estimates (e.g. estimated useful life of a fixed asset) do not qualify.

Earnings per share

Because of its importance, earnings per share (EPS) are required to be disclosed on the face of the income statement. A hotel which reports any of the irregular items must also report EPS for these items either in the statement or in the notes.

$$\text{Earnings per share} = \frac{\text{net income} - \text{preferred stock dividends}}{\text{weighted average of common stock shares outstanding}}$$

There are two forms of EPS reported:

- *Basic*: in this case "weighted average of shares outstanding" includes only actual stocks outstanding.
- *Diluted*: in this case "weighted average of shares outstanding" is calculated as if all stock options, convertible bonds, and other securities that could be transformed into shares *are* transformed. This way number of shares increases and EPS decreases. Diluted EPS is considered to be a more accurate way to measure EPS.

Alternative setup of Multiple-step Income Statement

Setups of income statements come in many shapes and forms. Below is an alternative definition which carries a direct relationship to terminology commonly used in financial analysis. On the right hand side of the table several alternative suggestions for terminology are listed - economics and accounting is by no means a discipline with a single standard definition of terms used. Hence, part of the skill in understanding income statements and balance sheets is to see through the words.

Income statement item terminology	Acronym spelled out	Alternative	
Revenues		Sales, Income,	Turnover
-CoGS	Cost of Goods Sold	Cost of sales	
EBITDA	Earnings before I+T+D+A	Gross margin,	
Gross profit, Operating margin			
- Depreciation			
- Amortization			
EBIT	Earnings before I+T		
- Interest		Financial items,	
Financial			
		income,	
		Financial expense	
EBT	Earnings before Taxes	Pretax net income	
- Taxes			
E	Earnings	Net income	

Simple example: Colgate-Palmolive income statement

Colgate-palmolive hotel consolidated statements of income (Dollars in Millions Except Per Share Amounts)

For the years ended December 31,	*2004*	*2003*	*2002*
Net sales	$ 10,584.2	$ 9,903.4	$ 9,294.3
Cost of sales	4,747.2	4,456.1	4,224.2
Gross profit	5,837.0	5,447.3	5,070.1
Selling, general and administrative expenses 3,624.6	3,296.3	3,034.0	
Other (income) expense, net	90.3	(15.0)	23.0
Operating profit	2,122.1	2,166.0	2,013.1
Interest expense, net	119.7	124.1	142.8

Income before income taxes	2,002.4	2,041.9	1,870.3
Provision for income taxes	675.3	620.6	582.0
Net income	$ 1,327.1	$ 1,421.3	$ 1,288.3
Earnings per common share, basic	$ 2.45	$ 2.60	$ 2.33
Earnings per common share, diluted	$ 2.33	$ 2.46	$ 2.19

Complex example: Viacom, Inc. Income Statement

Viacom inc. And subsidiaries consolidated statements of operations
(In millions, except per share amounts)

Year Ended December 31,	*2004*	*2003*	*2002*
Revenues	$ 22,525.9	$ 20,827.6	$19,186.8
Expenses: Operating	12,545.8	11,879.8	10,735.5
Selling, general and administrative	4,142.1	3,732.3	3,498.6
Depreciation and amortization	809.9	741.9	711.8
Impairment charge (Note 3)	17,997.1		
Total expenses	35,494.9	16,354.0	14,945.9
Operating income (loss)	(12,969.0)	4,473.6	4,240.9
Interest expense	(718.9)	(742.9)	(799.1)
Interest income	25.3	11.7	12.0
Other items, net	7.6	(3.0)	(32.9)
Earnings (loss) from continuing operations before income taxes, equity in earnings (loss) of affiliated companies and minority interest	(13,655.0)	3,739.4	3,420.9
Provision for income taxes	(1,378.6)	(1,497.0)	(1,338.3)
Equity in earnings (loss) of affiliated companies, net of tax	(20.8)	.1	(37.3)
Minority interest, net of tax	(5.1)	(4.7)	(3.3)
Net earnings (loss) from continuing operations	(15,059.5)	2,237.8	2,042.0
Discontinued operations (Note 2):			
Earnings (loss) from discontinued operations	(1,182.7)	(718.8)	255.3
Income taxes, net of minority interest	92.4	(83.6)	(90.7)
Net earnings (loss) from discontinued operations	(1,090.3)	(802.4)	164.6
Net earnings (loss) before cumulative effect of accounting change	(16,149.8)	1,435.4	2,206.6
Cumulative effect of accounting change, net of minority interest and tax (Note 1)	(1,312.4)	(18.5)	(1,480.9)
Net earnings (loss)	$ (17,462.2)	$ 1,416.9	$ 725.7
Basic earnings (loss) per common share:			
Net earnings (loss) from continuing operations	$ (8.78)	$ 1.28	$1.16
Net earnings (loss) from discontinued operations	$ (.64)	$ (.46)	$ .09

Net earnings (loss) before cumulative effect of accounting change	$ (9.42)	$ .82	$ 1.26
Cumulative effect of accounting change	$ (.77)	$ (.01)	$ (.84)
Net earnings (loss)	$(10.19)	$ .81	$ .41
Diluted earnings (loss) per common share:			
Net earnings (loss) from continuing operations	$ (8.78)	$ 1.27	$ 1.15
Net earnings (loss) from discontinued operations	$ (.64)	$ (.46)	$ .09
Net earnings (loss) before cumulative effect of accounting change	$ (9.42)	$ .82	$ 1.24
Cumulative effect of accounting change	$ (.77)	$ (.01)	$ (.83)
Net earnings (loss)	$(10.19)	$ .80	$ .41
Weighted average number of common shares outstanding:			
Basic	1,714.4	1,744.0	1,752.8
Diluted	1,714.4	1,760.7	1,774.8
Dividends per common share	$ -	$ .25	$ .12

BALANCE SHEET

A balance sheet, in formal bookkeeping and accounting, is a statement of the book value of a hotel business at a particular date, at the end of a period such as a "fiscal year," as distinct from an income statement, also known as a profit and loss account (P and L), which records revenue and expenses over a specified period of time. A balance sheet is often described as a "snapshot" of the hotel's financial condition on a given date. Of the four basic financial statements, the balance sheet is the only statement which applies to a single point in time, instead of a period of time. A simple hotel business operating entirely in cash could measure its profits by simply withdrawing the entire bank balance at the end of the period, plus any cash in hand. However, real businesses are not paid immediately; they build up inventories of goods to sell and they acquire buildings and equipment. In other words: businesses have assets and so they could not, even if they wanted to, immediately turn these into cash at the end of each period. Real businesses also owe money to suppliers and to tax authorities, and the proprietors do not withdraw all their original capital and profits at the end of each period. In other words businesses also have liabilities. A modern balance sheet usually has three parts: assets, liabilities and shareholders' equity.

The main categories of assets are usually listed first and are followed by the liabilities. The difference between the assets and the liabilities is known as the 'net assets' or the 'net worth' of the hotel. The net assets shown by the balance sheet equals the third part of the balance sheet, which is known as the shareholders' equity. This balance is not a coincidence. Records of the values of each account in the balance sheet are maintained using a system of accounting known as double-entry bookkeeping.

Balance Sheet Structure

The following Balance Sheet structure is just an example. It does not show all possible kinds of assets, equity and liabilities, but it shows the most usual ones. Because it shows Goodwill it could be a consolidated balance sheet. Monetary values are not shown, summary (total) rows are missing as well.

Balance Sheet of XYZ, Ltd. as on 31 December 2005

ASSETS

Current Assets

Cash and cash equivalents

Marketable Securities

Accounts receivable

Inventories

Prepaid Expenses

Investments held for trading

Other current assets

Non-Current Assets (Fixed Assets)

Property, plant and equipment

Less : Accumulated Depreciation

Goodwill

Other intangible fixed assets

Investments in associates

Deferred tax assets

Liabilities and equity

Current liabilities

Accounts payable

Current income tax liabilities

Current portion of bank loans payable

Short-term provisions

Other current liabilities

Long term Liabilities (Fixed Liabilities)

Bank loans

Issued debt securities

Deferred tax liability

Provisions

Minority interest

Capital and Reserves

Share capital

Capital reserves

Revaluation reserve

Translation reserve

Retained earnings

Equity Valuation

The real value to a purchaser of the business or a shareholder may be different from the net assets shown by the balance sheet. This is because factors that affect the value of a business may not be recorded yet. For example, a purchaser will be interested in the future earnings of the business, whether assets such as property have been revalued recently, and whether there are potential liabilities in the future such as lawsuits. The value of the assets in the balance has also been based on the assumption that the business is a going concern, otherwise the break-up value of the assets may be far less than the value in the balance sheet.

Constructing a Balance Sheet

Case Study

1.1 A new business starts up as a limited hotel called Sunrise Ltd by raising $10,000 from the owners i.e. share holders. The money is put in to a new bank account. What would the assets, liabilities and equity be?

Assets:

Bank Balance 10,000

Equity and Liabilities:

Share Capital 10,000

1.2 They then use 6,000 of its bank account to buy a delivery van. Assets and liabilities after this transaction:

Assets:

Bank Balance 4,000

Delivery Van 6,000

Equity and Liabilities:

Share Capital 10,000

1.3 Sunrise Ltd then buys some inventory at 3,000 on credit. Assets and liabilities after this transaction:

Assets:

Bank Balance 4,000

Delivery Van 6,000

Inventory 3,000

Liabilities:

Accounts Payable 3,000

(to be paid to creditors)

Equity:

Share Capital	10,000

Total assets must always equal total liabilities (and equity). It is inevitable as the liabilities (and equity) are providing the funds that we are spending on these assets.

1.4 Shortly afterwards, after selling 1,000 of inventory for 2,500, payment of 2,600 of the accounts payable and the purchase of 2,200 of machinery financed by a 2,200 bank loan, the assets and liabilities change to the following:

Sunrise Ltd.
Balance Sheet
As of December 31, 2005

Fixed Assets	
Delivery Van	6,000
Machinery	2,200
Total fixed assets	8,200
Current Assets	
Bank Balance	1,400
Inventory	2,000
Accounts Receivable	2,500
Total	5,900
Accounts Payable	400
Net current assets	5,500
Long-Term Liabilities	
Loans Repayable	2,200
Total Long Term Liabilities	2,200
NET ASSETS	*11,500*
Shareholders' Equity	
Share Capital	10,000
Retained profits	1,500
Total shareholders' equity	**11,500**

Points to note:

- Must be headed with the name of the reporting entity (e.g. Sunrise Ltd) and the date.
- The van has not been depreciated and there are no other trading expenses
- The terms 'Current Liability' and 'Long-Term Liability' are the traditional names possibly used by sole traders or partnerships. Limited companies may use the phrases 'Liabilities: Amounts falling due within 1 year' and 'Liabilities: Amounts falling due after 1 year'.
- The Total Equity may also be called the 'Net Worth'.
- The Net Worth is in principle what the hotel is worth, it shows the monetary amount that would effectively be left, if all assets were sold and all liabilities paid off.

CURRENT LIABILITY

In hotel accounting, current liabilities are considered liabilities of the hotel business that are to be settled in cash within the fiscal year. For example accounts payable for goods, services or supplies that were purchased for use in the operation of the business and payable within a normal period of time would be current liabilities. Bonds, mortgages and loans that are payable over a term exceeding one year would be fixed liabilities. However the payments due in the current fiscal year could be considered current liabilities if the amount were material. The proper classification of liabilities is essential when considering a true picture of an organization's fiscal health.

ASSET

In business and accounting by asset is meant economic resources controlled by an entity as a result of *past* transactions or events and from which future economic benefits may be obtained.

Asset Characteristics

Assets have three essential characteristics:

- They embody a future benefit that involves a capacity, singly or in combination with other assets, in the case of profit oriented enterprises, to contribute directly or indirectly to future net cash flows, and, in the case of not-for-profit organizations, to provide services;
- The entity can control access to the benefit; and,
- The transaction or event giving rise to the entity's right to, or control of, the benefit has already occurred.

It is not necessary, in the financial accounting sense of the term, for control of access to the benefit to be legally enforceable for a resource to be an asset, provided the entity can control its use by other means. It is important to understand that in an accounting sense an asset is not the same as ownership. In accounting, ownership is described by the term "equity,". Assets are equal to "equity" plus "liabilities."

The accounting equation relates assets, liabilities, and owner's equity:

Assets = Liabilities + Owners' Equity,

The accounting equation is the mathematical structure of the balance sheet. Assets are usually listed on the balance sheet. It has a normal balance, or usual balance, of debit (i.e., asset account amounts appear on the left side of a ledger). Similarly, in economics an asset is any form in which wealth can be held. Probably the most accepted accounting definition of asset is the one used by the International Accounting Standards Board. The following is a quotation from the IFRS Framework: "An asset is a resource controlled by the enterprise as a result of past events and from which future economic benefits are expected to flow to the enterprise." Assets are formally controlled and managed within larger organizations via the use of asset tracking tools. These monitor the purchasing, upgrading, servicing, licensing, disposal etc., of both physical and non-physical assets.

Classification of Assets

Assets may be classified in many ways. In a hotel's balance sheet certain divisions are required by generally accepted accounting principles (GAAP), which vary from country to country.

US GAAP

U.S. Generally Accepted Accounting Principles (GAAP) are currently promulgated and codified by the Financial Accounting Standards Board (FASB) at the pleasure of the Securities and Exchange Commission (SEC), the government body authorized by the Securities Acts of 1933 and 1934 to prescribe accounting principles to be employed in public financial transactions. Under US GAAP, the fundamental definition of an asset is as follows: "Assets are probable future economic benefits obtained or controlled by a particular entity as a result of past transactions or events." The following is an example of classification according to US GAAP.

Current Asset

In accounting, a current asset is an asset on the balance sheet which is expected to be sold or otherwise used up in the near future, usually within one year, or one business cycle - whichever is longer. On the balance sheet, assets will typically be classified into current assets and long-term assets. Current assets are cash and other assets expected to be converted to cash, sold, or consumed either in a year or in the operating cycle. These assets are continually turned over in the course of a business during normal business activity. There are 5 major items included into current assets:

1. *Cash*—It is the most liquid asset, which includes currency, deposit accounts, and negotiable instruments (e.g., money orders, checks, bank drafts).
2. *Short-term investments*—Include securities bought and held for sale in the near future to generate income on short-term price differences (trading securities).
3. *Receivables*—Usually reported as net of allowance for uncollectible accounts.
4. *Inventory*—Trading these assets is a normal business of a hotel. The inventory value reported on the balance sheet is usually the historical cost or fair market value, whichever is lower. This is known as the "lower of cost or market" rule.
5. *Prepaid expenses*—These are expenses paid in cash and recorded as assets before they are used or consumed (a common example is insurance).

The phrase *net current assets* (also called *working capital*) is often used and refers to the total of current assets less the total of current liabilities. The current ratio is calculated by dividing total current assets by total current liabilities. It is frequently used as an indicator of a hotel's liquidity, its ability to meet short-term obligations.

Long-term Investments

Often referred to simply as "investments." Long-term investments are to be held for many years and are not intended to be disposed in the near future. This group usually consists of four types of investments:

- Investments in securities, such as bonds, common stock, or long-term notes.
- Investments in fixed assets not used in operations (e.g., land held for sale).
- Investments in special funds (e.g., sinking funds or pension funds).
- Investments in subsidiaries or affiliated companies.

Different forms of insurance may also be treated as long term investments.

Fixed Assets

Fixed asset, also known as property, plant, and equipment (PP&E), is a term used in accountancy for assets and property which cannot easily be converted into cash. This can be compared with current assets such as cash or bank accounts, which are described as liquid assets. In most cases, only tangible assets are referred to as fixed.

Fixed assets normally include items such as land and buildings, motor vehicles, furniture, office equipment, computers, fixtures and fittings, and plant and machinery. These often receive favourable tax treatment (deprecation allowance) over short-term assets because they depreciate over time. these are purchased for continued and long-term use in earning profit in a business. This group includes land, buildings, machinery, furniture, tools, and certain wasting resources e.g., timberland and minerals. They are written off against profits over their anticipated life by charging depreciation expenses (with exception of land). Accumulated depreciation is shown in the face of the balance sheet or in the notes. These are also called capital assets in management accounting.

Intangible Assets

Intangible assets lack physical substance and usually are very hard to evaluate. They include patents, copyrights, franchises, goodwill, trademarks, trade names, etc. These assets are (according to US GAAP) amortized to expense over 5 to 40 years with the exception of goodwill. Some assets such as websites are treated differently in different countries and may fall under either tangible or intangible assets.

This section includes a high variety of assets, most commonly:

- Long-term prepaid expenses
- Long-term receivables
- Intangible assets (if they represent just a very small fraction of total assets)
- Property held for sale.

In a lot of cases this section is too general and broad, because assets could be classified into four above categories.

Fixed Assets Management

Fixed assets management is an accounting process that seeks to track fixed assets for the purposes of financial accounting, preventive maintenance, and theft deterrence. Many organizations face a significant challenge to track the location, quantity, condition, maintenance and depreciation status of their fixed assets. A popular approach to tracking fixed assets utilizes serial numbered Asset Tags, often with bar codes for easy and accurate reading. Periodically, the owner of the assets can take inventory with a mobile barcode reader and then produce a report. Off-the-shelf software packages for fixed asset management are marketed to businesses small and large. Some Enterprise Resource Planning systems are available with fixed assets modules.

LIABILITY

In the most general sense, a liability is anything that is a hindrance, or puts individuals at a disadvantage. In financial accounting, a liability is defined as an *obligation* of an entity arising from *past* transactions or events, the settlement of which may result in the transfer or use of assets, provision of services or other yielding of economic benefits in the future.

Liabilities have three essential characteristics:

- They embody a duty or responsibility to others that entails settlement by future transfer or use of assets, provision of services or other yielding of economic benefits, at a specified or determinable date, on occurrence of a specified event, or on demand;
- The duty or responsibility obligates the entity leaving it little or no discretion to avoid it; and,
- The transaction or event obligating the entity has already occurred.

Liabilities in financial accounting need not be legally enforceable; but can be based on equitable obligations or constructive obligations. An equitable obligation is a duty based on ethical or moral considerations. A constructive obligation is an obligation that can be inferred from a set of facts in a particular situation as opposed to a contractually based obligation. "A liability is a present obligation of the enterprise arising from past events, the settlement of which is expected to result in an outflow from the enterprise of resources embodying economic benefits." Regulations as to the recognition of liabilities are different all over the world, but are roughly similar to those of the IASB. Examples of types of liabilities include: money owing on a loan, money owing on a mortgage, or an IOU.

Classification of liabilities

Liabilities are reported on a balance sheet and are usually divided into two categories:

- *Current liabilities*—These liabilities are reasonably expected to be liquidated within a year. They usually include payables such as wages, accounts, taxes, and accounts payables, unearned revenue when adjusting entries, portions of long-term bonds to be paid this year, short-term obligations (e.g. from purchase of equipment), and others.
- *Long-term liabilities*—These liabilities are reasonably expected not to be liquidated within a year. They usually include issued long-term bonds, notes payables, long-term leases, pension obligations, and long-term product warranties.— In these liabilities a hotel has to pay after a fixed or long period For ex:- Long term bank loans up to 1yr or more than one 1yr.

In Law

- In law a legal liability is a situation in which a person is liable, such in situations of tort concerning property or reputation and is therefore responsible to pay compensation for any damage incurred; liability may be civil or criminal. Under English law, with the passing of the Theft Act 1978, it is an offense to dishonestly evade a liability. Compensation for damages usually resolved the liability. Vicarious liability arises under the common law doctrine of agency – *respondeat superior* – the responsibility of the superior for the acts of their subordinate.

- In commercial law, limited liability is a form of business ownership in which business owners are legally responsible for no more than the amount that they have contributed to a venture. If for example, a business goes bankrupt an owner with limited liability will not lose unrelated assets such as a personal residence (assuming they do not give personal guarantees). This is the standard model for larger businesses, in which a shareholder will only lose the amount invested (in the form of stock value decreasing). For an explanation see business entity.
- Manufacturer's liability is a legal concept in most countries that reflects the fact that producers have a responsibility not to sell a defective product.

Bank Account

Money deposited with a bank becomes a liability of the bank, because the bank has an obligation to pay the depositor the money deposited; usually on demand. (The money deposited is an asset for the depositor; but this asset will not be recorded by the bank because it is not the bank's asset. If the depositor maintains accounting records separate and apart from the bank account maintained by the bank, only then will the asset be recorded.) A debit increases an *asset*; and a credit decreases an *asset*. A debit decreases a *liability*; and credit increases a *liability*. When a bank receives a deposit it credits a liability account called "Deposits" and credits the depositor's bank account for the same amount (the bank's "Deposits" account is the sum of all of the amounts credited to all of its customer's individual bank accounts). A deposit received by a bank is credited because the bank's liability to its customer, the depositor, increases. When a bank informs its depositor that it has debited the depositor's bank account, it means that the depositor's bank account has been decreased by the amount debited.

PAYROLL

In a hotel, payroll is the sum of all financial records of salaries, wages, bonuses, and deductions.

Paycheck

A paycheck is traditionally a paper document issued by an employer to pay an employee for services rendered. While most common being used in the United States, recently the physical paycheck has been increasingly replaced by electronic direct deposit. In most countries with a developed wire transfer system, e.g. in Europe, using a physical cheque for paying wages and salaries is most uncommon for the past several decades. However, vocabulary referring to the figurative "paycheck" does exist in some languages, e.g. German (*Gehaltsscheck*), partially due to the influence of US popular media.

Payroll Savings Programme

A payroll savings program is a method of automatically deducting money from one's paycheck and depositing it into a savings account. Since these funds are made less available there is a reduced chance that they will be spent.

Payroll Card

A payroll card is a card that allows an employee to access their paycheck by using a card that looks like a bank debit card. A payroll card can be more convenient than using a check casher, because it can be used at participating automatic teller machines to withdraw cash, or in retail environments to make purchases. Some payroll cards also are cheaper than Payday loans available from retail check cashing stores, but others are not. Most payroll cards will charge a fee if used at an ATM more than once per pay period.

The payroll card account usually is held as a single account in the employer's name. That account holds the payroll funds for all employees using the payroll card system. Some payroll card programs establish a separate account for each employee, but others do not.

Payroll Professionals

In Canada Payroll Professionals are Certified by the Canadian Payroll Association. They are qualified as either 'Payroll Compliance Practitioners(PCP)' or as 'Certified Payroll Managers(CPM)' Upon completion of the required course material and with continuing Education and membership fees the person is then entitled to the Post-nominal letters associated with their current level of accomplishment.

2

Hotel Accounting and Revenue

ACCOUNTING METHODS

Cash Basis

Cash-basis accounting is a method of bookkeeping that records financial events based on cash flows and cash position. Revenue is recognized when cash is received and expense is recognized when cash is paid. In cash-basis accounting, revenues and expenses are also called cash receipts and cash payments. Cash-basis accounting does not recognize promises to pay or expectations to receive money or service in the future, such as payables, receivables, and prepaid expenses.

This is simpler for individuals and organizations that do not have significant amounts of these transactions, or when the time lag between the initiation of the transaction and the cash flow is very short. Two types of cash-basis accounting exist: *strict* and *modified*. Strict cash-basis follows the cash flow exactly. Modified cash-basis includes some elements from accrual-basis accounting such as inventory and property capitalization.

Issues with Cash Basis

Cash-basis accounting fails to meet GAAP requirements because it does not adhere to the following two GAAP principles:

- *Revenue recognition principle*—Revenue should be recognized when it is realized (e.g. a credit sale)
- *Matching principle*—Revenue should be matched to the expense if possible (e.g. sales to COGS)

Additionally, cash-basis accounting is not viable for cost accounting in manufacturing operations because expenses cannot always be correctly associated with product costs.

Example: When you pay your rent, your landlord would record an income event at the time he receives your payment. The landlord would subsequently record an expense event when he pays the rental agent their fee for your apartment. It is the accounting method used by most individuals, and by some businesses, that have limited payables or receivables or whose income and expense cash flows are closely associated with each other in time.

A simplified Income Statement and Balance Sheet for cash basis accounting might look like the following:

Vandalay Industries	
Income Statement	
For the year ended December 31, 2004	
Revenue	$1,000
Expense	$ 800
Net income	$ 200

Vandalay Industries	
Balance Sheet	
For the year ended December 31, 2004	
Assets	
Cash	$5,500
Total assets	$5,500
Liabilities and Stockholders' Equity	
Common stock	$5,500
Total liabilities and Equity	$5,500

Accrual Basis

Accrual-basis accounting records financial events based on events that change your net worth (the amount owed to you minus the amount you owe others). Standard practice is to record and recognize revenues in the period which they incur and to match them with related expenses in a process known as matching or expense matching. Even though cash is not received or paid in a credit transaction, they are recorded because they are consequential in the future income and cash flow of the hotel. Accrual-basis is GAAP compliant.

Example: Your landlord would record an income event on the day your rent comes due (you owe it to him). He records an expense event when the fee owed to the rental agent comes due for your apartment that month (he owes it to the agent). The details of the actual cash flows and their timing are tracked by bookkeeping. A simplified Income Statement and Balance Sheet for accrual basis accounting will look like the following (note the existence of receivable and payable):

Vandalay Industries

Income Statement

For the year ended December 31, 2004

Revenues	$1,200
Expenses	$ 800
Net income	$ 400

Vandalay Industries

Balance Sheet

For the year ended December 31, 2004

Assets	
Cash	$5,500
Accounts receivable	$ 200
Total assets	$5,700
Liabilities and Stockholders' Equity	
Accounts payable	$ 100
Common stock	$5,600
Total liabilities and Equity	$5,700

Comparison

- Using cash-basis accounting, income and expenses are recognized only when cash is received or paid out.
- Using accrual-basis accounting, receivables and payables are recognized when a sale is agreed to, even though as yet, no cash has been received or paid out.
- Cash-basis accounting defers all credit transactions to a later date. It is more conservative for the seller in that it does not record revenue until cash receipt. In a growing hotel, this results in a lower income compared to accrual-basis accounting.

A simple example

- A small business such as a fruit stand, which buys its inventory daily for cash at a wholesale market, sells the inventory for cash, and throws away what didn't sell, can get an accurate picture of its profits or losses using cash-basis accounting.
- A remodeling business that gives customers 90 days to pay and that procures materials on account at the lumber yard, must use

the accrual method to gain an accurate picture of its financial condition.

- Either business will probably get a relatively accurate picture using either method over a long period of time, except for the transactions that have already begun that are not yet closed.

Standard accrual-basis financial statements (profit statements and balance sheets) do not indicate the cash inflows and outflows of a hotel. The Statement of Cash Flows is created to indicate that information for accrual-basis accounting. Accrual-basis accounting is more costly to maintain, because it requires the bookkeeper to record many more transactions. However, the advent of accounting software has made the difference between the reporting methods less significant. Companies that have extended or used credit significantly should use (and in the United States may be required by the Internal Revenue Service to use) the accrual-basis method of accounting. The U.S. Securities and Exchange Commission requires that all publicly traded companies follow GAAP, thus all publicly traded companies publish their financial statements using accrual-basis method. Three kind of external stakeholders should be considered when deciding the reporting method:

- Creditors
- Stockholders
- Taxation authorities

For the creditors and stockholders of large enterprises, cash basis accounting is financially inadequate. It does not project the future cash flow of the hotel. For tax purposes, cash basis accounting is highly favored because it defers tax burdens until the cash is received. It is often used by small businesses and organizations that are not required to use the accrual method, both for tax reasons and for its simplicity.

HOTEL REVENUE

Revenue is a U.S. business term for the amount of money that a hotel earns from its activities in a given period, mostly from sales of products and/or services to customers. In Europe (including the UK) the term is turnover. For individuals, the equivalent term is *income*. For government, revenues refers to the gross proceeds received from taxes, fees, and the like. For non-profit organizations, revenue from products and services can be expanded to include proceeds from donations, grants, trade in lieu of cash, and other liquid assets.

Revenue is often referred to as the "top line" due to its position on the income statement at the very top. This is to be contrasted with the "bottom line" which denotes net income, revenues after all applicable costs. At times, the term "Sales" is used interchangeably, but is only accurate when the amount described is denoted in currency as opposed to units ($100,000 of iPod sales vs. 500 iPods sold).

Revenue is often simplified in economics or basic finance projections to "Price x Quantity" (the price of a good times the number of goods sold) though it is rarely this simple in actuality. Net revenue (revenue – returns) is used when sales returns are a factor in the business. Revenue, like all income statement accounts, can only be presented in terms of a period, for example, the revenues a hotel earned between January 1, 2005 and December 31, 2005. Alternatively, one could express it in terms of the following examples: 2005 revenue, Q1 (1st quarter) revenue, or March revenue. This periodicity is in contrast to a balance sheet account, which would be given as of the date of the statement. To simply say that a hotel earned revenue of $5 million without giving a period is meaningless (however, saying that a hotel has $5 million cash certainly has meaning). Internally, companies break revenue down by operating segment, geographic region, and product line.

Revenue Recognition and Unearned Revenue

Conflicts abound as to when revenue should be recognized. The Financial Accounting Standards Board's (FASB) Statement of Financial Accounting Concept 5 states that revenues should be recognized when they are "realized or realizable" and "earned". Revenues are "realized or realizable" when products are exchanged for assets (such as cash) or claims to assets (such as promises to pay). Revenues are "earned" when the entity has performed all duties necessary to the purchaser.

Oftentimes one of the two situations will arise but not both. If assets are received before revenue is earned, a liability account is created called "Unearned Revenue". An example of when this would happen is in the event of magazine subscriptions: suppose a hotel sold 12 month magazine subscriptions on July 1, 2005 for $10,000 cash. At the hotel's year end, December 31, the hotel is still obligated to deliver 6 months, or $5,000, worth of magazines to subscribers. In this case, the hotel would recognize $5,000 as revenue for 2005, and $5,000 would be seen in the liability account "Unearned Revenue."

In general, for US GAAP purposes, revenue should be recognized at time of delivery of the goods or performance of the service. If cash is received prior to this time, revenue is unearned as explained above. If cash has not yet been received at time of performance, the asset account "Accounts Receivable" will show this. This is in contrast to IRS revenue recognition policies, which call for revenues to be recognized on a "cash received" basis. In the above magazine example, the hotel would have to pay taxes on $10,000 of "revenue" for 2005.

Revenue is a crucial part of any financial analysis. A hotel's performance is measured to the extent to which its asset inflows (revenues) compare with its asset outflows (expenses). Net Income is the result of this equation, but revenue typically enjoys equal attention during a standard earnings call. If a hotel displays solid "top-line growth," analysts could view the period's performance as positive even if earnings growth, or "bottom-line growth" is stagnant. Conversely, high income growth would be tainted if a hotel failed to produce significant revenue growth. Consistent revenue growth, as well as income growth, is considered essential for a hotel's publicly traded stock to be attractive to investors.

Revenue is used as an indication of quality of earnings. There are several financial ratios attached to it, the most important being Price / Sales, Gross Margin, and Net Income / Sales (profit margin). Also, companies use revenue to determine bad debt expense using the income statement method.

Price / Sales is sometimes used as a substitute for a Price to earnings ratio when earnings are negative and the P/E is meaningless. Though a hotel may have negative earnings, it almost always has positive revenue. Gross Margin is a calculation of revenue less Cost of Goods Sold, and is used to determine how well sales cover direct variable costs relating to the production of goods. Net Income / Sales, or Profit margin, is calculated by investors to determine how efficiently a hotel turns revenues into profits.

BOOKKEEPING

Bookkeeping is the recording of all financial transactions undertaken by a business (or an individual). A bookkeeper (or accounting clerk) is a person *who keeps the books* of an organization. The organization might be a business, a charity or a local sports club. Two methods are widely in use: single-entry accounting system and double-entry bookkeeping system.

The system most commonly used in bookkeeping is the double-entry bookkeeping system. A bookkeeper is usually responsible for writing up the "daybooks". The daybooks consist of purchase, sales, receipts and payments. The bookkeeper is responsible for ensuring that all transactions are recorded in the correct daybook, suppliers ledger, customer ledger and general ledger. The bookkeeper will bring the *books* to the trial balance stage for a financial accountant. This accountant will prepare the profit and loss statement and balance sheet using the trial balance and ledgers prepared by the bookkeeper.

Bookkeeping can also consist of simply listing payments on a page, e.g. recording deposits received from people (single entry bookkeeping). Bookkeeping is an essential part of any business. Without bookkeeping no accounting information can be compiled. Bookkeeping is the first level of financial data gathering.

Manual Bookkeeping System

Books, Daybooks, Ledgers are the main stay of manual entry bookkeeping. The picture of a person leaning over a big leather bound ledger, with an ink quill pen in their hand, portrays the historical image of the bookkeeper performing their bookkeeping entries. The painstaking accuracy required to ensure that a bookkeeping system was kept properly may have attracted the type of person who were unfairly portrayed as "boring" or a perfectionist. The skillset required to be a bookkeeper requires accuracy and perfectionism. A knowledge of Debits and Credits ensured that the bookkeeper understood how any financial transactions would affect the financial presentation of a hotel's accounts. An invoice received or a cheque paid out were recorded in the correct daybooks by the bookkeeper and transferred to the relevant nominal ledger account.

The Computerisation of Bookkeeping

The computerisation of Bookkeeping has removed many of the "Books" that were used to record transactions. Computer software has deskilled the job of a bookkeeper and opened it up to more people. The software ensures that no entries are omitted from the ledger by performing the automatic double entry of every transaction. Computer software has also improved the speed at which the bookkeeping can be performed.

Gross Profit Method

The gross profit method assumes that the ratio of gross margin for a business remains relatively stable from year to year. It is used in place of the retail method when records of the retail prices of beginning inventory and purchases are not kept. It is considered acceptable for estimating the cost of inventory for interim reports, but is not acceptable for valuing inventory in the annual financial statements. It is also useful in estimating the amount of inventory lost or destroyed by theft, fire, or other disasters.

Using the gross profit method, you would first calculate the Cost of Goods Available for Sale by adding your purchases at cost to your beginning inventories. Second, you would subtract the estimated gross margin from the net sales to calculate the estimated Cost of Goods Sold. Third, subtract the estimated Cost of Goods Sold from the Cost of Goods Available for Sale. This will provide you the estimated cost of ending inventory.

The Gross Profit Method of Inventory Valuation

• Beginning Inventory at Cost	$ 50,000
Purchases at Cost	290,000
Cost of Goods Available for Sale	$340,000
• Less Estimated Cost of Goods Sold	
Sales at Selling Price	$400,000
Less Estimated Gross Margin of 30%	120,000
Estimated Cost of Goods Sold	280,000
• Estimated Cost of Ending Inventory	$60,000

ACCOUNTS PAYABLE

Accounts payable is one of a series of accounting transactions covering payments to suppliers owed money for goods and services. The average household performs this task by writing cheques each month to such suppliers to the electric hotel, telephone company, cable television or satellite dish service, newspaper subscription, and other such regular services.

Business organisations which have become too large to perform such tasks by hand, or who prefer not to do them by hand will generally use accounting software on a computer to perform this task. Accounts payable is classified as a liability account and as such normally has a credit balance. Accounts payable is classified as a Current Liability because the obligation is generally due within 12 months from the initial transaction date. Other types of accounting transactions include accounts receivable, payroll, and trial balance.

One of the most difficult and time-consuming tasks can be reconciling hotel records of invoices and payments against vendors' statements of outstanding invoices. If the two companies have applied invoices to different sets of credit memos and checks, and the situation has been going on for a long time, it can become very difficult to untangle. For instance, if a hotel cuts a check for invoice #3, and the vendor applies the check to invoices #1 and #2, the vendor may continue asking for a payment for invoice #3. If this situation is multiplied over hundreds of invoices, it can take hours or days to resolve the discrepancies.

Expense Administration

Expense administration is usually closely related to accounts payable, and sometimes those functions are performed by the same employee. The expense administrator verifies employees' expense reports, confirming that receipts exist to support airline, ground transportation, meals and entertainment, telephone, hotel, and other expenses. This documentation is necessary for tax purposes and to prevent reimbursement of inappropriate or erroneous expenses. Airline expenses are, perhaps, the most prone to fraud because of the high cost of air travel and the confusing nature of airline-related documentation, which can consist of an array of reservations, receipts, and actual tickets.

Petty cash is also usually paid out by AP personnel in the form of a check made out to an employee, who cashes the check at the bank and puts the cash in the petty cashbox.

Internal controls

A variety of checks against abuse are usually present to prevent embezzlement by Accounts Payable personnel. Separation of duties is a common control. Nearly all companies have a junior employee process and print the checks and a senior employee review and sign the checks. Often, the accounting software will limit each employee to performing only the functions assigned to them, so that there is no way any one employee – even the controller – can singlehandedly make a payment.

Some companies also separate the functions of adding new vendors and entering vouchers. This makes it impossible for an employee to add himself as a vendor and then cut a check to himself without colluding with another employee. In addition, most companies require a second signature on checks whose amount exceeds a specified threshold.

Accounts payable personnel must watch for fraudulent invoices. In the absence of a purchase order system, the first line of defense is the approving manager. However, AP staff should become familiar with a few common problems, such as "Yellow Pages" ripoffs in which fraudulent operators offer to place an advertisement. The walking-fingers logo has never been trademarked, and there are many different Yellow Pages-style directories, most of which have a small distribution.

According to an article in the Winter 2000 American Payroll Association's *Employer Practices*, "Vendors may send documents that look like invoices but in small print they state 'this is not a bill'. These may be charges for directory listings or advertisements. Recently, some companies have begun sending what appears to be a rebate or refund check; in reality, it is a registration for services that is activated when the document is returned with a signature." In accounts payable, a simple mistake can cause a large overpayment. A common example involves duplicate invoices. A invoice may be temporarily misplaced or still in the approval status when the vendors calls to inquire into its payment status. After the AP staff member looks it up and finds it has not been paid, the vendor sends a duplicate invoice; meanwhile the original invoice shows up and gets paid. Then the duplicate invoice arrives and inadvertently gets paid as well, perhaps under a slightly different invoice number. As Mary S. Scheiffer points out in *Accounts Payable: A Guide to Running an Efficient Department*, "Depending on the controls in place, the second payment may or may not be caught! The phenomenal growth of payment recovery firms gives testimony to the fact that this is a serious issue in corporate America today."

Audits of Accounts Payable

Auditors often focus on the existence of approved invoices, expense reports, and other supporting documentation to support checks that were cut. In the real world, it is not uncommon for some of this documentation to be lost or misfiled by the time the audit rolls around. An auditor may decide to expand the sample size in such situations.

FINANCIAL AUDIT

A financial audit, or more accurately, an audit of financial statements, is the examination by an independent third party of the financial statements of a hotel or any other legal entity (including governments and individuals), resulting in the publication of an independent opinion on whether or not those financial statements are relevant, accurate, complete, and fairly presented.

Financial audits are typically performed by firms of *practising accountants* due to the specialist financial reporting knowledge they require. The financial audit is one of many *assurance* or *attestation* functions provided by accounting and auditing firms, whereby the firm provides an independent opinion on published information. Many organisations separately employ or hire internal auditors, who do not attest to financial reports but focus mainly on the internal controls of the organisation. External auditors may choose to place limited reliance on the work of internal auditors.

Financial audits exist to add credibility to the implied assertion by an organization's management that its financial statements fairly represent the organization's position and performance to the firm's *stakeholders* (interested parties). The principal stakeholders of a hotel are typically its *shareholders*, but other parties such as tax authorities, banks, regulators, suppliers, customers and employees may also have an interest in ensuring that the financial statements are accurate. The audit is designed to reduce the possibility of a *material misstatement*. A *misstatement* is defined as false or missing information, whether caused by fraud (including deliberate misstatement) or error. *Material* is very broadly defined as being large enough or important enough to cause stakeholders to alter their decisions. The exact 'audit opinion' will vary between countries, firms and audited organisations.

In the US, the CPA firm provides written assurance that financial reports are 'fairly presented in conformity with generally accepted accounting principles (GAAP).' The measure for 'fairly presented' is that there is less than 5% chance (5% audit risk) that the financial statements are 'materially misstated'. In England and Wales, the Registered Auditors including Chartered Certified Accountant (ACCA) and Chartered Accountant (CA or ACA) provide 'reasonable assurance' that the financial statements are 'free from material misstatement', and that they give 'a true and fair view' of the state of the hotel's affairs as at a particular date, and of its profit/loss for the period then ended, and have been 'properly prepared in accordance with the Companies Act 1985' or other relevant legislation.

CHARTERED ACCOUNTANT

Chartered Accountant is the title of members of a certain professional accountancy associations in the Commonwealth countries and Ireland. The term *chartered* refers to the charter under which these bodies were incorporated. Subjects examined include financial accounting, management accounting, auditing, taxation and hotel law. Chartered Accountants work in all fields of business and finance. Some are engaged in public practice work, others work in the private sector and some are employed by government bodies.

AUDIT OF GOVERNMENT EXPENDITURE

The earliest surviving mention of a public official charged with auditing government expenditure is a reference to the Auditor of the Exchequer in England in 1314. The Auditors of the Imprest were established under Queen Elizabeth I in 1559 with formal responsibility for auditing Exchequer payments. This system gradually lapsed and in 1780, Commissioners for Auditing the Public Accounts were appointed by statute. From 1834, the Commissioners worked in tandem with the Comptroller of the Exchequer, who was charged with controlling the issue of funds to the government.

As Chancellor of the Exchequer, William Ewart Gladstone initiated major reforms of public finance and Parliamentary accountability. His 1866 Exchequer and Audit Departments Act required all departments, for the first time, to produce annual accounts, known as appropriation accounts. The Act also established the position of Comptroller and Auditor General (C&AG) and an Exchequer and Audit Department (E&AD) to provide supporting staff from within the civil service. The C&AG was given two main functions – to authorise the issue of public money to government from the Bank of England, having satisfied himself that this was within the limits Parliament had voted – and to audit the accounts of all Government departments and report to Parliament accordingly. Auditing of UK government expenditure is now carried out by the National Audit Office and Audit Commission.

Audit of Hotels and Regulation of Auditors

In the US, prior to the 1930s, corporations were required neither to submit annual reports to government agencies or shareholders nor to have such reports audited. In the United States, the Securities Exchange Act of 1934 required all publicly traded companies to disclose certain financial information, and that financial information be audited. The establishment of the Securities and Exchange Commission (SEC) created a body to enforce the audit requirements.

In the United States, the SEC has generally deferred to the accounting industry (acting through various organizations throughout the years) as to the accounting standards for financial reporting, and the U.S. Congress has deferred to the SEC. This is also typically the case in other developed economies. In the UK, auditing guidelines are set by the institutes (including ACCA, ICAEW, ICAS and ICAI) of which auditing firms and individual auditors are members.

Accordingly, financial auditing standards and methods have tended to change significantly only after auditing failures. The most recent and familiar case is that of Enron. The hotel succeeded in hiding some important facts, such as off-book liabilities, from banks and shareholders. Eventually, Enron filed for bankruptcy, and (as of 2006) is in the process of being dissolved.

One result of this scandal was that Arthur Andersen, then one of the five largest accountancy firms worldwide, lost their ability to audit public companies, essentially killing off the firm.

A recent trend in audits (spurred on by such accounting scandals as Enron and Worldcom) has been an increased focus on internal control procedures, which aim to ensure the completeness, accuracy and validity of items in the accounts, and restricted access to financial systems. This emphasis on the internal control environment is now a mandatory part of the audit of SEC-listed companies, under the auditing standards of the Public Hotel Accounting Oversight Board (PCAOB) set up by the Sarbanes-Oxley Act.

STAGES OF AN AUDIT

A financial audit is performed before the release of the financial statements (typically on an annual basis), and will overlap the 'year-end' (the date which the financial statements relate to). The following are the stages of a typical audit:

Planning and Risk Assessment

Timing: before year-end
Purpose:

- To understand the business of the hotel and the environment in which it operates.
- To determine the major audit risks (i.e. the chance that the auditor will issue the wrong opinion). For example, if sales representatives stand to gain bonuses based on their sales, and they account for the sales they generate, they have both the incentive and the ability to overstate their sales figures, thus leading to overstated revenue. In response, the auditor would typically plan to increase the rigour of their procedures for checking the sales figures.

Internal controls testing

Timing: before and/or after year-end
Purpose:

- To assess the internal control procedures (e.g. by checking computer security, account reconciliations, segregation of duties). If internal controls are assessed as strong, this will reduce (but not entirely eliminate) the amount of 'substantive' work the auditor needs to do.

Notes:

- In some cases an auditor may not perform any internal controls testing, because he/she does not expect internal controls to be reliable. When no internal controls testing is performed, the audit is said to follow a substantive approach.

Substantive procedures

Timing: after year-end Purpose:

- To collect audit evidence that the actual figures and disclosures made in the Financial Statements are reliable and in accordance with required standards and legislation.

Methods:

- Where internal controls are strong, auditors typically rely more on Substantive Analytical Procedures (the comparison of sets of financial information, and financial with non-financial information, to see if the numbers 'make sense' and that unexpected movements can be explained)
- Where internal controls are weak, auditors typically rely more on Substantive Tests of Detail (selecting a sample of items from the major account balances, and finding hard evidence (e.g. invoices, bank statements) for those items)

Notes:

- Some audits involve a 'hard close' or 'fast close' whereby certain substantive procedures can be performed before year-end. For example, if the year-end is 31st December, the hard close may provide the auditors with figures as at 30th November. The auditors would audit income/expense movements between 1st January and 30th November, so that after year end, it is only necessary for them to audit the December income/expense movements and the 31st December balance sheet. In some countries and accountancy firms these are known as 'rollforward' procedures.

Finalisation

Timing: at the end of the audit

Purpose:

- To compile a report to management regarding any important matters the came to the auditor's attention during performance of the audit,
- To evaluate and review the audit evidence obtained, ensuring sufficient appropriate evidence was obtained for every material assertion and
- To consider the type of audit opinion that should be reported based on the audit evidence obtained.

SIGNIFICANT AUDIT FIRMS

These firms are the 'Big 4' multinational accountancy firms which audit the majority of large quoted/listed companies. In addition to providing audits, they also provide other services including tax advice and strategic consultancy.

Firm	2005 global revenue (US dollars)
PricewaterhouseCoopers (corporate website)	20.3bn
Deloitte (corporate website)	18.2bn
Ernst and Young (corporate website)	16.9bn
KPMG (corporate website)	15.7bn

Commercial Relationships versus Objectivity

One of the major issues faced by private auditing firms is the need to provide independent auditing services while maintaining a business relationship with the audited hotel. The auditing firm's responsibility to check and confirm the reliability of financial statements may be limited by pressure from the audited hotel, who pays the auditing firm for the service. The auditing firm's need to maintain a viable business through auditing revenue may be weighed against its duty to examine and verify the accuracy, relevancy, and completeness of the hotel's financial statements.

ACCOUNTS RECEIVABLE

Accounts receivable is one of a series of accounting transactions dealing with the billing of customers who owe money to a person, hotel or organization for goods and services that have been provided to the customer by the hotel. This is typically done in a one person organization by writing an invoice and mailing or delivering it to each customer. On a hotel's balance sheet, accounts receivable is the amount that customers owe a business. Sometimes called trade receivables, they are classified as current assets. To record a journal entry for a sale on account, one must debit a receivable and credit a revenue account. When the customer pays off their accounts, one debits cash and credit the receivable in the journal entry. The ending balance on the trial balance sheet for accounts receivable is always debit.

Business organizations which have become too large to perform such tasks by hand (or small ones that could but prefer not to do them by hand) will generally use accounting software on a computer to perform this task. Associated accounting issues include recognizing accounts receivable, valuing accounts receivable, and disposing of accounts receivable. Accounts receivable departments use the *Sales Ledger*. Other types of accounting transactions include accounts payable, payroll, and trial balance. Since not all customer debts will be collected, businesses typically record an allowance for bad debts which is subtracted from total accounts receivable. When accounts receivable are not paid, some companies turn them over to collection agencies. However, many debtors still do not pay; in those cases, some creditors turn to collection attorneys.

AMORTIZATION (BUSINESS)

Amortization is the distribution of a single lump-sum cash flow into many smaller cash flow installments, as determined by an amortization schedule. Unlike other repayment models, each repayment installment consists of both principal and interest. Amortization is chiefly used in loan repayments (a common example being a mortgage) and in sinking funds. Payments are divided into equal amounts for the duration of the loan, making it the simplest repayment model. A greater amount of the payment is applied to interest at the beginning of the amortization schedule, while more money is applied to principal at the end. The amortization calculator formula is: $(1-v^n)/r$, where n = number of years, v = 1/(1+r), and r = interest rate / 100.

Divide by (1+r) if a payment is due at the beginning.

Another method of writing this kind of formula is:

$$A = P\frac{i(1+i)^m}{(1+i)^m - 1}$$

where: *P* = principal amount borrowed *i* = periodic interest rate *m* = number of periods each year (vs."t"= number of periods over the life of the loan, or t=n*m) *A* = periodic payment. Negative amortization (also called deferred interest) occurs if the payments made do not cover the interest due. The remaining interest owed is added to the outstanding loan balance, making it larger than the original loan amount.

In Accounting

In accounting, amortization refers to expensing the acquisition cost less the residual value of intangible assets such as trademarks and copyrights in a systematic manner over their estimated useful economic lives so as to reflect their consumption, expiration, obsolescence or other decline in value as a result of use or the passage of time. A corresponding concept for tangible assets is depreciation. Methodologies for allocating amortization to each accounting period are generally the same as for depreciation. However, many intangible assets such as goodwill or certain brands may be deemed to have an indefinite useful life and are therefore not subject to amortization.

Amortization is recorded in the financial statements of an entity as a reduction in the carrying value of the intangible asset in the balance sheet and as an expense in the income statement. Under International Financial Reporting Standards, guidance on accounting for the amortization of intangible assets is contained in International Accounting Standard 38, Intangible Assets. Under United States generally accepted accounting principles, the primary guidance is contained in Statement of Financial Accounting Standards No. 142, Goodwill and Other Intangible Assets.

ANNUAL REPORT

An annual report is a document which a hotel presents at its Annual General Meeting for approval by its shareholders. The report is made up of reports and of financial statements, including the following:

- Chairman's report
- CEO's report
- Auditor's report on the financial statements
- Auditor's report on corporate governance
- Balance sheet
- Statement of changes in equity
- Income statement
- Cash Flow statement
- Notes to the financial statements
- Mission statement
- Accounting policies
- Corporate governance statement of compliance
- Statement of directors' responsibilities

Other information deemed relevant to stakeholders may also be included, such as a report on operations for manufacturing firms. In the case of larger companies, it is usually a sleek, colorful, high gloss publication. The details provided in the report are of use to investors in gaining an understanding of the hotel's financial position and future direction. The report is usually compiled in compliance with IFRSs and/or the domestic GAAP, as well as domestic legislation (e.g. the SOX in the U.S.). In the United States, a more-detailed version of the report, called a Form 10-K, is submitted to the U.S. Securities and Exchange Commission.

THROUGHPUT

In communication networks, throughput is the amount of digital data per time unit that is delivered to a certain terminal in a network, from a network node, or from one node to another, for example via a communication link. The throughput is usually measured in bit per second (bit/s or bps). The system throughput or aggregate throughput is the sum of the data rates that are delivered to all terminals in a network.

Often maximum throughput is implied by the term throughput. The maximum throughput of a node or communication link is synonym to its capacity. The maximum throughput is defined as the asymptotic throughput when the load (the amount of incoming data) is very large. In packet switched systems where the load and the throughput are equal (where there are no packet drops), the maximum throughput may be defined as the load in bit/s when the delivery time (the latency) asymptotically reaches infinity.

Channel Utilization

The channel utilization in percentage is the achieved throughput related to the physical data rate in bit/s of a digital communication channel (also known as the network access connection speed, the digital bandwidth or the channel capacity). For example, if the the throughput is 70 Mbit/s in a 100 Mbit/s Ethernet connection, the channel utilization is 70%. In a point-to-point or point-to-multipoint communication link, where only one terminal is transmitting, the maximum throughput is often equivalent to or very near the physical data rate (the channel capacity), since the channel utilization can be almost 100% in such a network, except for a small inter-frame gap.

For example in Ethernet, the interframe gap is 12 bytes, and the maximum frame size 1538 bytes (1500 byte payload + 12 byte interframe gap + 8 byte preamble + 14 byte header + 4 Byte trailer). This corresponds to a maximum channel utilization of (1538–12)/1538•100% = 99.2%, or a maximum throughput of 99.2 Mbit/s in a 100 Mbit/s Ethernet connection.

In a computer network, the throughput that is achieved from one computer to another may be lower than the maximum throughput, and than the network access channel capacity, for several reasons, for example:

- The channel capacity may be shared by other users. If a bottle neck communication link physical data rate *R* is shared by *N*, every user typically achieves a throughput of approximately *N*/*R* if fair queuing best-effort communication is assumed.
- Flow control, for example in the TCP protocol, affects the throughput if the bandwidth delay product is larger than the TCP window, i.e. the buffer size. In that case the sending computer must wait for acknowledgement of the data packets before it can send more packets.
- Packet loss due to Network congestion. Packets may be dropped in switches and routers when the packet queues are full due to congestion.
- Packet loss due to bit errors.
- TCP congestion avoidance controls the data rate. So called "slow start" occurs in the beginning of a file, and after packet drops caused by router congestion or bit errors in for example wireless links.
- Scheduling algorithms in routers and switches. If fair queuing is not provided, users that send large packet will get higher bandwidth. Some users may be prioritized in a weighted fair queuing (WFQ) algorithm if differentiated or guaranteed quality of service (QoS) is provided.
- Ethernet "backoff" waiting time after collisions.

Throughput, Goodput and Overhead

The maximum throughput is often an unreliable measurement of perceived speed, for example the file transmission speed in bits per seconds.

As pointed out above, the achieved throughput is often lower than the maximum throughput. Also, the protocol overhead affect the perceived speed.

The throughput is not a well-defined measure when it comes to how to deal with protocol overhead. The most simple definition is the number of bits per second that are physically delivered. A typical example where this definition is practised is an Ethernet network. In this case the maximum throughput is the gross bitrate or raw bitrate.

However, in schemes that include forward error correction codes (channel coding), the redundant error code is normally excluded from the throughput. An example in modem communication, where the throughput typically is measured in the interface between the PPP protocol and the circuit switched modem connection. In this case the maximum throughput is often called net bitrate or useful bitrate.

To determine the actual speed of a network or connection, the goodput measurement definition may be used. For example in file transmission, the goodput corresponds to the file size (in bits) divided by the file transmission time. The goodput is the amount of useful information that is delivered per second to the application layer protocol. Dropped packets, packet retransmissions and protocol overhead are not counted. Because of that, the goodput is lower than the throughput. Technical factors that affect the difference are presented in the goodput article.

Throughput over Analog Channels

The maximum throughput of a point-to-point or point-to-multipoint physical transmission medium, is equal to or near the channel capacity. This is affected by modulation method and physical layer protocol overhead such as error correction coding, bit synchronization and equalizer training sequences. The maximum throughput may be related to the analog bandwidth of a physical transmission medium, measured in Hertz. The link spectral efficiency in bit/s/Hz is the maximum throughput divided by the analog bandwidth. It is a measure of the efficiency of the digital transmission scheme.

In wireless networks or cellular systems, the system spectral efficiency in bit/s/Hz/area unit, bit/s/Hz/site or bit/s/Hz/cell, is the maximum system throughput (aggregate throughput) divided by the analog bandwidth and some measure of the system coverage area.

Throughput and Latency

Normally throughput and latency are opposed goals. To improve latency you typically want to increase how much the computer checks to see if you are trying to interact. This checking overhead slows you down. However, there is one very common exception to this rule. Network protocols and programs tend to synchronize both ends regularly. If these synchronizations are slow, then throughput can suffer tremendously.

The perceived speed is mostly based on the speed of requests made or responsiveness. As such, responsiveness has far less to do with throughput than latency. To illustrate this, consider a truck full of magnetic tape en route from Moscow to Paris. The time or latency it takes to deliver the data may be several days, but the amount or throughput of data delivered will exceed the throughput of a broadband connection. In contrast, the broadband connection, which has a throughput many times less than that of the truck, has a relatively low latency and can deliver smaller amounts of data much faster. For a user, surfing the Internet for instance, the latter which has a lower latency is perceived as "faster".

Latency is measured from the time a request (e.g. a single packet) leaves the client to the time the response (e.g. An Acknowledgment) arrives back at the client from the serving entity. The unit of latency is time. Throughput on the other hand is the amount of data that is transferred over a period of time. For example if over ten seconds twenty packets are transferred then the throughput would be 20/10=2 packets per second. Throughput can have many units (for example: "bits/second," "bytes/second," or "packets/second"), but it is always measured in a volume-per-time ratio.

Throughput Accounting

Throughput accounting (TA) is an alternative to cost accounting proposed by Eliyahu M. Goldratt. It is not based on Standard Costing or Activity Based Costing (ABC). Throughput Accounting is not costing and it does not allocate costs to products and services. It can be viewed as business intelligence for profit maximization. Conceptually throughput accounting seeks to increase the velocity at which products move through an organization by eliminiating bottlenecks within the organization.

Cost (or Management) accounting is an organization's internal method used to measure efficiency. Since no one outside the organization uses such internal accounts for investment or other decisions, any methods that an organization finds helpful can be used. Outside parties to a business depend on accounting reports prepared by financial (public) accountants who apply Generally Accepted Accounting Practices (GAAP) issued by the Financial Accounting Standards Board (FASB) and enforced by the U.S. Securities and Exchange Commission (SEC) and other regulatory agencies. Throughput accounting improves profit performance with better management decisions by using measurements that more closely reflect the effect of decisions on three critical monetary variables (throughput, inventory, and operating expense — defined below).

When cost accounting was developed in the 1890's, Labour was the largest fraction of product cost and workers might not know how many hours they would work in a week when they reported on Monday morning. Cost accountants, therefore, concentrated on how efficiently managers used Labour since it was their most important variable resource. Now, however, workers who come to work on Monday morning almost always work 40 hours or more; their cost is fixed rather than variable. Many managers are still evaluated on their Labour efficiencies, though, and many "downsizing," "rightsizing," and other Labour reduction campaigns are based on them.

Goldratt argues that, under current conditions, Labour efficiencies lead to decisions that harm rather than help organizations. Throughput accounting, therefore, removes standard cost accounting's reliance on efficiencies in general and Labour efficiency in particular from management practice. Many cost and financial accountants agree with Goldratt's critique, but they have not agreed on a replacement of their own and there is enormous inertia in the installed base of people trained to work with existing practices.

The recent development of TA is constraints accounting, which focuses more strongly on the role of the constraint in decision making.

The Concept of Throughput Accounting

Goldratt's alternative begins with the idea that each organization has a goal and that better decisions increase its value. The goal for a profit maximizing firm is easily stated, to increase profit, now and in the future. Throughput accounting applies to not-for-profit organizations too, but they have to develop a goal that makes sense in their individual cases. Throughput Accounting also pays particular attention to the concept of bottlenecks in the manufacturing or servicing processes.

Throughput accounting uses three measures of income and expense:

- *Throughput* (T) is the rate at which the system produces "goal units." When the goal units are money (in for-profit businesses), throughput is sales revenues less the cost of the raw materials (T = S – RM). Note that T only exists when there is a sale of the product or service. Producing materials that sit in a warehouse does not count. ("Throughput" is sometimes referred to as "Throughput Contribution" and has similarities to the concept of "Contribution" in Marginal Costing which is sales revenues less "variable" costs - "variable" being defined according to the Marginal Costing philosophy.)
- *Investment* (I) is the money tied up in the system. This is money associated with inventory, machinery, buildings, and other assets and liabilities. In earlier TOC documentation, the "I" was interchanged between "Inventory" and "Investment." The preferred term is now only "investment." Note that TOC recommends inventory be valued strictly on totally variable cost associated with creating the inventory, not with additional cost allocations from overhead.
- *Operating expense* (OE) is the money the system spends in generating "goal units." For physical products, OE is all expenses except the

cost of the raw materials. OE includes maintenance, utilities, rent, taxes, payroll, etc.

Organizations that wish to increase their attainment of The Goal should therefore require managers to test proposed decisions against three questions. Will the proposed change:

Increase Throughput? How?

Reduce Investment (Inventory) (money that cannot be used)? How?

Reduce Operating expense? How?

The answers to these questions determine the effect of proposed changes on system wide measurements:

Net profit (NP) = Throughput – Operating Expense = T–OE

Return on investment (ROI) = Net profit / Investment = NP/I

Productivity (P) = Throughput / Operating expense = T/OE

Investment turns (IT) = Throughput / Investment = T/I

These relationships between financial ratios as illustrated by Goldratt are very similar to a set of relationships defined by DuPont and General Motors financial executive Donaldson Brown about 1920. Brown did not advocate changes in management accounting methods, but instead used the ratios to evaluate traditional financial accounting data. Throughput Accounting is an important development in modern accounting that allows managers to understand the contribution of constrained resources to the overall profitability of the enterprise.

3

Debit and Credit

CREDIT (FINANCE)

Credit as a financial term, used in such terms as credit card, refers to the granting of a loan and the creation of debt. Any movement of financial capital is normally quite dependent on credit, which in turn is dependent on the reputation or creditworthiness of the entity which takes responsibility for the funds. A similar usage is in commercial trade, where *credit* is used to refer to the approval for delayed payments for goods purchased. Sometimes if a person has financial instability or difficulty, credit is not granted. Companies frequently offer credit to their customers as part of the terms of a purchase agreement. Organizations that offer credit to their customers frequently employ a credit manager. Credit is denominated by a unit of account. Unlike money (by a strict definition), credit itself cannot act as a unit of account. However, many forms of credit can readily act as a medium of exchange. As such, various forms of credit are frequently referred to as *money* and are included in estimates of the money supply.

Credit is also traded in the market. The purest form is the "Credit Default Swap" market, which is essentially a traded market in credit insurance. A credit default swap represents the price at which two counterparties will exchange this risk — the protection "seller" takes the risk of default of the credit in return for a payment, commonly denoted in basis points (one basis point being 1/100 of a percent) of the notional amount to be referenced, while the protection "buyer" pays this premium and in the case of default of the underlying (a loan, bond or other receivable), delivers this receivable to the protection seller and receives from the seller the par amount (i.e., is made whole).

DEBITS AND CREDITS AND DEBT

Debit and Credit are formal bookkeeping and accounting terms that have opposite meanings and come from Latin. Debit comes from *debere,* which means "to owe". The Latin *debitum* means "debt". Credit comes from the Latin word *credere,* which means "to believe". It is more common to use the terms in the plural, Debits and Credits. Debit is abbreviated as *Dr.*, while credit is abbreviated as *Cr.*

"Debit" also refers to the left side of a general ledger account, while "Credit" refers to the right side. Due to the proliferation of bookkeeping and accounting computer software, it is now common for Debits to be mistakenly treated as positive values and Credits to be mistakenly treated as negative values. This allows for mathematical calculations. This has lead to confusion as people do not understand why a Sales amount is treated as an negative value (Credit) and an expense is treated as a positive value (Debit). If the value of the debits are greater than the value of the credits, then the balance on the account is a debit and should not be described as a positive value balance.

Debits or Credits are neither positive or a negative values. The balance on an account is either a debit or a credit not a positive or a negative value. Asset and expense accounts increase in value when debited and decrease when credited. Whereas liability, equity, and revenue accounts decrease in value when debited and increase when credited.

This distinction is somewhat counterintuitive, until the nature of those accounts is more closely scrutinized. For example, revenue is coded as a credit. After recording a day's sales invoices, the hotel will have credited a certain amount in revenue, but the customers ledger will hold a debit balance being the amount of the unpaid invoices. To fully understand this see Double-entry bookkeeping system where Debits and Credits form the core of that system.

For instance, the journal entry for paying the telephone bill might look like this:

Description	*Debits*	*Credits*
Phone expense	$200	
Cash		$200

The telephone company would record the exact same transaction (from their side) like this:

Description	*Debits*	*Credits*
Cash	$200	
Revenue		$200

Confusion also arises where the term debit is also informally referred to as a "charge" as in a charge card or Debit Card and that Credit is a limit set or an amount granted by a hotel to its customers as in a credit limit. They are used in a different context in these two cases.

It is often assumed that a debit decreases a balance, and a credit increases it, because this is how the terms are used on bank statements and using a debit card decreases the balance in one's bank acco7unt. However, this is because bank statements are traditionally written from the bank's perspective, where the customer's account is a liability. By withdrawing money, the customer is decreasing the bank's liability. Since liability accounts normally have a credit balance, the withdrawal of cash from a banking account is reflected on the bank's balance sheet as a debit.

TRADE CREDIT

Trade credit exists when one provides goods or services to a customer with an agreement to bill them later, or receive a shipment or service from a supplier under an agreement to pay them later. It can be viewed as an essential element of capitalization in an operating business because it can reduce the required capital investment to operate the business if it is managed properly. Trade credit is the largest use of capital for a majority of business to business (B2B) sellers in the United States and is a critical source of capital for a majority of all businesses. For example, Wal-Mart, the largest retailer in the world, has used trade credit as a larger source of capital than bank borrowings; trade credit for Wal-Mart is 8 times the amount of capital invested by shareholders. (Trade credit is the second largest source of capital for Wal-Mart; retained earnings is the largest.)

There are many forms of trade credit in common use. Various industries use various specialized forms. They all have, in common, the collaboration of businesses to make efficient use of capital to accomplish various business objectives. *For example:* Let's say you operate an ice cream stand under a franchise which agrees to provide you with ice cream stock under the terms Net 60 with a ten percent discount on payment within 30 days, and a 20 % discount on payment within 10 days. This means that you have 60 days to pay the invoice in full. If you sell a sufficient amount of ice cream at your markup within a week, then you can dispatch a cheque for 80 % of the invoice, and make an extra 20 % on the ice cream sold. However, if sales are slow, leading to a month of low cash flow, then you may decide to pay 90 % within 30 days or use the money another 30 days and pay the full invoice amount within 60 days.

The ice cream distributor can do the same thing. Receiving trade credit from milk and sugar suppliers on terms of Net 30, 2 % discount, if paid within ten days, means he is apparently taking a loss or disadvantageous position in this web of trade credit balances. Why would he do this? First, remember he has a substantial markup on the ingredients and other costs of production of the ice cream he sells to you. There are many reasons and ways to manage trade credit terms for the benefit of a business. The ice cream distributor may be well capitalized either by steady profits or recent new investments and may be looking to expand his markets. In this case he is being aggressive in attempting to locate new customers or to help them get established. Having experienced a few customers going out of business from cash flow instabilities he has decided on financial terms to accomplish two things:

- Allow startup ice cream parlors the ability to mismanage their investment in inventory for a while, while learning their markets without having a dramatic negative balance in their till or bank account, which could put them out of business. This is in effect, a short term business loan made to help expand the distributor's market and customer base.

By tracking who pays, and when, the distributor can see potential problems developing and take steps to reduce or increase the allowed amount of trade credit he extends to prospering or faltering businesses. This limits the exposure to losses from customers going bankrupt who would never pay for the ice cream delivered. It is better to have a $5,000 loss than a $30,000 loss.

PETTY CASH

Hotel Businesses often need small amounts discretionary funds in the form of cash known as petty cash for expenditures where it is not practical to make the disbursement by check. The most common way of accounting for these expenditures is to use the imprest system. The initial fund would be created by issuing a check for the desired amount. Usually $100 would be sufficient for most small business needs, however larger businesses may have several thousand dollars in discretionary funds available as petty cash. The entry for this initial fund would be to debit Petty Cash and credit cash.

As expenditures are made, the custodian of the fund will reimburse employees and secure a petty cash voucher in return. At any given time the total of cash on hand plus reimbursed vouchers must equal the original fund. When the fund gets low the custodian submits the vouchers for reimbursement. Assuming the vouchers add up to $80 and that the majority of expenditures were for office supplies, an $80 check is issued and an $80 debit towards office expenses is marked. Once the check is cashed, the custodian has cash at the original amount.

Oversight of petty cash is important because of the potential for abuse. Examples of petty cash controls include a limit (such as 10% of the total fund) on disbursements and monthly audits by someone other than the custodian. Use of petty cash is sufficiently widespread that vouchers for use in reimbursement are available at any office supply store.

CASH FLOW STATEMENT

People and groups interested in cash flow statements include:

- Accounting personnel, who need to know whether the organization will be able to cover payroll and other immediate expenses
- Potential lenders/creditors, who want a clear picture of a hotel's ability to repay
- Potential investors who need to judge whether the hotel is financially sound

- Potential employees or contractors who need to know whether the hotel will be able to afford compensation

Cash flow statements are particularly important for start-up companies with limited liquid assets. These companies are vulnerable to devastating cash shortages, even when Accounts Receivable balances point to long-term financial health.

Statement of Cash Flows

Statement of Cash Flow for the period 12/31/2005 to 12/31/2006

Cash flow from operations (CFO)	+/– x x
Cash flow from investing (CFI)	+/– y y
Cash flow from financing (CFF)	+/– z z
Equals change in cash account	= change of cash flow
+ Beginning of period cash	+ Beginning cash
= Ending cash balance	= Ending cash

Operating Activities

Operating activities include the production, sales and delivery of the hotel's product as well as collecting payment from its customers. This could include purchasing raw materials, building inventory, advertising and shipping the product. Items under Operating activities include:

- Net income from income statement
- Depreciation
- Non-cash items
- Deferred tax
- Interest amortization
- Accrual items, such as wages payable
- Working Capital

Investing activities

Investing activities focus on the purchase of the long-term assets a hotel needs in order to make and sell its products, and the selling of any long-term assets that are no longer needed by the hotel. Items under Investing Activities include:

- Capital expenditures, includes purchases of equipment on account.
- Investments.

Financing activities

Financing activities include the influx of cash from investors such as banks and shareholders, as well as the outflow of cash to investors as the hotel generates income. Other activities which impact the long-term liabilities and equity of the hotel are also listed in the financing activities section of the cash flow statement. Items under the Financing activities section include:

- Dividends paid
- Sale purchase of stock
- Net borrowings

Preparation Methods

Direct Method

Shows the major classes of gross cash receipts and payments. This method starts with Net Income and mirrors the Income Statement while also including Current Assets and Current Liabilities.

Indirect Method

Shows the net profit or loss as a starting point and makes adjustments for all transactions of a non-cash items

COST OF SERVICES DONE

In hotel accounting, the cost of services done (also, cost of sales or cost of revenue) describes the *direct* expenses incurred in producing a particular good for sale, including the actual cost of materials that comprise the good, and direct Labour expense in putting the good in salable condition. Cost of goods sold does *not* include indirect expenses such as office expenses, accounting, shipping department, advertising, and other expenses that can not be attributed to a particular item for sale.

Subtracting the *cost of goods sold* from the amount billed when selling the good (*sales revenue*) produces the *gross profit* on the good. The *net profit*, what most people understand as the business' income or profit, is determined by subtracting the *cost of goods sold* and the *indirect expenses* from the *sales revenue*.

Accounting method

The revenue from merchandise sold must be matched with the cost of goods sold. Cost of sales or cost of goods sold is the identification of the cost of those items sold in the most recent accounting period. It can be done by specific identification, taking inventory, or different methods using estimates such as the "retail" method.

Cost of Goods sold is also the determining factor in arriving at *gross profit* and is determined under the periodic method as follows:

Sales		$100,000
Cost of Goods Sold		
Inventory 01/01/03	$ 5,000	
Purchases	45,000	
Direct Labour	30,000	
	80,000	
Less: Inventory 12/31/03	10,000	
Net Cost of Goods Sold	70,000	
Gross Profit on Sales	$30,000	

To determine the net profit, one would then compute the indirect expenses such as office expenses, light, heat, etc. Determining the cost of goods sold is the first step in arriving at the net profit.

If the cost of goods sold is too high gross profit will not support the indirect expenses and will result in a loss for the accounting period.

EARNINGS MANAGEMENT

According to Healy and Wahlen (1999), "Earnings Management" occurs when managers use judgement in financial reporting and in structuring transactions to alter financial reports to either mislead some stakeholders about the underlying economic performance of a hotel or to influence contractual outcomes that depend on reported accounting numbers. Earnings management usually involves the artificial increase (or decrease) of revenues, profits, or earnings per share figures through aggressive accounting tactics. Aggressive earnings management is a form of fraud and differs from reporting error.

Management wishing to show earnings at a certain level or following a certain pattern seek loopholes in financial reporting standards that allow them to adjust the numbers as far as is practicable to achieve their desired aim or to satisfy projections by financial analysts. These adjustments amount to fraudulent financial reporting when they fall 'outside the bounds of acceptable accounting practice'. Drivers for such behaviour include market expectations, personal realisation of a bonus, and maintenance of position within a market sector. In most cases conformance to acceptable accounting practices is a matter of personal integrity. Aggressive earnings management becomes more probable when a hotel is affected by a downturn in business.

Earnings management is seen as a pressing issue in current accounting practice. Part of the difficulty lies in the accepted recognition that there is no such thing as a single 'right' earnings figure and that it is possible for legitimate business practices to develop into unacceptable financial reporting.

It is relatively easy for an auditor to detect error but earnings management can involve sophisticated fraud that is covert. The requirement for management to assert that the accounts have been prepared properly offers no protection where those managers have already entered into conscious deceit and fraud. Auditors need to distinguish fraud from error by identifying the presence of intention.

The main forms of earnings management are as follows:

- Unsuitable revenue recognition
- Inappropriate accruals and estimates of liabilities
- Excessive provisions and generous reserve accounting
- Intentional minor breaches of financial reporting requirements that aggregate to a material breach.

ENGAGEMENT LETTER

An engagement letter defines the legal relationship (or engagement) between a professional firm (e.g., law, investment banking, consulting, advisory or accountancy firm) and its client(s). This letter states the terms and conditions of the engagement, principally addressing the scope of the engagement and the terms of compensation for the firm. Most engagement letters follow a standard format. The example given below refers to the engagement of an accountancy firm.

Standard format for letters of Engagement

- *Addressee*: Typically addressed to the senior management (e.g. CEO) of the client.
- *Identification of the service to be rendered*: One type of service is a financial statement audit. Provided in this section is a brief descri ption of the nature of the particular service. Other services that are planned for the audit (e.g. evaluation of internal control, preparation of regulatory reports) are also identified in this section.
- *Specification of the responsibilities of the auditor of the hotel*: This section refers to the specific professional standards and responsibilities of the auditor.
- *Constraints on the accounting firm*: For example, timing of access to client facilities and accounting records may delay the engagement.
- *Deadlines*: This section lays out the estimated date of completion and release of the financial statements, as well as the general guidelines for the timing of the audit work.
- *Description of any assistance to be provided by the client*: Typically, the client's personnel will prepare some schedules (e.g. bank reconciliations) and retrieve documents from files. The letter should

describe the assistance of client personnel. If the assistance is not provided and the auditors must complete the work themselves, this section of the letter would provide justification for additional fees to the client.

- *Interactions with specialists, internal auditors, and the predecessor auditor needed to conduct the audit*: Some specialists needed on an audit may include engineers to verify the stage of completion of electronic components, real estate appraisers to appraise realizable value of real estate used as collateral for loans, actuaries to evaluate the funding requirements and future cash flows associated with pensions or post-retirement health costs, and attorneys to evaluate the likely disposition of contingent losses arising from litigation.
- *A disclaimer*: Describing the limits of the audit. Typically this expresses that an audit is not designed to detect all forms of fraud or illegal acts; rather, an audit checks the financial position of a client with reference to generally accepted accounting principles.
- *A description of the basis for fees*: This may include a fixed fee or an estimate of fees based on expected completion time and billing rates of firm employees assigned to the engagement.
- Ownership and accessibility of the auditor's files to outsiders.

EXPENSE

In hotel accounting, an expense represents an event in which an asset is used up or a liability is incurred. In terms of the accounting equation, expenses reduce owners' equity. The official definition of *expense* used by International Accounting Standards Board is (quotation from IFRS Framework):

> *Expenses are decreases in economic benefits during the accounting period in the form of outflows or depletions of assets or incurrences of liabilities that result in decreases in equity, other than those relating to distributions to equity participants. [F.70]*

One specific use of the term in accounting is whether a particular expenditure is classified as an expense, which is reported immediately to the investing public in the business's income statement; or whether it is classified as a capital expenditure or an expenditure subject to depreciation, which is not. These latter types of expenditures are reported as expenses eventually, but not immediately, by businesses that use accrual-basis accounting, meaning all large businesses.

In investing, one controversy that mounted throughout 2002 and 2003 was whether companies should report the granting of stock options to employees as an expense on the income statement, or should not report this at all in the income statement, which is what had previously been the norm.

OWNERSHIP EQUITY

In hotel business accounting, ownership equity is the owners' interest in all assets after all liabilities are paid. There is a greater discussion at shareholders' equity (when the owners are shareholders). Ownership equity is also known as *equity, risk capital,* and *liable capital.* In a bankruptcy court, creditors have the first claim on assets, and ownership equity is the last or residual claim against assets, paid only after all other creditors are paid. In real estate the owner's equity in a property is the difference between the market price of a property and the owner's mortgage debt, or the owner's 'home equity loan'.

EQUIVALENT ANNUAL COST

In finance the equivalent annual cost (EAC) is the cost per year of owning and operating an asset over its entire lifespan. EAC is often used as a decision making tool in capital budgeting when comparing investment projects of unequal lifespans. For example if project A has an expected lifetime of 7 years, and project B has an expected lifetime of 11 years it would be improper to simply compare the net present values (NPVs) of the two projects, unless neither project could be repeated. EAC is calculated by dividing the NPV of a project by the *present value of an annuity* factor. Equivalently, the NPV of the project may be multiplied by the *loan repayment factor.*

EAC=NPV

The use of the EAC method implies that the project will be replaced by an identical project.

A Practical Example

A manager must decide on which machine to purchase:

Machine A

Investment cost $50,000

Expected lifetime 3 years

Annual maintenance $13,000

Machine B

Investment cost $150,000

Expected lifetime 8 years

Annual maintenance $7,500

The cost of capital is 5%.

The EAC for machine A is: ($50,000*$A_{3,5}$)+$13,000=$31,360

The EAC for machine B is: ($150,000*$A_{8,5}$)+$7,500=$30,780

Where A is the loan repayment factor for t years and 5% cost of capital.

The conclusion is to invest in machine B since it has a lower EAC.

Alternative method:

The manager calculates the NPV of the machines:

Machine A EAC=$85,400*$A_{3,5}$=$31,360

Machine B EAC=$19,847*$A_{8,5}$=$30,780

The result is the same, although the first method is easier it is essential that the annual maintenance cost is the same each year.

Alternatively the manager can use the NPV method under the assumption that the machines will be replaced with the same cost of investment each time. This is known as the *chain method* since 8 repetitions of machine A are chained together and 3 repetitions of machine B are chained together. Since the time horizon used in the NPV comparison must be set to 24 years (3*8=24) in order to compare projects of equal length, this method can be slightly more complicated than calculating the EAC. In addition, the assumption of the same cost of investment for each link in the chain is essentially an assumption of zero inflation, so a real interest rate rather than a nominal interest rate is commonly used in the calculations.

FREE CASH FLOW

Free cash flow measures a firm's net increase in

- Cash from operations (this includes the reduction for interest),
- Less the dividends paid to preferred shareholders, and
- Less expenditures necessary to maintain assets.

Increases in non-cash current assets may, or may not be deducted, depending on whether they are considered to be maintaining the status quo, or to be investments for growth.

Problems with CapX

- The expenditures for maintenance of assets is only part of the capx reported on the Statement of Cash Flows. It must be separated from the expenditures for growth purposes. This split is not a requirement under GAAP, and is not audited. Management is free to disclose maintenance capx or not. Therefore this input to the calculation of free cash flow is easy to manipulate. Since it is a very large number, maintenance capx's questionable validity is the basis for some people's dismissal of 'free cash flow'.
- A second problem with the maintenance capx measurement is its intrinsic 'lumpyness'. By their nature, expenditures for capital assets that will last decades are infrequent, but costly when they occur. 'Free cash flow', in turn, will be very different from year to year. No particular year will be a 'norm' that can be expected to be repeated.

Uses of the metric

- Free cash flow measures the ease with which businesses can grow and pay dividends to shareholders. Even profitable businesses may have negative cash flows. Their requirement for increased financing will result in increased financing costs reducing future income. It is easier to grow with organic cash flows than with additional financing.

- According to the discounted cash flow valuation model, the intrinsic value of a hotel is the present value of all future free cash flows, plus the cash proceeds from its eventual sale. The presumption is that the cash flows are used to pay dividends to the shareholders. Bear in mind the lumpyness discussed above.
- Some investors prefer using free cash flow instead of net income to measure a hotel's financial performance, because free cash flow is more difficult to manipulate than net income. The problems with this presumption are itemized at cash flow and return of capital.
- The payout ratio is a metric used to evaluate the sustainability of distributions from REITs, Oil and Gas Royalty Trusts, and Income Trust. The distributions are divided by the free cash flow. Distributions may include any of income, flowed-through capital gains or return of capital.

This metric is used only by shareholders. Debt holders are not concerned with maintaining the operating capital assets, or with growing the business. Nor are they concerned with taxes paid since their payments come first. The appropriate metric for debt holders is EBITDA.

GAIN

In electronics, gain is usually taken as the mean ratio of the signal output of a system to the signal input of the system. A gain of five would imply that either the voltage or power is increased by a factor of five. It has wide application in amplifiers.

Logarithmic units and Decibels

In electronics, it is common to use logarithmic units to measure gain. Originally, the bel was used:

$$\text{Gain} = \log_{10}(P_2/P_1) \text{ bel}$$

where P1 and P2 are the input and output *powers* respectively.

Using the bel unit, however, results in small numbers, so the decibel (one tenth of a bel) became popular in its place. As there are ten decibels (dB) in a bel:

$$\text{Gain} = 10 * \log_{10}(P_2/P_1) \text{ dB}$$

(A similar unit using natural logarithms is called the neper.)

When gain is calculated using voltage instead of power, making the substitution ($P=V^2/R$), the formula is:

- $\text{Gain} = 10 * \log ((V_2^2/R) / (V_1^2/R)) \text{ dB}$

- Gain = 10 * log $((V_2/V_1)^2)$ dB
- Gain = 20 * log (V_2/V_1) dB

This formula only holds true if the load impedances are identical. In many modern electronic devices, output impedances are low enough and input impedances high enough that load can be ignored without significantly affecting the calculation.

Example: If an amplifier produces an output of 1 volt into a 1 ohm load, then it is providing 1 watt of output power. If the amplifier is then altered to produce an output of 10 volts into the same load, it is now providing 100 watts of output power ($P = V^2/R$). Therefore:

voltage gain = 10 times (10 dB)

power gain = 100 times (20 dB)

A gain of factor 1 or (equivalent to 0 dB) where both input and output are at the same voltage level is also known as *unity gain.*

INTEREST

Interest is the "rent" paid to borrow money. The lender receives a compensation for deferring their own consumption. The original amount lent is called the "principal," and the percentage of the principal which is paid/payable over a period of time is the "interest rate."

Calculations

Simple interest: Add up all the interest paid/payable in a period. Divide that by the principal at the beginning of the period. E.g. on $100 (principal):

- Credit card debt where $1/day is charged. 1/100 = 1%/day.
- Corporate bond where $3 is due after six months, and another $3 is due at year end. (3+3)/100 = 6%/year.
- Certificate of deposit (GIC) where $6 is paid at year end. 6/100 = 6%/year.

There are three problems with simple interest.

- The time periods used for measurement can be different, making comparisons wrong. You cannot say the 1%/day credit card interest is 'equal' to a 365%/year GIC.
- The time value of money means that $3 paid every six months hurts more than $6 paid only at year end. So you cannot 'equate' the 6% bond to the 6% GIC.
- When interest is due, but not paid, it must be clear what happens. Does it remain 'interest payable', like the bond's $3 payment after six months? Or does it get added to the original principal, like the 1%/day on the credit card? Each time it is added to the principal it 'compounds'. The interest from that time forward is calculated on

that (now larger) principal. The more frequent the compounding, the faster the principal grows, and the greater the interest.

Compound interest: In order to solve these three problems, there is a convention that interest rates will be disclosed as if the term is one year and the compounding is yearly. The discussion at compound interest shows how to convert to and from the different measures of interest.

Real interest: This is calculated as (nominal interest rate) - (inflation). It attempts to measure the value of the interest in units of stable purchasing power.

Cumulative interest/return: This calculation is (FV/PV)-1. It ignores the 'per year' convention and assumes compounding at every payment date. It is usually used to compare two long term opportunities. Since the difference in rates gets magnified by time, so the speaker's point is more clearly made.

Rule of 78: Some consumer loans calculate interest by the "Rule of 78" or "Sum of digits" method. Seventy-eight is the sum of the numbers 1 through 12, inclusive. And the practice enabled quick calculations of interest in the pre-computer days. In a loan with interest calculated per the Rule of 78, the total interest over the life of the loan is calculated as either simple or compound interest and amounts to the same as either of the above methods. Payments remain constant over the life of the loan; however, payments are allocated to interest in progressively smaller amounts. In a one-year loan, in the first month, 12/78 of all interest owed over the life of the loan is due; in the second month, 11/78; progressing to the twelfth month where only 1/78 of all interest is due. The practical effect of the Rule of 78 is to make early pay-offs of term loans more expensive. Approximately 3/4 of all interest due on a one year loan is collected by the sixth month, and pay-off of the principal then will cause the effective interest rate to be much higher than than the APY used to calculate the payments.

The United States outlawed the use of "Rule of 78" interest in loans over five years in term. Certain other jurisdictions have outlawed application of the Rule of 78 in certain types of loans, particularly consumer loans. *Rule of 72*: The "Rule of 72" is a "quick and dirty" method for finding out how fast money doubles for a given interest rate. For example, if you have an interest rate of 6%, it will take 72/6 or 12 years for your money to double, compounding at 6%. This is an approximation that starts to break down above 10%.

DEBT

Debt is that which is owed; usually referencing assets owed, but the term can cover other obligations. In the case of assets, debt is a means of using future purchasing power in the present before a summation has been earned. Some companies and corporations use debt as a part of their overall corporate finance strategy. A debt is created when a creditor agrees to loan a sum of assets to a debtor. In modern society, debt is usually granted with expected repayment; in many cases, plus interest. Historically, debt was responsible for the creation of indentured servants.

Payment

Before a debt can be had, both the debtor and the creditor must agree on the manner in which the debt will be repaid, known as the standard of deferred payment. This payment is usually denominated as a sum of money in units of currency, but can sometimes be denominated in terms of goods. Payment can be made in increments over a period of time, or all at once at the end of the loan agreement.

Types of debt

There are numerous types of debt, including basic loans, syndicated loans, bonds, and promissory notes. Debt, especially large sums of debt, can also be secured through a mortgage or other security interest over some of the debtor's property, in which case the creditor will have some rights over that property in the event that the debtor becomes unable to repay the debt and defaults on the loan.

A basic loan is the simplest form of debt. It consists of an agreement to lend a principal sum for a fixed period of time, to be repaid by a certain date. In commercial loans interest, calculated as a percentage of the principal sum per annum, will also have to be paid by that date. A syndicated loan is a loan that is granted to companies that wish to borrow more money than any single lender is prepared to risk in a single loan, usually many millions of dollars. In such a case, a syndicate of banks can each agree to put forward a portion of the principal sum.

A bond is a debt security issued by certain institutions such as companies and governments. A bond entitles the holder to repayment of the principal sum, plus interest. Bonds are issued to investors in a marketplace when an institution wishes to borrow money. Bonds have a fixed lifetime, usually a number of years; with long-term bonds, lasting over 30 years, being less common. At the end of the bond's life the money should be repaid in full. Interest may be added to the end payment, or can be paid in regular instalments (known as coupons) during the life of the bond. Bonds may be traded in the bond markets, and are widely used as relatively safe investments in comparison to stocks.

Accounting debt

In national accounting debts are added according to those who are indebted. Household debt is the debt held by households. "National" or Public debt is the debt held by the various governmental institutions (federal government, states, cities ...). Business debt is the debt held by businesses. Financial debt is the debt held by the financial sector (from one financial institution to another). Total debt is the sum of all those debts, excluding financial debt to prevent double accounting. These various types of debt can be computed in debt/GDP ratios. Those ratios help to assess the speed of variations in the indebtness and the size of the debt due. For example the USA has a high consumer debt and a low public debt, while in European countries the opposite tends to be true.

There are differences in the accounting of debt for private and public agents. If a private agent promises to pay something later, it has a debt, and this debt is enforceable by public agents. If a public body passes a law stating that it'll pay something later (a kind of promise), it keeps the right to change the law later (and not to pay). This is why for instance the money governments promised to pay for retirements does not show up in the public debt assessment, whereas the money private companies promised to pay for retirements do.

Securitization

Securitization occurs when a hotel groups together assets or receivables and sells them in units to the market through a trust. Any asset with a cashflow can be securitized. The cash flows from these receivables are used to pay the holders of these units. Companies often do this in order to remove these assets from their balance sheets and monetize an asset. Although these assets are "removed" from the balance sheet and are supposed to be the responsibility of the trust, that does not end the hotel's involvement. Often the hotel maintains a special interest in the trust which is called an "interest only strip" or "first loss piece". Any payments from the trust must be made to regular investors in precedence to this interest. This protects investors from a degree of risk, making the securitization more attractive. The aforementioned brings into question whether the assets are truly off balance sheet given the hotel's exposure to losses on this interest.

Debt, Inflation and the Exchange rate

As noted above, debt is normally denominated in a particular monetary currency, and so changes in the valuation of that currency can change the effective size of the debt. This can happen due to inflation or deflation, so it can happen even though the borrower and the lender are using the same currency. Thus it is important to agree on standards of deferred payment in advance, so that a degree of fluctuation will also be agreed as acceptable. It is for instance common to agree to "US dollar denominated" debt.

The form of debt involved in banking accounts for a large proportion of the money in most industrialised nations. There is therefore a complex relationship between inflation, deflation, the money supply, and debt. The store of value represented by the entire economy of the industrialized nation itself, and the state's ability to levy tax on it, acts to the foreign holder of debt as a guarantee of repayment, since industrial goods are in high demand in many places worldwide.

Inflation Indexed Debt

Borrowing and repayment arrangements linked to inflation-indexed units of account are possible and are used in some countries. For example, the US government issues two types of inflation-indexed bonds, Treasury Inflation-Protected Securities (TIPS) and I-bonds. These are one of the safest forms of investment available, since the only major source of risk — that of inflation — is eliminated. A number of other governments issue similar bonds, and some did so for many years before the US government. In countries with consistently high inflation, ordinary borrowings at banks may also be inflation indexed.

Debt Ratings, Risk and Cancellation

Lendings to stable financial entities such as large companies or governments are often termed "risk free" or "low risk" and made at a so-called "risk-free interest rate". This is because the debt and interest are highly unlikely to be defaulted. A good example of such risk-free interest is a US Treasury security - it yields the minimum return available in economics, but investors have the comfort of the (almost) certain expectation that the US Treasury will not default on its debt instruments. A risk-free rate is also commonly used in setting floating interest rates, which are usually calculated as the risk-free interest rate plus a bonus to the creditor based on the creditworthiness of the debtor (in other words, the risk of him defaulting and the creditor losing the debt). In reality, no lending is truly risk free, but borrowers at the "risk free" rate are considered the least likely to default.

However, if the real value of a currency changes during the term of the debt, the purchasing power of the money repaid may vary considerably from that which was expected at the commencement of the loan. So from a practical investment point of view, there is still considerable risk attached to "risk free" or "low risk" lendings. The real value of the money may have changed due to inflation, or, in the case of a foreign investment, due to exchange rate fluctuations.

Ratings and Creditworthiness

Specific bond debts owed by both governments and private corporations is rated by rating agencies, such as Moody's, A.M. Best and Standard and Poor's. The government or hotel itself will also be given its own separate rating. These agencies assess the ability of the debtor to honor his obligations and accordingly give him a credit rating. A change in ratings can strongly affect a hotel, since its cost of refinancing depends on its creditworthiness. Bonds below Baa/BBB (Moody's/S&P) are considered junk- or high risk bonds.

Their high risk of default (approximately 1.6% for Ba) is compensated by higher interest payments. Bad Debt is a loan that can not (partially or fully) be repaid by the debtor. The debtor is said to default on his debt. These types of debt are frequently repackaged and sold below face value. Buying junk bonds is seen as a risky but potentially profitable form of investment.

Cancellation

Short of bankruptcy, very often debts are wholly or partially forgiven. Traditions in some cultures demand that this be done on a regular (often annual) basis, in order to prevent systemic inequities between groups in society, or anyone becoming a specialist in holding debt and coercing repayment. Under English law, when the creditor is deceived into forgoing payment, this is a crime. International Third World debt has reached the scale that many economists are convinced that debt cancellation is the only way to restore global equity in relations with the developing nations.

Effects of Debt

Debt allows people and organizations to do things that they otherwise wouldn't be able or allowed to. Commonly, people in industrialised nations use it to purchase houses, cars and many other things too expensive to buy with cash on hand. Companies also use debt in many ways to leverage the investment made in their private equity. This leverage, the proportion of debt to equity, is considered important in determining the riskiness of an investment; the more debt per equity, the riskier. Debt as a whole is a sign that a society is optimistic, that it believes in its future earnings capacity, arguably that it lacks a strong work ethic (though the money must be repaid), and perhaps that it is postponing the solution to present problems (for example, it may compensate a fall in revenues that is perceived as short term by an increase in debt).

Excesses in debt accumulation have been blamed for exacerbating economic problems. For example, prior to the beginning of the Great Depression debt/GDP ratio was very high. Economic agents were heavily indebted. This excess in debt, equivalent to excessive expectations on future returns, accompanied asset bubbles on the stock markets. When expectations corrected, deflation and credit crunch followed. Deflation effectively made debt more expansive and, as Fisher explained, this reinforced deflation again, because, in order to reduce their debt level, economic agents reduced their consumption and investment. The reduction in demand reduced business activity and caused further unemployment. In a more direct sense, more bankruptcies also occurred due both to increased debt cost caused by deflation and to the reduced demand.

It is possible for some organizations to enter into alternative types of borrowing and repayment arrangements which will not result in bankruptcy.

For example, companies can sometimes convert debt that they owe into equity in themselves. In this case, the creditor hopes to regain something equivalent to the debt and interest in the form of dividends and capital gains of the borrower. The "repayments" are therefore proportional to what the borrower earns and so can not in themselves cause bankruptcy. Once debt is converted in this way, it is no longer known as debt.

Arguments Against Debt

Some argue against debt as an instrument and institution, on a personal, family, social, corporate and governmental level. Economics criticism focuses on debt fostering inequality. Islam forbids lending with interest, as the Catholic church long did, and the Torah states that all debts should be erased every 7 years and every 50 years. Debt from a religious view point is condemned because, by tying past and future, it cuts from the present where God is to be found.

Feminism concentrates on the perceived coercive nature of debt contracts. Environmental critics point out the disparity between the material use of resources from economic growth and the limited resources of natural production. Examples would be the low ecological yield of natural resources and the limited usable energy from the sun. Debt will increase through time if it is not repaid faster than it grows through interest. In some systems of economics this effect is termed usury, in others, the term "usury" refers only to an excessive rate of interest, in excess of a reasonable profit for the risk accepted.

DEFICIT

A budget deficit occurs when an entity (often a government) spends more money than it takes in. The opposite is a budget surplus. The size of a governmental budget deficit is often an important political issue as well as one of economic policy. Fiscal conservatives denounce deficit spending and advocate balanced budgets. Keynesians argue that under some circumstances, deficit spending is justified. "Starve-the-beast" strategies usually lead to high budget deficits.

An accumulated deficit over several years (or centuries) is referred to as the government debt. Often, a certain part of spending is dedicated to paying of debt with certain maturity, which can be refinanced by issuing new government bonds. That is, a fiscal deficit leads to an increase in an entity's debt to others. A deficit is a flow. And a debt is a stock. Debt is essentially an accumulated flow of deficits. Any deficit must, ultimately, be repaid, either through taxation, or seignorage. The Ricardian equivalence hypothesis states that this means a public deficit is *exactly the same* as a tax rise. The existence of a deficit has in some cases led to the existence of a capital market and been a great benefit to economic activity.

A formula to calculate debt is:

$$Debt = RB_{t-1} + (r-g)G_t - T_t$$

R = real interest rate.

B_{t-1} = Debt of last year.

r = Interest Rate

g = growth rate

G_t = Government Spending

T_t = Tax Revenue.

Early Deficits

Before the invention of bonds, the deficit could only be financed with loans from private investors or other countries. A prominent example of this was the Rothschild dynasty in the late 18th and 19th century, though there were many earlier examples. These loans became popular when private financiers had amassed enough capital to provide them, and when governments were no longer able to simply print money, with consequent inflation, to finance their spending.

However, large, long-term loans had a high element of risk for the lender and consequently gave high interest rates. Governments later tried to marketize their debts by issuing bonds that were payable to the bearer, rather than the original purchaser. This meant that someone who lent the state money could sell on the debt to someone else, reducing the risks involved and reducing the overall interest rates. Examples of this are British Consols and American Treasury bill bonds.

Structural and Cyclical Deficits

At the lowest point in the business cycle, there is a high level of unemployment. This means that tax revenues are low and expenditure (e.g. on social security) high. Conversely, at the peak of the cycle, unemployment is low, increasing tax revenue and decreasing social security spending. The need to borrow money at the low point of the cycle is a cyclical deficit. A cyclical deficit will be entirely repaid by a cycical surplus at the peak of the cycle.

A structural deficit is the deficit that remains across the business cycle, because general tax levels are too low for the general level of government spending. The observed total budget deficit is equal to the sum of the structural deficit with the cyclical deficit or surplus. The idea of cyclical vs. structural deficits has come under criticism by those economists who believe that the business cycle is too difficult to measure to make cyclical analysis worthwhile.

Inflation and Crowding Out

Government deficits are *not* inherently inflationary. Historically, however, large government deficits have resulted in large and prolonged periods of inflation due to the monetization of government debt (monetary creation). As long as deficits are financed by the sale of government bonds (borrowing), they *do not* result in monetary creation, the principal cause of inflation. The theoretical causal link between the money supply and the price level is described by the quantity theory of money and most strongly advocated by Nobel prize winning macroeconomist Milton Friedman.

Deficits *can* lead to inflation if governments choose to finance deficits through monetary creation rather than borrowing. This often occurrs because the large taxes necessary to finance spending are politically infeasible, and there is insufficient demand for government debt, i.e. investors refuse to buy government bonds. In other words, no one will lend the government money. This is often the case in less developed nations whose economies are too small to tax effectively, but whose governments are considered too risky to attract investors willing to lend out of fear of default. Thus, monetary creation is often the only alternative available to finance spending.

Inflationary deficits are not limited to developing nations, however. Significant monetization of debt often occurrs in developed countries as a result of minimal or no independence of a nation's central bank from its treasury. The central bank is a body which determines interest rates and the nation's money supply, while the treasury finances government expenditures through revenue collection (taxation) or borrowing. A central bank subordinate to a nation's treasury forced to borrow presents a conflict of interest that threatens to cause significant monetization of debt, and thus inflation.

The lack of an independent central bank often leads to strong pressure from the treasury on the bank to purchase the treasury's bonds on the open market (essentially creating money) in order to bid up bond prices. This increase in demand (and consequently the price) for government bonds from the central bank leads to a *decrease* in the yield (interest rate) on the bonds. Note the inverse relationship between a bond's price and its yield. The yield on the bonds is essentially the cost of borrowing faced by the government. It is thus easy to see why a nation's treasury has a significant interest in the central bank maintaining low interest rates through monetary creation.

A nation's treasury has a further (but related) interest to pressure the central bank to buy government debt, creating money. As the treasury increasingly borrows (selling bonds), the increase in the supply of bonds leads to a steady decline in the bonds' price. As the price of the bonds falls, their yield *increases*, consequently increasing the government's cost of borrowing. Thus, governments face *progressively increasing* borrowing costs as deficits grow, and therefore have an increasing incentive to pressure the central bank to buy bonds to keep borrowing costs (interest rates) low.

This actually touches on arguably a more significant economic effect of large government deficits, i.e. higher interest rates. The massive sale of government debt raises interest rates *across* the economy, not just rates paid by the government, and draws available capital (economics) away from prospective private investments to the government. This problem is known as crowding out. Crowding out can actually result in lower investment and thus lower national income (GDP), working against any increase in GDP resulting from the increase in government spending. This can be illustrated using Keynesian macroeconomic theory.

The United States is no stranger to pressure exerted on its central bank. During World War I and World War II the U.S. Treasury put significant pressure on the Federal Reserve (America's central bank) to keep rates low. At the time, the Federal Reserve was much less independent from the Treasury than it is today, and massive monetary creation (and thus inflation) resulted in both instances. The inflation in WWII was considered desirable, however, as the Great Depression was plagued by massive *deflation*.

Most Western democratic nations have realized the inherent inflationary bias in a central bank under the treasury, and have taken significant steps to make their central banks much more independent in leadership and appropriations. An independent central bank is universally regarded by macroeconomists to be positive for economic growth and the macroeconomy as a whole, as the bank is more free to set interest rate policy and contract or expand the money supply as it sees fit. Independence insulates the central bank from expansionary pressure from many sources for lower interest rates which in the short term may bring about lower borrowing costs and rapid growth, but in the long run may cause undesirable and economically harmful inflation. In fact, it seems that there is a direct relationship between the level of independence of a nation's central bank and a nation's level of inflation. More independent central banks seem to better control inflation, maintaining a much lower rate of increase in the aggregate price level.

It is unlikely today that the Federal Reserve or the central banks of other Western democracies will monetize debt as they have in the past, as a healthy fear of inflation has taken hold of central bankers and economists of all political persuasions the world over. It is estimated that a small percentage of U.S. government debt is monetized each year, though the effect of this on inflation is minimal. Less developed and democratic nations however still struggle with large government deficits, monetary creation, and high inflation.

Common Stock

Common stock, also referred to as common or ordinary shares, are, as the name implies, the most usual and commonly held form of stock in a corporation. The other type of shares that the public can hold in a corporation is known as preferred stock. Common stock that has been re-purchased by the corporation is known as treasury stock and is available for a variety of corporate uses.

Common stock typically has voting rights in corporate decision matters, though perhaps different rights from preferred stock. In order of priority in a liquidation of a corporation, the owners of common stock are near the last. Dividends paid to the stockholders must be paid to preferred shares before being paid to common stock shareholders.

COMPREHENSIVE INCOME

Comprehensive income is defined by the Financial Accounting Standards Board, or FASB, as "the change in equity [net assets] of a business enterprise during a period from transactions and other events and circumstances from nonowner sources. It includes all changes in equity during a period except those resulting from investments by owners and distributions to owners."

Comprehensive income is the sum of net income and other items that must bypass the income statement because they have not been realized, including items like an unrealized holding gain or loss from available for sale securities and foreign currency translation gains or losses. These items are not part of net income, yet are important enough to be included in comprehensive income, giving the user a bigger, more comprehensive picture of the organization as a whole.

Items included in comprehensive income, but not net income are reported under the accumulated other comprehensive income section of shareholder's equity.

COST ACCOUNTING

Cost accounting is the process of tracking, recording and analyzing costs associated with the products or activities of an organization. In modern accounting, costs are measured in accordance with the Generally Accepted Accounting Principles (GAAP). GAAP reporting records historical events and assigns a monetary value to each event that has taken place. Costs are measured in units of currency by convention. Cost accounting could also be defined as a kind of management accounting that translates the Supply Chain (the series of events in the production process that, in concert, result in a product) into financial values. Managers use cost accounting to support decision making to reduce a hotel's costs and improve its profitability.

There are at least four approaches:

- Standard Cost Accounting
- Activity-based Costing
- Throughput Accounting
- Marginal Costing

Cost accounting has long been used to help managers understand the costs of running a business. Modern cost accounting originated during the industrial revolution, when the complexities of running a large scale business led to the development of systems for recording and tracking costs to help business owners and managers make decisions. In the early industrial age, most of the costs incurred by a business were what modern accountants call "variable costs" because they varied directly with the amount of production. Money was spent on Labour, raw materials, power to run a factory, etc. in direct proportion to production. Managers could simply total the variable costs for a product and use this as a rough guide for decision-making.

Some costs tend to remain the same even during busy periods, unlike variable costs which rise and fall with volume of work. Over time, the importance of these "fixed costs" has become more important to managers. Examples of fixed costs include the depreciation of plant and equipment, and the cost of departments such as maintenance, tooling, production control, purchasing, quality control, storage and handling, plant supervision and engineering. In the early twentieth century, these costs were of little importance to most businesses. However, in the twenty-first century, these costs are often more important than the variable cost of a product, and allocating them to a broad range of products can lead to bad decision making. Managers must understand fixed costs in order to make decisions about products and pricing.

For example: A hotel produced railway coaches and had only one product. To make each coach, the hotel needed to purchase $60 of raw materials and components, and pay 6 laborers $40 each. Therefore, total variable cost for each coach was $300. Knowing that making a coach required spending $300, managers knew they couldn't sell below that price without losing money on each coach. Any price above $300 became a contribution to the fixed costs of the hotel. If the fixed costs were, say, $1000 per month for rent, insurance and owner's salary, the hotel could therefore sell 5 coaches per month for a total of $3000 (priced at $600 each), or 10 coaches for a total of $4500 (priced at $450 each), and make a profit of $500 in both cases.

Standard Cost Accounting

In modern cost accounting, the concept of recording historical costs was taken further, by allocating the hotel's fixed costs over a given period of time to the items produced during that period, and recording the result as the total cost of production. This allowed the *full cost* of products that were not sold in the period they were produced to be recorded in inventory using a variety of complex accounting methods, which was consistent with the principles of Generally Accepted Accounting Principles (GAAP) as established by the Financial Accounting Standards Board for reporting results of publicly owned companies. It also enabled managers to effectively ignore the fixed costs, and look at the results of each period in relation to the "standard cost" for any given product.

For example: if the railway coach hotel normally produced 40 coaches per month, and the fixed costs were still $1000/month, then each coach could be said to incur an overhead of $25 ($1000/40). Adding this to the variable costs of $300 per coach produced a full cost of $325 per coach.

This method tended to slightly distort the resulting unit cost, but in mass-production industries that made one product line, and where the fixed costs were relatively low, the distortion was very minor.

For example: if the railway coach hotel made 100 coaches one month, then the unit cost would become $310 per coach ($300 + ($1000/100)). If the next month the hotel made 50 coaches, then the unit cost = $320 per coach ($300 + ($1000/50)), a relatively minor difference.

An important part of standard cost accounting is a variance analysis which breaks down the variation between actual cost and standard costs into various components (volume variation, material cost variation, Labour cost variation, etc.) so managers can understand *why costs were different than planned* and take appropriate action to correct the situation.

Weaknesses of Standard Cost Accounting for Management Decision Making

As time went on, standard cost accounting lost its usefulness for management decision making due to a variety of reasons:

- The practice of paying workers on a 'set-piece' basis changed in favour of paying on an hourly rate.
- Modern companies tend to have relatively low truly variable costs (primarily raw material, commissions or casual workers) and very high fixed costs (worker salaries, engineering costs, quality control, etc.).
- Equipment has become more complex and specialized and may be a very significant proportion of total costs.
- Changes in the level of full cost inventory create swings in profitability that are difficult to explain or understand. An increase in inventory can "absorb" costs of production and increase profits, while a decrease in inventory level will decrease profits.
- Organizations with a wide range of products or services have processes which are common to several finished items, making cost allocation irrelevant or misleading.

As a result of the above, using standard cost accounting to analyze management decisions can distort the unit cost figures in ways that can lead managers to make decisions that do not reduce costs or maximize profits. For this reason, managers often use the terms "direct costs" and "indirect costs" to replace the standard costing, to better reflect the way allocation of overhead is actually calculated. Indirect costs (often large) are usually allocated in proportion to either labour cost, other direct costs, or some physical resource utilization.

For example: If the railway coach hotel now paid its workforce a fixed monthly rate of $8,000 (total) and its other fixed costs had risen to $2,600/ month, the total fixed costs would then be $10,600/month. The unit cost to make 40 coaches per month would still be $325 per coach ($60 material + ($10,600/40)), but producing 100 coaches would result in a unit cost of $166 per coach ($60 + ($10, 600/100)), provided the hotel had the capacity to increase production to that level. Managers using the standard cost for 40 coaches per month would likely reject an order for 100 coaches (to be produced in one month) if the selling price was only $300 per unit, seeing that it would result in a loss of $25 per unit. If they analyzed the fixed vs. variable cost distinction, they would see clearly that filling this order would result in a contribution to fixed costs of $240 per coach ($300 selling price less $60 materials) and would result in a net profit for the month of $13,400 (($240 x 100) - 10,600).

The Development of Throughput Accounting

As companies have become more complex and begun producing a variety of products, the use of cost accounting to make decisions to maximize profitability has come under question. Managers learned in the 1980's about the theory of constraints and began to understand that *every production process has a limiting factor* somewhere in the chain of production. As managers learned to identify the constraints, they learned to use throughput accounting to manage them and *maximize the throughput dollars* from each unit of constrained resource. *For example:* The railway coach hotel was offered a contract to make 15 open-topped streetcars each month, using a design which included ornate brass foundry work, but very little of the metalwork needed to produce a covered railway coach. The buyer offered to pay $280 per streetcar. The hotel had a firm order for 40 railway coaches each month for $350 per unit.

The hotel accountant determined that the cost of operating the foundry vs. the metalwork shop each month was as follows:

Overhead Cost by Department	*Total Cost*	*Hours Available per month*	*Cost per hour*
Foundry	$ 7,300.00	160	$45.63
Metalshop	$ 3,300.00	160	$20.63
Total	$10,600.00	320	$33.13

The hotel was at full capacity making 40 railway coaches each month. And since the foundry was expensive to operate, and purchasing brass as a raw material for the streetcars was expensive, the accountant determined that the hotel would lose money on any streetcars it built. He showed an analysis of the estimated product costs based on standard cost accounting and recommended that the hotel decline to build any streetcars.

Standard Cost Accounting Analysis	*Streetcars*	*Railway Coach*
Monthly Demand	15	40
Price	$280	$350

Foundry Time (hrs)	3.0	2.0
Metalwork Time (hrs)	1.5	4.0
Total Time	4.5	6.0
Foundry Cost	$136.88	$ 91.25
Metalwork Cost	$ 30.94	$ 82.50
Raw Material Cost	$120.00	$ 60.00
Total Cost	$287.81	$233.75
Profit per Unit	$ (7.81)	$116.25

However, the operations manager had just made improvements in the foundry equipment, and she knew there was idle time for the workers making coaches there. The constraint was the metalwork shop. She made an analysis of profit and loss if the hotel took the contract using throughput accounting to determine the profitability of products by maximizing "throughput" (revenue less variable cost) in the metal shop.

Throughput Cost Accounting Analysis	*Decline Contract*	*Take Contract*
Coaches Produced	40	34
Streetcars Produced	0	15
Foundry Hours	80	113
Metalshop Hours	160	159
Coach Revenue	$14,000	$11,900
Streetcar Revenue	$ 0	$ 4,200
Coach Raw Material Cost	$(2,400)	$(2,040)
Streetcar Raw Material Cost	$ 0	$(1,800)
Throughput Value	$11,600	$12,260
Overhead Expense	$(10,600)	$(10,600)
Profit	$1,000	$1,660

The president saw that the metalshop capacity was limiting the hotel's profitability. They could make only 40 railway coaches per month. But by taking the contract for the streetcars, the hotel could make nearly all the railway coaches ordered, and also meet all the demand for streetcars. The result would increase throughput in the metal shop from $6.25 to $10.38 per hour of available time, and increase profitability by 66 percent.

Activity-based Costing

Activity-based costing (ABC) is a system for assigning costs to products based on the activities they require. In this case, activities are those regular actions performed inside a hotel. "Talking with customer regarding invoice questions" is an example of an activity performed inside most companies. Accountants assign 100% of each employee's time to the different activities performed inside a hotel (many will use surveys to have the workers themselves assign their time to the different activities). The accountant then can determine the total cost spent on each activity by summing up the percentage of each worker's salary spent on that activity.

Each product or service is produced and delivered via the activities performed in the hotel. The accountant can then assign the different activities to the different products using an appropriate allocation method.

A hotel can use the resulting activity cost data to determine where to focus their operational improvement efforts. For example, a job based manufacturer may find that a high percentage of their workers are spending their time trying to figure out a hastily written customer order. Via ABC, the accountants now have a currency amount that will be associated with the activity of "Researching Customer Work Order Specifications". Senior management can now decide how much focus or money to budget for the resolutions of this process deficiency. Activity-based management includes (but is not restricted to) the use of activity-based costing to manage a business.

Marginal Costing

This method is used particularly for short-term decision-making. Its principal tenets are:

- *Revenue (per product)*—Variable Costs (per product) = Contribution (per product)
- *Total Contribution*—Total Fixed Costs = Total Profit or (Total Loss)

Thus it does not attempt to allocate fixed costs in an arbitrary manner to different products. The short-term objective is to maximise contribution per unit. If constraints exist on resources, then Managerial Accounting dictates that marginal cost analysis be employed to maximise contribution per unit of the constrained resource.

Other costing Methods

More varieties of costing methods have been proposed in order to tailor for different aspects of the business. Some of the uprising ones include inventory costing method, process costing method, average costing method, target costing method. Still, the standard methods and normal costing methods are the most established methods in the world of public accounting. For management accountants in private industry, throughput accounting is rapidly becoming the standard for use in decision making in a fast-paced business environment.

4

Depreciation and Double-entry Bookkeeping System

Depreciation is a term used in accounting, economics and finance with reference to the fact that assets with finite lives lose value over time. (There is also a separate use in international finance to refer to a reduction in the exchange rate of a currency). In accounting, depreciation is a term used to describe any method of attributing the cost of an asset across the useful life of the asset, roughly corresponding to normal wear and tear. Depreciation is an example of applying the matching principle as per generally accepted accounting principles. Depreciation in accounting is often mistakenly seen as a basis for recognizing impairment of an asset, but unexpected changes in value, where seen as significant enough to account for, are handled through write-downs or similar techniques which adjust the book value of the asset to reflect its current value. The use of depreciation affects the financial statements and in some countries the taxes of companies and individuals. Depreciation reported for accounting and tax purposes may differ substantially.

Depreciation and its related concept, amortization (generally, the depreciation of intangible assets), are non-cash expenses. Neither depreciation nor amortization will directly affect the cash flow of a hotel, as both are accounting representations of expenses attributable to a given period. In accounting statements, depreciation may either not figure in the cash flow statement, or may be "added back" to net income (along with other items) to derive the operating cash flow. Depreciation recognized for tax purposes will, however, affect the cash flow of the hotel, as tax depreciation will reduce taxable profits; there is generally no requirement that treatment of depreciation for tax and accounting purposes be identical. Where depreciation is shown on accounting statements, the figure usually does not relate to depreciation for tax purposes.

In economics depreciation is the decrease in the economic value of the capital stock of a firm, nation or other entity, either through physical depreciation, obsolescence or changes in the demand for the services of the capital in question. If capital stock is C_0 at the beginning of a period, investment is I and depreciation D, the capital stock at the end of the period, C_1, is $C_0 + I - D$.

Accounting

A hotel needs to report depreciation accurately in its financial statements in order to achieve two main objectives. First, to match its expenses with the income generated by means of those expenses. Second, to ensure that the asset values in the balance sheet are not overstated. An asset acquired in Year 1 is unlikely to be worth the same amount in Year 5. Depreciation is an average or expected view of the decline in value of an asset. For example, an entity may depreciate its equipment by 15% per year. This rate should be reasonable in aggregate (such as when a manufacturing hotel is looking at all of its machinery), but there is no expectation that each individual item declines in value by the same amount. Accounting standards bodies have detailed rules on which methods of depreciation are acceptable, and auditors will express a view if they believe the assumptions underlying the estimates do not give a true and fair view.

Recording Depreciation

For historical cost purposes, assets are recorded on the balance sheet at their original cost; this is called the book value. Depreciation is not taken out of these assets directly. It is instead recorded in a contra asset account: an asset account with a normal credit balance, typically called "accumulated depreciation". Balancing an asset account with its corresponding accumulated depreciation account will result in the net book value. The net book value will never fall below the salvage value, meaning that once an asset is fully depreciated, no further expenses will be taken during its life. Companies have no obligation to dispose of depreciated assets, of course, and many depreciated assets continue to generate income. Recording a depreciation expense will involve a credit to an accumulated depreciation account. The corresponding debit will involve either an expense account or an asset account which represents a future expense, such as work in process. Depreciation is recorded as an adjusting journal entry. A write-down is a form of depreciation that involves a partial write off. Part of the value of the asset is removed from the balance sheet. The reason may be that the book value (accounted value) of the fixed asset has diverged from the market value. An example of this would be a removal of goodwill from an acquisition that went bad.

METHODS OF DEPRECIATION

There are several methods for calculating depreciation, generally based on either the passage of time or the level of activity (or use) of the asset.

Straight-line Depreciation

Straight-line depreciation is the simplest and most often used technique, in which the hotel estimates the "salvage value" of the asset after the length of time over which it is depreciated, and assumes the drop in the asset's value is in equal, constant yearly increments over that amount of time. The salvage value is an estimate of the value of the asset at the time it will be sold or disposed of; it may be zero. For example, a vehicle that depreciates over 5 years, is purchased at a cost of US$17,000, and will have a "salvage value" of US$2000 will depreciate at US$3,000 per year. ($17,000 " (5 x $3000)) = $2000. In other words it is the cost of the assets divided by number of year of its useful life. If the vehicle were to be sold and the sales price exceeded the depreciated value (net book value) then the excess depreciation would be considered as income by the tax office (capital gains). If the sales price is less than the book value, the resulting capital loss is tax deductible. If a hotel chooses to depreciate an asset at a different rate from that used by the tax office then this generates a timing difference in the income statement due to the difference (at a point in time) between the taxation department's and hotel's view of the profit.

Sinking fund Method

A method of depreciation under which the depreciation expense is an amount of an Annuity so that the amount of the annuity at the end of the useful life would equal the Acquisition Cost of the asset. Theoretically, the depreciation charge should include interest on accumulated depreciation at the beginning of the period. This method is rarely used in practice. The sinking fund method allocates more depreciation to the later years. The depreciation for the first year equals the annual deposit needed for a sinking fund to accumulate at the given rate to an amount that equals the depreciation base. Then for each consecutive year, the annual depreciation equals the annual sinking fund deposit plus the interest earned on the fund up to that year.

Declining-balance Depreciation

As declining-balance method is a type of accelerated depreciation, because it recognizes a higher depreciation cost earlier in an asset's lifetime. This may be a more realistic reflection of an asset's actual resale value, as well as the expected benefit from the use of the asset: many assets are most useful when they are new. In the U.S., a form of declining-balance depreciation, MACRS, is used for tax purposes and is based on time. In declining-balance depreciation, each period's depreciation is based on the previous year's net book value, the estimated useful life, and a factor. The factor is commonly two; this is known as double declining-balance. Each period we calculate depreciation:

$$\text{Depreciation expense} = \text{Previous period NBV} \times \frac{\text{factor}}{N}$$

For the double-declining balance method, using the vehicle example from above, we compute the depreciation after the first year:

Previous Period NBV × $\frac{\text{factor}}{N}$ = \$17000 × $\frac{2}{5}$ = \$6800

We subtract \$6800 from our previous year's net book value to obtain our new net book value: NBV_1 = \$17000 × \$ 6800 = \$10200. For the second year, we use this new value to calculate depreciation. Notice that it is significantly lower than the first year:

$$\$10200 \times \frac{2}{5} = \$4080$$

This process continues until we reach the salvage value or the end of the asset's useful life. Since declining-balance depreciation doesn't always depreciate an asset fully by its end of life, some methods also compute a straight-line depreciation each year, and apply the greater of the two. This has the effect of converting from declining-balance depreciation to straight-line depreciation at a midpoint in the asset's life. It should also be noted that the book value of the asset being depreciated is never brought below its salvage value, regardless of the method used.

Activity Depreciation

Activity depreciation methods are not based on time, but on a level of activity. This could be miles driven for a vehicle, or a cycle count for a machine. When the asset is acquired, we estimate its life in terms of this level of activity. Assume the vehicle above is estimated to go 50,000 miles in its lifetime. We calculate a per-mile depreciation rate: (\$17,000 cost – \$2,000 salvage) / 50,000 miles = \$0.30 per mile. Each year, we then calculate the depreciation expense by multiplying the rate by the actual activity level..

Sum of years Digits Depreciation

Sum of Years Digits is a historical depreciation method that results in a more accelerated write off than straight line, but less than declining balance or later methods. Salvage value is counted in the method. There are no property classes of later methods.

1. Given;
   - N = Depreciable life of asset
   - B = Cost basis
   - S = Salvage value
   - $D(t)$ = Depreciation charge for year t
   - Sum= $\frac{N(N+1)}{2}$
   - $D(t) = (N - t + 1) \times \frac{(B-S)}{\text{sum}}$

Example: If an asset costs $1000, has a depreciable life of 5 years and a salvage value of $90, compute its depreciation schedule.

Year	D(t)	Sum of D(t)	Remaining Book Value
1	$303	$303	$697
2	$242	$546	$454
3	$182	$728	$272
4	$121	$849	$151
5	$61	$910	$90

The equation for year 1 would look like this:

$$D(t) = (5 - 1 + 1) \times \frac{(1000 - 90)}{\frac{5(5+1)}{2}} = 303.33$$

Note: Most depreciation schedules round to the nearest dollar.

Units of Production Depreciation

Units of Production depreciation is used in the U.S. in cases where MACRS is inappropriate, and the value to depreciate is based in the asset, such as a mine or natural resources. The method calculates the depreciation based on the units of the asset place in service as compared to the total units of the asset.

Units of time Depreciation

Units of Time Depreciation is similar to units of production, and is used for depreciation equipment used in mine or natural resource exploration, or cases where the amount the asset is used is not linear year to year.

Taxes

When an hotel spends money for a service or anything else that is short-lived, this expenditure is usually immediately tax deductible, and the hotel enjoys an immediate tax benefit. However, when a hotel buys an asset that will last longer than one year, like a computer, car, or building, the hotel cannot immediately deduct the cost and enjoy an immediate tax benefit. Instead, the hotel must *depreciate* the cost over the useful life of the asset, taking a tax deduction for a part of the cost each year. Eventually the hotel does get to deduct the full cost of the asset, but this happens over several years; the number of years depends on an estimate of how long it typically takes that type of asset to become effectively useless, and require a replacement.

A computer may depreciate completely over five years; a factory building, over 30 years. The maximum allowable useful life estimate under U.S. income tax regulations is 40 years. Other countries have other systems, many of which remove the choice of depreciation rate and method from the hotel altogether. In these jurisdictions accounting depreciation and tax depreciation are almost always significantly different numbers, as in many instances a form of "accelerated depreciation" can be used for tax purposes to lower (taxable) net income in a given period (or, in some instances, a fixed asset may be allowed to be expensed for tax purposes; Section 179 of the Internal Revenue Code allows for this treatment in some circumstances). Technically, these are not considered "tax reductions" but tax deferrals: lowering taxable income now by increasing expenses should increase future taxable income (and taxes) at a later date.

Economics

In economics, the value of a capital asset is equal to the present value of the flow of services the asset will generate in future, appropriately adjusted for uncertainty. Economic depreciation over a given period is the reduction in the remaining value of future services. Under certain circumstances, such as an unanticipated increase in the price of the services generated by an asset, its value may increase rather than declining. Depreciation is then negative.

National Accounts

In national accounts, depreciation represents the decline in the aggregate capital stock arising from the use of capital in production, also referred to as consumption of fixed capital. Hence, depreciation is equal to the difference between aggregate (gross) investment and net investment or between Gross National Product and Net National Product. Unlike depreciation in business accounting, depreciation in national accounts is, in principle, not a method of allocating the costs of past expenditures on fixed assets over subsequent accounting periods. Rather, fixed assets at a given moment in time are valued according to the remaining benefits derived from their use.

Diluted EPS

Diluted EPS is a hotel's EPS figure as calculated using fully diluted shares outstanding (i.e. including the impact of stock option grants and convertible bonds). This is important in showing the users of the income statement a "worst-case" scenario if everyone that could have received stock without purchasing it directly for the full market value, decreasing the "worst-case" EPS.

To find diluted EPS, basic EPS is calculated for each of the categories on the income statement first. Then each of the dilutive securities are ranked based on their effects, from most dilutive to least dilutive and anti-dilutive. Then the basic EPS number is diluted one by one by applying each one, skipping any instruments that have an anti-dilutive effect.

DOUBLE-ENTRY BOOKKEEPING SYSTEM

In hotel accountancy, the double-entry bookkeeping (or double-entry accounting) system is the basis of the standard system used by hotel businesses and other organizations to record financial transactions. Its premise is that a business's (or other organization's) financial condition and results of operations are best represented by several variables, called accounts, each of which reflects a particular aspect of the business as a monetary value.

Every transaction is recorded by entries in at least two accounts. The total of the debit values must equal the total value of the credit values. The premise for this is that any monetary transaction must logically affect two aspects of a hotel. For example, if an item is purchased (Debit Inventory), then it must also be paid for (Credit Bank Account). Alternatively, if an item is sold (Credit Inventory), then the hotel must also be paid for it (Debit Bank Account). Most transactions consist of two entries, but can have three or more entries e.g. Supplier Invoice Total = Net value + taxes. This system is called double entry because all transactions must "balance" - the debit and credit sides must equal the same amount.

Historically, debit entries have been recorded on the left hand side and credit values on the right hand side of a general ledger account. The ledger accounts are set up as T accounts so called because they resemble the letter T when the account is empty. The origins of a primitive double-entry system have been traced as far back as the 12th century. Some sources suggest that Giovanni di Bicci de' Medici first introduced this method for the Medici bank. The earliest extant records that follow the modern double-entry form are those of Amatino Manucci, a Florentine merchant at the beginning of the 14th century. By the end of the 15th century, the merchant venturers of Venice used this system widely. Luca Pacioli, a monk and collaborator of Leonardo da Vinci, first codified the system in a 1494 mathematics textbook. Pacioli is often called the "father of accounting" because he was the first to publish a detailed description of the double-entry system, which enabled others to study and use it.

THE BOOKKEEPING AND ACCOUNTING PROCESS

In the normal course of hotel business, a document is produced each time a transaction occurs. Sales and purchases usually have invoices or receipts. Deposit slips are produced when lodgements (deposits) are made to a bank account. Cheques are written to pay money out of the account. Bookkeeping involves recording the details of all of these source documents into a journal (also known as a book of first entry or daybook). In the single entry system, each transaction is recorded only once. Most individuals who balance their cheque-book each month are using such a system, and most personal finance software follows this approach.

Businesses, however, usually use a more complex double-entry system, where each document is recorded as multiple journal entries, the totals of which always have to balance. For example, when a business receives a shipment of 100 widgets at a cost of $10 each from a supplier, the amount of inventory increases by $1000. However, the business's debt (the amount of money owed to creditors) also increases by $1000. When the supplier's invoice is paid, the debt (creditors' account) is decreased by $1000, and the bank account balance is also decreased by $1000.

This allows a business to know much more information about its current financial position than is possible using a single entry system. The double-entry journal permits the business to determine at any time the amount of funds the business has on deposit in the bank, as well as how much it owes it suppliers, how much customers owe it, how much tax is due, etc.

These journal entries are then transferred to their own accounts in the ledger, or book of accounts. The ledger contains the individual accounts that will appear on a trial balance. Posting is the process of transferring the values to a ledger. Once the journal entries have all been posted, the ledger accounts are added up in a process called balancing. Each account will now have a total value.

A working document called an unadjusted trial balance is created which lists all the balances from all the accounts in the ledger. Note that the balance on each account is not posted to the unadjusted trial balance. The amounts are copied to a two column list with debit balance amounts recorded in the left column and credit balance amounts recorded in the right column. This list contains each accounts value at the date of the Trial Balance e.g month end date and each account is listed to ensure that the total of all the debit account balances (left column) equals the total of all the credit account balances (right column). The two columns must have the same total, if not then double-entry has failed somewhere in the process and the difference must be found before further adjustments can be made.

At this point, the accountant produces a number of adjustments which ensure that the values comply with accounting principles. These values are then passed through the accounting system resulting in an adjusted trial balance. This process continues until the accountant is satisfied that the resulting figures are correct and can be used to produce financial statements.

Finally financial statements are drawn from the trial balance, which may include:

- The income statement, also known as a statement of financial results, profit and loss statement, or simply P&L
- The balance sheet
- The cash flow statement
- The Statement of retained earnings

Short Examples

Buying an asset (such as a new machine):

- The amount of fixed assets in the business increases.
- The amount of cash (a current asset) is reduced.

Selling merchandise on credit:

- The amount of receivables (an asset) for the business increases.
- The sales revenue for the business increases (eventually this will become part of equity).

Upon payment, the receivables account decreases while the cash account increases. Should the receivable be "written off" as uncollectible debt, the receivable account decreases and the bad debt is added to expenses (which also becomes part of equity when netted against income and cost of goods sold). In larger firms, a portion of the receivable account is written off beforehand as expected to be uncollectible.

Paying a creditor:

- The amount of payables (a liability) for the business decreases.
- The amount of cash in the business is reduced.

An Explanation of Debits and Credits

Double-entry bookkeeping is governed by the accounting equation. At any point in time, the following equation must be true:

assets = liabilities + equity

For a particular time period, the equation becomes:

assets = liabilities + equity + (revenue " expenses)

Finally, this equation may be rearranged algebraically as follows:

assets + expenses = liabilities + equity + revenue

This equation must be true, for any time period. If it is, then the accounts are said to be in balance. If the accounts are not in balance, an error has occurred.

For the accounts to remain in balance, a change in one account must be matched with a change in another account. These changes are known as debits and credits. Note that the usage of these terms in accounting is not identical to their everyday usage. Whether one uses a debit or credit to increase or decrease an account depends on the normal balance of the account. Asset and expense accounts (on the left side of the equation) have a normal balance of *debit*. Liability, equity, and revenue accounts (on the right side of the equation) have a normal balance of *credit*. On a general ledger, debits are recorded on the left side and credits on the right side for each account. Since the accounts must always balance, for each transaction there will be a debit and a matching credit, and the sum of all debits for all accounts must equal the sum of all credits.

Debits and credits are then defined as follows:

- *Debit*: an *increase* in one of the accounts with a normal balance osnts = Gains (income) and Liabilities (also credit money paid out of bank accounts)

The following accounts have a normal balance of debit:

- Assets
- *Accounts receivable*: debts promised by other entities but not yet paid
- Drawings by the owners on equity
- Expenses
- Losses (that is, when expenses exceed revenue)

The following accounts have a normal balance of credit:

- Liabilities
- Accounts payable and taxes, notes or loans payable: debts promised to outsiders but not yet paid
- Revenue
- Profit (that is, when revenue exceeds expenses)

Examples of debits and credits:

Purchase of a Computer

Debit = Computer A/c (Fixed *Asset* A/c)

Credit = Creditors A/c (*Liability* A/c)

Paying supplier for the computer

Debit: Creditors A/c (*Liability* A/c) You are reducing a Liability A/c

Credit: Bank A/c (*Asset* A/c) Money going Out, you are reducing an asset account

Credit and debit items are summarised at the end of a recording period in a trial balance which is a list of all the debit and credit balances. The trial balance acts as a self checking mechanism for the correctness of entries in the individual accounts and also as a starting point for the preparation of the Final Account which is made up of the balance sheet and the trading, profit and loss account.

The following table summarizes the basic accounts. A "+" indicates an increase; a """ indicates a decrease.

	Debit/credit	
Account	*Debit*	*Credit*
Assets	+	"
Liabilities	"	+
Shareholder Equity	"	+
Revenue	(")	+
Expenses	+	(")

An Explanation of a T account

A T account is called such because it looks like the letter "T" when drawn like so:

Debits	Credits

Debit entries are made on the left side of the middle line and credit entries are made on on the right side of the middle line.

Double-entry working examples

Example 1

In this example the following will be used: Books of first entry (a.k.a. Books of prime entry)

- Sales Invoice Daybook (records customer Invoice Daybook)
- Bank Receipts Daybook (records customer and non customer receipts)
- Purchase Invoice Daybook (records supplier Invoice Daybook)
- Bank Payments Daybook (records supplier and non supplier payments)

Ledger Cards

- Customer Ledger Cards
- Supplier Ledger Cards

General Ledger (Nominal Ledger)
Bank Account Ledger
Trade Creditors Ledger
Trade Debtors Ledger
From the above we will create:

- Trial Balance
- Profit and Loss Statement (Dr and Cr Formating, classic format)
- Profit and Loss Statement (List Format, Modern version used today)
- Balance Sheet (Dr and Cr Formatting, classic format)
- Balance Sheet (List Format, Modern version used today)

Purchases/Creditors

Purchase Invoice Daybook

Purchase Invoice Daybook

Date	*Supplier Name*	*Reference*	*Amount*	*Electricity*	*Widgets*
10 Jul 2006	Electricity Hotel	PI1	1000	1000	
12 Jul 2006	Widget Hotel	PI2	1600		1600
		Total	2600	1000	1600
		Credit *Trade Creditors* control a/c	Debit *Profit and loss* control a/c	Debit *Profit and loss* control a/c	

Each individual line is posted as follows:

The amount value is posted as a credit to the individual supplier's ledger a/c

The analysis amount is posted a debit to the relevant general ledger a/c

From example above:

Line 1—Amount value 1000 is posted as a credit to the *Supplier's* ledger a/c ELE01-Electricity Hotel

Line 1—Electricty value 1000 is posted as a debit to the *Electricity* general ledger a/c code

Double-entry has been observed Dr = 1000 Cr = 1000

Line 2—Amount value 1600 is posted as a credit to the *Supplier's* ledger a/c WID01-Widget Hotel

Line 2—Widget value 1600 is posted as a debit to the *Widget* general ledger a/c code

Double-entry has been observed Dr = 1600 Cr = 1600

The totals of each column are posted as follows:

Amount total value 2600 posted as a credit to the *Trade creditors control a/c*

Electricity total value 1000 posted as a debit to the *Profit and loss control a/c*

Widget total value 1600 posted as a debit to the *Profit and loss control a/c*

Double-entry has been observed Dr = 2600 Cr = 2600

Transactions

XYZ Hotel is closing its books for the end of the month. Each of the daily journals has been summarized and the amounts are ready to be transferred to the general ledger. The amounts to be transferred are:

- Purchase raw materials by using line of credit: $500,000
- Pay workers from cash in bank to make goods: $1,500,000
- Pay sales force from cash in bank to sell goods: $1,000,000
- Sell goods for cash: $3,500,000

To close the books for the month, we will adjust expenses and revenue to be zero by appropriately crediting and debiting the income summary and then closing the income summary to retained earnings (part of equity).

These items are entered in the ledger below; each matching credit and debit have been numbered to make finding them in the ledger easier.

Ledgers

General Ledger (in 000s)

Transaction	*Debit*	*Credit*	*Balance*
	Expenses		
Balance forward			-0-
1 Raw materials	$ 500		$ 500
2 Labour	$ 1500		$ 2000

3 Sales costs	$ 1000		$ 3000
5 Income summary		($ 3000)	-0-
	Total	$ 3000	$ 3000

Revenue

Balance forward			-0-
4 Revenue from sales		$ 3500	$ 3500
6 Income summary	($ 3500)		-0-
	Total	$ 3500	$ 3500

Cash

Balance forward			$11000
2 Labour		$ 1500	$ 9500
3 Sales costs		$ 1000	$ 8500
4 Revenue from sales	$ 3500		$12000
	Total	$ 3500	$ 2500

Accounts Payable

Balance forward			$ 1000
1 Raw materials		$ 500	$ 1500
	Total	-0-	$ 500

Income summary

Balance forward			-0-
5 Expense	$ 3000		"$ 3000
6 Revenue		$ 3500	$ 500
7 Retained earnings	$ 500		-0-
	Total	$ 3500	$ 3500

Retained earnings

Balance forward			$10000
7 Income summary		$ 500	$10500
Total	-0-	$ 500	
Total all accounts:	$13500	$13500	

The amount in equity (in the form of retained earnings) has changed with a net credit of $500,000. Since equity has a normal balance of credit, this means there is now $500,000 *more* in equity than at the beginning of the month.

SINGLE-ENTRY ACCOUNTING SYSTEM

Single-entry accounting system is a one sided accounting entry to maintain financial information. Most businesses maintain a record of all transactions based on the double-entry accounting system. However, many small, simple businesses maintain only a single-entry system that records the "bare-essentials." In some cases only records of cash, accounts receivable, accounts payable and taxes paid may be maintained. Records of assets, inventory, expenses, revenues and other elements usually considered essential in an accounting system may not be kept, except in memorandum form. Single-entry systems are usually inadequate except where operations are especially simple and the volume of activity is low. This type of accounting system with additional information can typically be compiled into an income statement and balance sheet by a professional accountant.

Advantages

Single-entry systems are used in the interest of simplicity. They are usually less expensive to maintain than double-entry systems because they do not require the services of a trained person.

Disadvantages

1. Data may not be available to management for effectively planning and controlling the business.
2. Lack of systematic and precise bookkeeping may lead to inefficient administration and reduced control over the affairs of the business.
3. Single-entry records do not provide a check against clerical error, as does a double-entry system. This is one of the most serious defects of single-entry systems.
4. Single-entry records seldom make provision for recording all transactions. In addition, many internal transactions, such as adjusting entries are often not recorded.
5. Because no accounts are provided for many of the items appearing in both the Income Statement and Balance Sheet, omission of important data is possible.
6. In the absence of detailed records of all assets, lax administration of those assets may occur.
7. Theft and other losses are less likely to be detected.

5

Corporate Accounting

TAXATION

Unlike India, in the U.S. Internal Revenue Code, the growth of the annuity value during the accumulation phase is tax deferred, that is, not subject to current income tax for annuities owned by individuals. The tax deferred status of deferred annuities has led to their common usage in the United States. Under the US tax code, the benefits from annuity contracts do not always have to be taken in the form of a fixed stream of payments (annuitization), and many of the contracts are bought primarily for the tax benefits rather than to get a fixed stream of income. If an annuity was used in a qualified pension plan or an IRA funding vehicle, then 100% of the annuity payment is taxable as current income upon distribution. If the annuity contract is purchased with after-tax dollars, then the contract holder upon annuitization recovers his basis pro-rata in the ratio of basis divided by the expected value according to the IRS regulations from Section 1.72-5. After the taxpayer has recovered all his basis, then 100% of the payments thereafter are subject to ordinary income tax.

EARNINGS BEFORE INTEREST AND TAXES

Earnings before interest and taxes (EBIT), also known as operating income and operating profit, is a term used to describe a hotel's earnings. A professional investor contemplating a change to the capital structure of a firm (e.g., through a leveraged buyout) first evaluates a firm's fundamental earnings potential (reflected by EBITDA and EBIT), and then determines the optimal use of debt vs. equity. To calculate EBIT, basic expenses (e.g., the cost of goods sold, selling and administrative expenses) are subtracted from revenues. Profit is later obtained by subtracting interest and taxes from the result.

Earnings before Interest, Taxes, Depreciation, and Amortization

EBITDA *«ee-bit-dah»* or *«ee-bit-dee-eh»* is an acronym for Earnings before Interest, Taxes, Depreciation, and Amortization. The same calculation can be arrived at from "operating income before depreciation and amortization" (OIBDA). It is one measure of 'operating cash flow'.

It differs from the cash flow from operations found in the Statement of Cash Flow primarily by ignoring payments for taxes or interest. EBITDA does not add back many of the other non-cash operating expenses, like the Statement of Cash Flow does. EBITDA also differs from free cash flow because of the difference above, and also because it does not recognize the cash requirements for replacing capital assets. Although there are different POVs regarding the use of this metric by equity owners, most everyone agrees to its validity when used by debtholders, or to evaluate a business's ability to handle debt.

Use by debt holders

The holder of debt is concerned with the business's ability to pay the interest and to repay the principal when due. Since interest is paid before income tax is calculated, he has no interest in taxes. The debtholder is not interested in whether the business can replace its assets when they wear out, so he can ignore both capital expenditures and their amortization. EBITDA measures the cash earnings that he can expect to be applied to interest and debt retirement.

There are two EBITDA metrics used.

- The interest coverage ratio is used to determine a firm's ability to pay interest on outstanding debt. It is calculated : EBITDA /Interest Expense. The greater the year-to-year variance in EBITDA, the greater the multiple should be.
- The measure of the pay-back period for a debt is : Debt/EBITDA. The longer the payback period, the greater the risk.

The ratios can be customized by reducing Debt by any cash on the balance sheet or by deducting maintenance capx from EBITDA to form a measure closer to free cash flow.

Use by Equity Owners –pro

A hotel's Net Income is distorted by decisions that the hotel made in previous years. This is because of the differences between accrual accounting and cash basis accounting. Some purchases are depreciated or amortized over 20 years or more, with a negative impact on the Net Income long after the actual financial effects of the purchases have ceased. The EBITDA does not suffer this distortion, so investors can get a better idea of how profitable the hotel really is

Depreciation of capital expenditures is a particularly strong factor. For example, if a hotel spends $99 million in new desktop computers for all its employees, the hotel will often decide to depreciate the purchase over their expected lifetime of three years. This way, in the first year, when the hotel calculates its "income" number, it pretends that it has only spent $33 million that year on desktop computers. The hotel's income number paints a more rosy and optimistic picture than actually occurred that year. In each of the second and third years, the hotel also pretends that it has spent $33 million per year on desktop computers. Hence, the hotel's financial picture was probably healthier than indicated by the income number, since the $33 million had actually already been paid out.

Capital expenditures typically vary from year to year. Accrual accounting accounts for this by spreading the expense of capital investments over the years in which they will be generating value for the hotel. EBITDA removes this effect. Investors can use EBITDA to approximate the fundamental earning power of the hotel's operations while separately factoring in the projected capital expenditures needed to maintain those operations. This is valuable because of the time value of money principle. (An expenditure is less costly if it is to be made several years into the future, because during the interim period the firm can use the cash for that expenditure to generate income in other ways.) Because EBITDA is measured before interest (which vary with the amount of debt financing), it approximates the hotel's earnings potential as if financed with zero debt. It corrects for the differences between hotels' valuations due to their capital structure. If the investor can change the capital structure of a firm (e.g., through a leveraged buyout) he first evaluates a firm's fundamental earnings potential (reflected by EBITDA or EBIT), and then determines the optimal use of debt vs. equity.

Use by equity owners-con

In layman's terms, EBITDA is called "Earnings, before all the bad stuff". Warren Buffett famously asked, "Does management think the tooth fairy pays for capital expenditures?" People who understand the how's and why's of accounting think that Net Income is a better measure of a business' performance than EBITDA.

The basic debate over the value of accrual vs. cash accounting comes down to the question. "When you bought your Christmas presents in December 2001, did you consider them to be a 2001 expense? Or did you consider them to only show up in 2002 when you made the January credit card payment? Most people acknowledge the costs in 2001, even though there was no cash transaction.

Depreciation

The same argument applies to the purchase of long-life capital assets. You can consider depreciation to be either:

- The allocation of the original cost, at a later date, when the asset was used to generate revenue. The time-value-of-money (same argument used above) means that the depreciation UNDERSTATES the cost.

- The amount of cash required to be retained in order to finance the eventual replacement asset. Since inflations is the basis for time-value-of-money, the amounts set aside today must be invested and grow in value in order to pay the inflated price in the future. Or
- The decrease in value of the balance sheet asset since the last reporting period. Assets wear out with use. A hotel with old assets is not worth as much as a hotel with new ones.

No matter which POV you choose, non-cash expenses are 'real' costs. This amount of cash received from sales is only a return of capital. No matter that the proponents of EBITDA claim to separately consider the future requirements for capital asset replacements, none due in public. When management is free to create their own estimate, their numbers are never justified with details and always low-balled beyond belief. Depreciation is not an exact measure, but it is beyond management manipulation, and supported by disclosed math calculations.

Interest

The only reason to ignore interest and financing expenses is if the investor CAN in fact create his own personal leverage that will equalize the leverage between different investments. No investors can. In the big picture, investors lever their portfolio, not individual stock positions. Even if long-term leverage could be equalized, most businesses use extensive short term debt to finance 1-2-3 month cash requirements. The investor can never replicate these cash flows. If the investor separately measures the hotel's leverage and combines this metric with EBITDA, it would be valid. But leverage rates are rarely quoted in the media. Even sophisticated investors do not know how to weigh the trade-offs between the two metrics.

Taxes

There is no excuse for ignoring taxes. Management is payed to manage taxes, just like other expenses. This is why they incorporate in tax havens. The less money going to taxes, the more is left for equity owners.

Manipulation

The major argument for EBITDA is that is beyond management manipulation. Yet once management is told this is the metric they will be judged by, they immediately find ways to manipulate it.

Unprofitable Businesses

When comparing businesses with no profits, their potential to make profit is more important than their Net Loss. Since taxes on losses will be misleading in this context, taxes can be ignored. Capital expenditures and their related debt result in fixed costs. These are of less importance than the variable costs that can be expected to grow with increasing sales volume, in oder to cover the fixed costs. So depreciation and interest costs are of less importance. It is likely than an unprofitable business is burning cash (has a negative cash flow), so investors are most concerned with "how long the cash will last before the business must get more financing" (resulting in debt or equity dilution). For these reasons EBITDA is the metric most appropriate.

Be clear that EBITDA is not used as a valuation metric in these circumstances. It is a starting point on which future growth is applied and future profitability discounted back to the present. Equity owners only benefit from net profits, after all the expenses are paid. During the dot com bubble companies promoted their stock by emphasizing either EBITDA or pro forma earnings in their financial reports, and explaining away the (often poor) "income" number. This would involve ignoring one-time write-offs, asset impairments and other costs deemed to be non-recurring. Because EBITDA (and its variations) are not measures generally accepted under U.S. GAAP, the U.S. Securities and Exchange Commission requires that companies registering securities with it (and when filing its periodic reports) reconcile EBITDA to net income in order to avoid misleading investors. A negative EBITDA figure is not meaningful when consideration valuation multiples (namely Enterprise Value/EBITDA).

STOCK

In financial markets, stock is the capital raised by a corporation through the issuance and distribution of shares. A person or organisation which holds at least a partial share of stocks is called a shareholder. The aggregate value of a corporation's issued shares is its market capitalization. In the United Kingdom and Australia, the term *share* is used the same way, but *stocks* there refer to either a completely different financial instrument, the bond, or more widely to all kinds of marketable securities.

Type of stock

There are several types of stock.

Common Stock

Common stock, also referred to as common shares or ordinary shares, are, as the name implies, the most usual and commonly held form of stock in a corporation. Shareholders of common stock have voting rights in corporate decision matters. It is the residual corporate interest that bears the ultimate risks of loss and receives the benefits of success.

Preferred Stock

Preferred stock, sometimes called preference shares, have priority over common stock in the distribution of dividends and assets. Most preferred shares provide no voting rights in corporate decision matters. However, some preferred shares have special voting rights to approve certain extraordinary events (such as the issuance of new shares, or the approval of the acquisition of the hotel), or to elect directors.

Dual Class Stock

Dual class stock is shares issued for a single hotel with varying classes indicating different rights on voting and dividend payments. Each kind of shares has its own class of shareholders entitling different rights.

Treasury stock

Treasury stock is shares that have been bought back from the public. Treasury Stock is considered issued, but not outstanding.

STOCK DERIVATIVES

A stock derivative is any financial claim which has a value that is dependent on the price of the underlying stock. Futures and options are the main types of derivatives on stocks. The underlying security may be a stock index or an individual firm's stock, e.g. single-stock futures. Stock futures are contracts where the buyer, or long, takes on the obligation to buy on the contract maturity date, and the seller, or short takes on the obligation to sell. Stock index futures are generally not delivered in the usual manner, but by cash settlement. A stock option is a class of option. Specifically, a call option is the right (*not* obligation) to buy stock in the future at a fixed price and a put option is the right (*not* obligation) to sell stock in the future at a fixed price. Thus, the value of a stock option changes in reaction to the underlying stock of which it is a derivative. The most popular method of valuing stock options is the Black Scholes model.

Apart from call options granted to employees, most stock options are transferable. The first hotel to issue shares of stock was the Dutch East India Hotel, in 1602. The innovation of joint ownership made a great deal of Europe's economic growth possible following the Middle Ages. The technique of pooling capital to finance the building of ships, for example, made the Netherlands a maritime superpower. Before adoption of the joint-stock corporation, an expensive venture such as the building of a merchant ship could be undertaken only by governments or by very wealthy individuals or families.

SHAREHOLDER

A shareholder or *stockholder* is an individual or hotel (including a corporation) that legally owns one or more shares of stock in a joint stock hotel. Companies listed at the stock market strive to enhance shareholder value. Stockholders are granted special privileges depending on the class of stock, including the right to vote (usually one vote per share owned) on matters such as elections to the board of directors, the right to share in distributions of the hotel's income, the right to purchase new shares issued by the hotel, and the right to a hotel's assets during a liquidation of the hotel. However, stockholder's rights to a hotel's assets are subordinate to the rights of the hotel's creditors. This means that stockholders typically receive nothing if a hotel is liquidated after bankruptcy (if the hotel had had enough to pay its creditors, it would not have entered bankruptcy), although a stock may have value after a bankruptcy if there is the possibility that the debts of the hotel will be restructured.

Stockholders or shareholders are considered by some to be a partial subset of stakeholders, which may include anyone who has a direct or indirect equity interest in the business entity or someone with even a non-pecuniary interest in a non-profit organization. Thus it might be common to call volunteer contributors to an association stakeholders, even though they are not shareholders. Although directors and officers of a hotel are bound by fiduciary duties to act in the best interest of the shareholders, the shareholders themselves normally do not have such duties towards each other. However, in a few unusual cases, some courts have been willing to imply such a duty between shareholders. For example, in California, majority shareholders of closely held corporations have a duty to not destroy the value of the shares held by minority shareholders. The largest shareholders (in terms of percentages of companies owned) are often mutual funds, and especially passively managed exchange-traded funds.

Application

The owners of a hotel may want additional capital to invest in new projects within the hotel. They may also simply wish to reduce their holding, freeing up capital for their own private use. By selling shares they can sell part or all of the hotel to many part-owners. The purchase of one share entitles the owner of that share to literally share in the ownership of the hotel a fraction of the decision-making power, and potentially a fraction of the profits, which the hotel may issue as dividends.

In the common case of a publicly traded corporation, where there may be thousands of shareholders, it is impractical to have all of them making the daily decisions required to run a hotel. Thus, the shareholders will use their shares as votes in the election of members of the board of directors of the hotel. In a typical case, each share constitutes one vote (except in a co-operative society where every member gets one vote regardless of the number of shares he holds). Corporations may, however, issue different classes of shares, which may have different voting rights. Owning the majority of the shares allows other shareholders to be out-voted - effective control rests with the majority shareholder (or shareholders acting in concert). In this way the original owners of the hotel often still have control of the hotel.

Shareholder Rights

Although ownership of 51% of shares does result in 51% ownership of a hotel, it does not give the shareholder the right to use a hotel's building, equipment, materials, or other property. This is because the hotel is considered a legal person, thus it owns all its assets itself. This is important in areas such as insurance, which must be in the name of the hotel and not the main shareholder.

In most countries, including the United States, boards of directors and hotel managers have a fiduciary responsibility to run the hotel in the interests of its stockholders. Nonetheless, as Martin Whitman writes:

> *"...it can safely be stated that there does not exist any publicly traded hotel where management works exclusively in the best interests of OPMI [Outside Passive Minority Investor] stockholders. Instead, there are both "communities of interest" and "conflicts of interest" between stockholders (principal) and management (agent). This conflict is referred to as the principal/agent problem. It would be naive to think that any management would forego management compensation, and management entrenchment, just because some of these management privileges might be perceived as giving rise to a conflict of interest with OPMIs."*

Even though the board of directors runs the hotel, the shareholder has some impact on the hotel's policy, as the shareholders elect the board of directors. Each shareholder typically has a percentage of votes equal to the percentage of shares he or she owns. So as long as the shareholders agree that the management (agent) are performing poorly they can elect a new board of directors which can then hire a new management team. In practice, however, genuinely contested board elections are rare. Board candidates are usually nominated by insiders or by the board of the directors themselves, and a considerable amount of stock is held and voted by insiders.

Owning shares does not mean responsibility for liabilities. If a hotel goes broke and has to default on loans, the shareholders are not liable in any way. However, all money obtained by converting assets into cash will be used to repay loans and other debts first, so that shareholders cannot receive any money unless and until creditors have been paid (most often the shareholders end up with nothing).

Means of Financing

Financing a hotel through the sale of stock in a hotel is known as equity financing. Alternatively, debt financing (for example issuing bonds) can be done to avoid giving up shares of ownership of the hotel. Unofficial financing known as trade financing usually provides the major part of a hotel's working capital (day-to-day operational needs). Trade financing is provided by vendors and suppliers who sell their products to the hotel at short-term, unsecured credit terms, usually 30 days. Equity and debt financing are usually used for longer-term investment projects such as investments in a new factory or a new foreign market. Customer provided financing exists when a customer pays for services before they are delivered, e.g. subscriptions and insurance.

TRADING

A stock exchange is an organization that provides a marketplace (either physical or virtual) for trading shares, where investors (represented by stock brokers) may buy and sell shares in a wide range of companies. A given hotel will usually list its shares by meeting and maintaining the listing requirements of a particular stock exchange. In the United States, through the inter-market quotation system, stocks listed on one exchange can also be bought or sold on several other exchanges, including relatively new internet-only exchanges. Stocks are broadly grouped into NYSE-listed and NASDAQ-listed stocks. Exchanges where NYSE-listed stocks may be bought are generally not the same group as the exchanges where NASDAQ-listed stocks may be bought. Many large foreign companies choose to list on a U.S. exchange as well as an exchange in their home country in order to broaden their investor base. These shares are called American Depository Receipts (ADRs) — or, in the case of companies such as UBS and Daimler Chrysler — "foreign ordinary shares."

The most common way to trade stock options is trading standardized options contracts that are listed by various futures and options exchanges — there are currently six exchanges in the United States that list standardized options contracts based on underlying stocks — The Philadelphia Stock Exchange (PHLX), American Stock Exchange (AMEX) and NYSE Arca in New York City, and the Chicago Board Options Exchange (CBOE) which are all open-outcry marketplaces, and the International Securities Exchange (ISE) and Boston Options Exchange (BOX) are electronic marketplaces. However, even for the non-electronic exchanges, competition and the introduction of automated execution (AutoEx) has led, by late 2006, to hybridization where all but the largest trades are executed electronically. In Europe the main exchanges where stock options are traded are Euronext.liffe and Eurex.

There are also over-the-counter options contracts that are traded not on exchanges, but between two independent parties. At least one of those parties is usually a large financial institution with a balance sheet big enough to underwrite such a contract. Large U.S. companies also list in foreign exchanges for the same reason. Although it makes sense for some companies to raise capital by offering stock on more than one exchange, in today's era of electronic trading, there is limited opportunity for private investors to make profit on pricing discrepancies between one stock exchange and another. As such, arbitrage opportunities disappear quickly due to the efficient nature of the market.

Buying

There are various methods of buying and financing stocks. The most common means is through a stock broker. Whether they are a full service or discount broker, they arrange the transfer of stock from a seller to a buyer. Most trades are actually done through brokers listed with a stock exchange, such as the New York Stock Exchange.

There are many different stock brokers from which to choose, such as full service brokers or discount brokers. The full service brokers usually charge more per trade, but give investment advice or more personal service; the discount brokers offer little or no investment advice but charge less for trades. Another type of broker would be a bank or credit union that may have a deal set up with either a full service or discount broker.

There are other ways of buying stock besides through a broker. One way is directly from the hotel itself. If at least one share is owned, most companies will allow the purchase of shares directly from the hotel through their investor relations departments. However, the initial share of stock in the hotel will have to be obtained through a regular stock broker. Another way to buy stock in companies is through Direct Public Offerings which are usually sold by the hotel itself. A direct public offering is an initial public offering in which the stock is purchased directly from the hotel, usually without the aid of brokers.

When it comes to financing a purchase of stocks there are two ways: purchasing stock with money that is currently in the buyers ownership, or by buying stock on margin. Buying stock on margin means buying stock with money borrowed against the stocks in the same account. These stocks, or collateral, guarantee that the buyer can repay the loan; otherwise, the stockbroker has the right to sell the stock (collateral) to repay the borrowed money. He can sell if the share price drops below the margin requirement, at least 50% of the value of the stocks in the account. Buying on margin works the same way as borrowing money to buy a car or a house, using the car or house as collateral. Moreover, borrowing is not free; the broker usually charges 8-10% interest.

Selling

Selling stock is procedurally similar to buying stock. Generally, the investor wants to buy low and sell high, if not in that order (short selling); although a number of reasons may induce an investor to sell at a loss.

As with buying a stock, there is a transaction fee for the broker's efforts in arranging the transfer of stock from a seller to a buyer. This fee can be high or low depending on which type of brokerage, discount or full service, handles the transaction. After the transaction has been made, the seller is then entitled to all of the money. An important part of selling is keeping track of the earnings. Importantly, on selling the stock, in jurisdictions that have them, capital gains taxes will have to be paid on the additional proceeds, if any, that are in excess of the cost basis.

Stock Price Fluctuation

The price of a stock fluctuates fundamentally due to the theory of supply and demand. Like all commodities in the market, the price of a stock is directly proportional to the demand. However, there are many factors on basis of which the demand for a particular stock may increase or decrease. These factors are studied using methods of fundamental analysis and technical analysis to predict the changes in the stock price.

Technology's Influence on Trading

Stock trading has evolved tremendously. Since the very first Initial Public Offering (IPO) in the 13th century owning shares of a hotel has been a very attractive incentive. Even though the origins of stock trading go back to the 13th century, the market as we know it today did not catch on strongly until the late 1800s.

Co-production between technology and society has led the push for effective and efficient ways of trading. Technology has allowed the stock market to grow tremendously, and society has encouraged the growth. Within seconds of an order for a stock, the transaction can now take place. Most recent advancements with trading have been due to the Internet. The Internet has allowed online trading. I

n contrast to the past where only those who could afford expensive stockbrokers, anyone who wishes to be active in the stock market can now do so at a very low cost per transaction. Trading can even be done through Computer-Mediated Communication (CMC) use of mobile devices such as handheld computers and cellular phones. These advances in technology have made day trading possible.

Option Naming Conventions

Stock option names are written in the following format: SYMBOL+MONTH+STRIKE

SYMBOL = Option Root Symbol

MONTH = Month the option expires

STRIKE = Strike price

Expiration Month Codes

Month	Call	Put
January	A	M
February	B	N

March	C	O
April	D	P
May	E	Q
June	F	R
July	G	S
August	H	T
September	I	U
October	J	V
November	K	W
December	L	X

Strike Price Codes

Code	**Strike Prices**					**Code**	**Strike Prices**					
A	5	105	205	305	405	505	N	70	170	270	370	470	570
B	10	110	210	310	410	510	O	75	175	275	375	475	575
C	15	115	215	315	415	515	P	80	180	280	380	480	580
D	20	120	220	320	420	520	Q	85	185	285	385	485	585
E	25	125	225	325	425	525	R	90	190	290	390	490	590
F	30	130	230	330	430	530	S	95	195	295	395	495	595
G	35	135	235	335	435	535	T	100	200	300	400	500	600
H	40	140	240	340	440	540	U	7.5	37.5	67.5	97.5	127.5	157.5
I	45	145	245	345	445	545	V	12.5	42.5	72.5	102.5	132.5	162.5
J	50	150	250	350	450	550	W	17.5	47.5	77.5	107.5	137.5	167.5
K	55	155	255	355	455	555	X	22.5	52.5	82.5	112.5	142.5	172.5
L	60	160	260	360	460	560	Y	27.5	57.5	87.5	117.5	147.5	177.5
M	65	165	265	365	465	565	Z	32.5	62.5	92.5	122.5	152.5	182.5

The basic Trades or Traded Stock Options

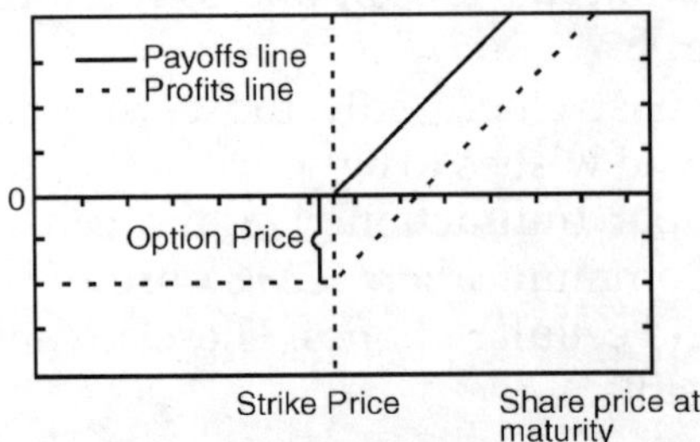

Payoffs and profits from a long call.

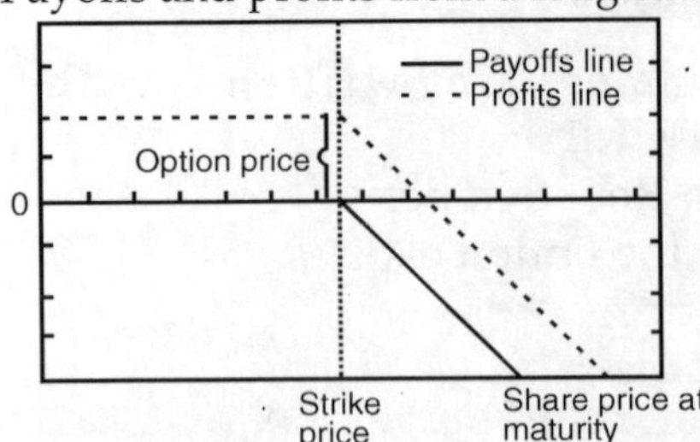

Payoffs and profits from a short call.

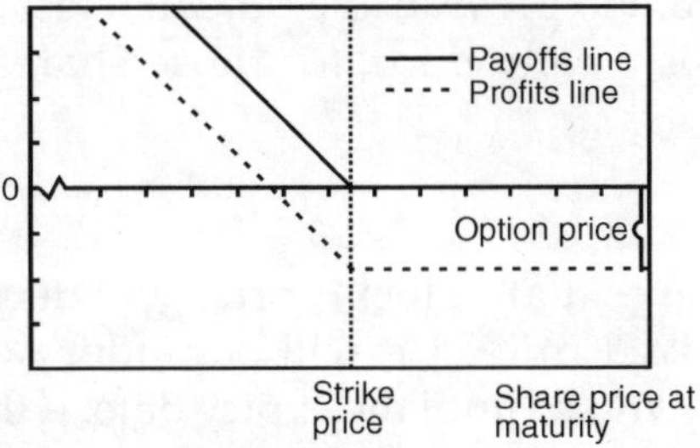

Payoffs and profits from a long put.

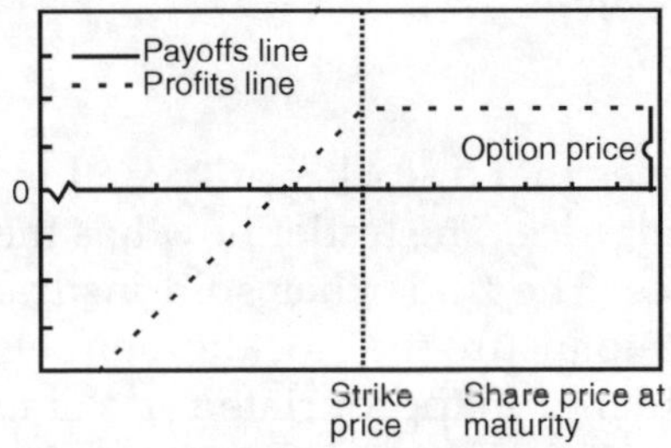

Payoffs and profits from a short put.

These trades are described from the point of view of a speculator. If they are combined with other positions, they can also be used in hedging.

Long Call

A trader who believes that a stock's price will increase may buy the right to purchase the stock (a call option) rather than just buy the stock. He would have no obligation to buy the stock, only the right to do so until the expiry date. If the stock price increases over the exercise price by more than the premium paid, he will profit. If the stock price decreases, he will let the call contract expire worthless, and only lose the amount of the premium. A trader might buy the option instead of shares, because for the same amount of money, he can obtain a larger number of options than shares. If the stock rises, he will thus realize a larger gain than if he had purchased shares. This is an example of the principle of leverage.

Short Call (Naked short call)

A trader who believes that a stock's price will decrease can short sell the stock or instead sell a call. Both tactics are generally considered inappropriate for small investors. The trader selling a call has an obligation to sell the stock to the call buyer at the buyer's option. If the stock price decreases, the short call position will make a profit in the amount of the premium. If the stock price increases over the exercise price by more than the amount of the premium, the short will lose money. Unless a trader already owns the shares which he may be required to provide, the potential loss is unlimited. However, such a trader who sells a call option for those shares he already owns has sold a covered call.

Long Put

A trader who believes that a stock's price will decrease can buy the right to sell the stock at a fixed price. He will be under no obligation to sell the stock, but has the right to do so until the expiry date. If the stock price decreases below the exercise price by more than the premium paid, he will profit. If the stock price increases, he will just let the put contract expire worthless and only lose his premium paid.

Short Put (Naked put)

A trader who believes that a stock's price will increase can sell the right to sell the stock at a fixed price. The trader now has the obligation to purchase the stock at a fixed price. The trader has sold insurance to the buyer of the put requiring the trader to insure the stockholder below the fixed price. This trade is generally considered inappropriate for a small investor. If the stock price increases, the short put position will make a profit in the amount of the premium. If the stock price decreases below the exercise price by more than the premium, the short position will lose money.

Introduction to Option Strategies

Combining any of the four basic kinds of option trades (possibly with different exercise prices) and the two basic kinds of stock trades (long and short) allows a variety of options strategies. Simple strategies usually combine only a few trades, while more complicated strategies can combine several.

Covered call — Long the stock, short a call. This has essentially the same payoff as a short put.

Straddle — Long a call and long a put with the same exercise prices (a long straddle), or short a call and short a put with the same exercise prices (a short straddle).

Strangle — Long a call and long a put with different exercise prices (a long strangle), or short a call and short a put with different exercise prices (a short strangle).

Bull spread — Long a call with a low exercise price and short a call with a higher exercise price, or long a put with a low exercise price and short a put with a higher exercise price.

Bear spread — Short a call with a low exercise price and long a call with a higher exercise price, or short a put with a low exercise price and long a put with a higher exercise price.

Butterfly — Butterflies require trading options with 3 different exercise prices. Assume exercise prices $X1 < X2 < X3$ and that $(X1 + X3)/2 = X2$

Long butterfly — long 1 call with exercise price X1, short 2 calls with exercise price X2, and long 1 call with exercise price X3. Alternatively, long 1 put with exercise price X1, short 2 puts with exercise price X2, and long 1 put with exercise price X3.

Short butterfly — short 1 call with exercise price X1, long 2 calls with exercise price X2, and short 1 call with exercise price X3. Alternatively, short 1 put with exercise price X1, long 2 puts with exercise price X2, and short 1 put with exercise price X3.

Box spreads — Any combination of options that has a constant payoff at expiration. For example combining a long butterfly made with calls, with a short butterfly made with puts will have a constant payoff of zero, and in equilibrium will cost zero. In practice any profit from these spreads will be eaten up by commissions (hence the name "alligator spreads").

Uses of Options

Contracts similar to options are believed to have been used since ancient times. In the real estate market, call options have long been used to assemble large parcels of land from separate owners, *e.g.* a developer pays for the right to buy several adjacent plots, but is not obligated to buy these plots and might not unless he can buy all the plots in the entire parcel. Film or theatrical producers often buy the right — but not the obligation — to dramatize a specific book or script. Lines of credit give the potential borrower the right — but not the obligation — to borrow within a specified time period.

Many choices, or embedded options, have traditionally been included in bond contracts. For example many bonds are convertible into common stock at the buyer's option, or may be called (bought back) at specified prices at the issuer's option. Mortgage borrowers have long had the option to repay the loan early.

Privileges were options sold over the counter in nineteenth century America, with both puts and calls on shares offered by specialized dealers. Their exercise price was fixed at a rounded-off market price on the day or week that the option was bought, and the expiry date was generally three months after purchase. They were not traded in secondary markets.

TREASURY STOCK

In the United Kingdom, treasury stocks refer to government bonds or gilts. The British equivalent of *treasury stock* as used in the United States is treasury share. In the United States, a treasury stock or reacquired stock is stock which is bought back by the issuing hotel. It reduces the number of outstanding stocks on the open market ("open market" including insiders' holdings). On the balance sheet, treasury stock is listed under shareholder equity as a negative number. Stock repurchases are often used as a tax-efficient method to put cash into shareholders' hands, rather than pay dividends.

Sometimes, companies do this when they feel that their stock is undervalued on the open market. Other times, companies do this to provide a "bonus" or incentive compensation plan for employees. Rather than receive cash, recipients receive an asset that might appreciate in value faster than cash saved in a bank account.

Limitations of treasury stock include:

Treasury stock does not pay a dividend

Treasury stock has no voting rights

Total treasury stock can not exceed the maximum proportion of total capitalization specified by law in the relevant country

After buyback, the hotel can either retire the shares (however, retired shares are not listed as treasury stock on the hotel's financial statements) or hold the shares for later resale. Buying back stocks reduces the number of outstanding shares. However, the smaller number of shares outstanding is not the reason why stock prices usually increase after announcements of buybacks. To see this, note that achoteling the decrease in the number of shares outstanding is a reduction in hotel assets, in particular, cash assets, which are used to buy back shares. The correct reason for the price jump is that by buying back its own shares, the hotel, who supposedly knows more about the true value of its stock than investors, sends a signal to investors that the stock is currently undervalued. The stock price increases as a response to this positive signal.

One way of accounting for treasury stock is with the cost method. In this method, the paid-in capital account is reduced in the balance sheet when the treasury stock is bought. When the treasury stock is sold back on the open market, the paid-in capital is either debited or credited if it is sold for more or less than the initial cost respectively. Another common way for accounting for treasury stock is the par value method. In the par value method, when the stock is purchased back from the market the books will reflect the action as a retirement of the shares. Therefore, common stock is debited and treasury stock is credited. However, when the treasury stock is resold back to the market the entry in the books will be the same as the cost method.

In either method, any transaction involving treasury stock cannot increase the amount of retained earnings. If the treasury stock is sold for more than cost, then the paid-in capital treasury stock is the account that is increased not retained earnings. In auditing financial statements, there is a common practice to check for this error to detect possible attempts to "cook the books".

If you believe in efficient market theory, a hotel buying back its stock should have no effect at all on its stock price. If the market fairly prices a hotel's shares at $50/share, if a hotel buys back 100 shares for $5000, it now has $5000 less cash but there are 100 fewer shares outstanding; the net effect should be that the value per share is unchanged. However, buying back shares does improve certain per-share ratios, such as price/earnings (earnings per share is increased due to fewer shares outstanding), but that is only because valuing a hotel's shares according to those ratios is not accurate when a hotel is holding a lot of cash. If a hotel's shares are underpriced, then a hotel can benefit its other shareholders by buying back shares. If a hotel's shares are overpriced, then a hotel is actually hurting its remaining shareholders by buying back stock.

One other reason for a hotel to buy back its own stock is to reward holders of stock options. Option holders are not rewarded by dividends, if issued, since holders of options have not invested any capital into the hotel. Option holders are often employees and executives of the hotel that benefit from the rise in stock. If you believe that share buyback programs increase the share value, at least temporarily, the option holder is the benficiary if she/he sells the options.

EARNINGS PER SHARE

Earnings per share (EPS) are the earnings returned on the initial investment amount. The FASB requires companies' income statements to report EPS for each of the major categories of the income statement: continuing operations, discontinued operations, extraordinary items, and net income. The EPS formula does not include preferred dividends for categories outside of continuing operations and net income as shown here. This formula also shows the most basic formula for earnings per share.

$$\text{Earnings per Share} = \frac{\text{Profit}}{\text{Weighted Average Common Shares}}$$

The EPS formula is shown here for Net Income and Continuing Operations (substitute income from continuing operations for net income).

$$\text{Earnings per Share} = \frac{\text{Net Income-preferred Dividends}}{\text{Weighted Average Common Shares}}$$

Note: Only dividends actually declared in the current year are subtracted. The exception is when preferred shares are cumulative, in which case annual dividends are deducted regardless of whether they have been declared or not. Dividends in arrears are not relevant when calculating EPS.

Earnings per share for continuing operations and net income are more complicated in that any preferred dividends are removed from net income before calculating EPS. Remember that preferred stock rights have precedence over common stock. If preferred dividends total $100,000, then that is money not available to distribute to each share of common stock. The value used for hotel earnings can either be the last twelve months' Net income (referred to as trailing twelve months, or ttm), or analysts' predictions for the next twelve months' net income (referred to as forward).

The number of shares used for the calculation can either be basic (only shares that are currently outstanding) or diluted (includes all shares that could potentially enter the market). Companies often use a weighted average of shares outstanding over the reporting term. (The weight refers to the time period covered by each share level) EPS can be calculated for the previous year ("trailing EPS"), for the current year ("current EPS"), or for the coming year ("forward EPS"). Note that last year's EPS would be actual, while current year and forward year EPS would be estimates.

PREFERRED STOCK

A preferred stock, also known as a preferred share or simply a preferred, is a share of stock carrying additional rights above and beyond those conferred by common stock. Unlike common stock, preferred stock usually has several rights attached to it:

- The core right is that of preference in dividends. Before a dividend can be declared on the common shares, any dividend obligation to the preferred shares must be satisfied.
- The dividend rights are often cumulative, such that if the dividend is not paid it accumulates in arrears.
- Preferred stock has a par value or liquidation value associated with it. This represents the amount of capital that was contributed to the corporation when the shares were first issued.
- Preferred stock has a claim on liquidation proceeds of a stock corporation, equivalent to its par or liquidation value. This claim is senior to that of common stock, which has only a residual claim.
- Almost all preferred shares have a fixed dividend amount. The dividend is usually specified as a percentage of the par value or as a fixed amount. For example Pacific Gas and Electric 6% Series A preferred. Unlike debt securities, however, a hotel is not legally required to pay preferred dividends and will not be in default for missing a preferred dividend payment.
- Variable preferreds are rare exceptions; their changing dividends depend on prevailing interest rates, or varying as a percentage of net income.
- Some preferred shares have special voting rights to approve certain extraordinary events (such as the issuance of new shares or the approval of the acquisition of the hotel) or to elect directors, but most preferred shares provide no voting rights associated with them. Some preferred shares only gain voting rights when the preferred dividends are in arrears.
- Usually preferred shares contain protective provisions which prevent the issuance of new preferred shares with a senior claim. Individual series of preferred shares may have a senior, pari-passu or junior relationship with other series issued by the same corporation.

The above list, although including several customary rights, is far from comprehensive. Preferred shares, like other legal arrangements, may specify nearly any right conceivable. Preferred shares normally carry a call provision, enabling the issuing corporation to repurchase the share at its (usually limited) discretion. Some corporations contain provisions in their charters authorising the issuance of preferred stock whose terms and conditions may be determined by the board of directors when issued. These "blank check" preferred shares are often used as takeover defense. These shares may be assigned very high liquidation value that must be redeemed in the event of a change of control or may have enormous supervoting powers.

Users

Preferred shares are more common in private companies, where it is more useful to distinguish between the control of and the economic interest in the hotel. Also, government regulations and the rules of stock exchanges discourage the issuance of publicly traded preferred shares. For example the Tel Aviv Stock Exchange prohibits listed companies from having more than one class of capital stock. A single hotel may issue several classes of preferred stock. For example, a hotel may undergo several rounds of financing, with each round receiving separate rights and having a separate class of preferred stock; such a hotel might have "Series A Preferred", "Series B Preferred", "Series C Preferred" and common stock.

Canada

Preferred shares represent a significant portion of Canadian capital markets, with over CAD 5-billion in preferred share issues in 2005.

Canadian issuers

Many issuers are financial organizations that may count capital raised in the preferred share market as Tier 1 capital, provided that the shares issued are perpetual. Another class of issuer are "Split Share Corporations".

Canadian investors

Investors in Canadian preferred shares are generally those who wish to hold fixed-income investments in a taxable portfolio. Preferential tax treatment of dividend income, as opposed to interest income, may in many cases result in a greater after-tax return than might be achieved with bonds.

United Kingdom issuers

Perpetual non-cumulative preference shares may be included as Tier 1 capital. Perpetual cumulative preferred shares are Upper Tier 2 capital. Dated preferred shares (normally having an original maturity of at least five years) may be included in Lower Tier 2 capital.

United States

In the United States issuance of publicly listed preferred stock is generally limited to financial institutions, REITs and public utilities. Because in the US dividends on preferred stock are not tax deductible (like interest expense), the effective cost of capital raised by preferred stock is 35% greater than issuing the equivalent amount of debt at the same interest rate. This has lead to the development of TRuPS (Trust-preferred security) which are essentially debt instruments with the same properties as preferred stock.

However, with a dividend tax of 15% and a top marginal tax rate of 35%, one dollar of dividend income taxed at these rates provides the same after-tax income as approximately $1.30 in interest. The size of the preferred stock market in the United States has been estimated as USD 200-billion, as of August, 2006, compared to USD 16-trillion for equities and USD 5-trillion for bonds.

Common types

There are various types of preferred stocks that are common to many corporations:

- *Cumulative Preferred Stock*—If the dividend is not paid, it will accumulate for future payment.
- *Non-cumulative Preferred Stock*—Dividend for this type of preferred stock will not accumulate if it is unpaid. This type is very rare, because the payment of dividends is always at the discretion of the board of directors.
- *Convertible Preferred Stock*—This type of preferred stock carries the option to convert into a common stock at a prescribed price.
- *Exchangable Preferred Stock*—This type of preferred stock carries the option to be exchanged for some other security upon certain conditions.
- *Participating Preferred Stock*—This type of preferred stock allows the possibility of additional dividend above the stated amount under certain conditions.
- *Perpetual Preferred Stock*—This type of preferred stock has no fixed date on which invested capital will be returned to the shareholder, although there will always be redemption privileges held by the corporation. Most preferred stock is issued without a set redemption date.
- *Puttable Preferred Stock*—These issues have a "put" privilege whereby the holder may, upon certain conditions, force the issuer to redeem shares.

P/E RATIO

The P/E ratio of a stock (also called its "earnings multiple", or simply "multiple", "P/E", or "PE") is used to measure how cheap or expensive its share prices is. The lower the P/E, the less you have to pay for the stock, relative to what you can expect to earn from it. It is a valuation ratio included in other financial ratios.

$$\text{P/E ratio} = \frac{\text{Price per Share}}{\text{Earnings per Share}}$$

The price per share (numerator) is the market price of a single share of the stock. The earnings per share (denominator) is the net income of the hotel for the most recent 12 month period, divided by number of shares outstanding. The EPS used can also be the "diluted EPS" or the "comprehensive EPS"

For example, if stock A is trading at $24 and the Earnings per share for the most recent 12 month period is $3, then the P/E ratio is 24/3=8. Stock A said to have a P/E of 8 (or a multiple of 8). Put another way, you are paying $8 for every one dollar of earnings.

It is probably the single most consistent red flag to excessive optimism and over-investment. It also serves, regularly, as a marker of business problems and opportunities. By relating price and earnings per share for a hotel, one can analyze the market's valuation of a hotel's shares relative to the wealth the hotel is actually creating.

One reason to calculate P/Es is for investors to compare the value of stocks, one stock with another. If one stock has a P/E twice that of another stock, it is *probably* a less attractive investment. But comparisons between industries, between countries, and between time periods may be dangerous. To have faith in a comparison of P/E ratios, one should compare comparable stocks.

DETERMINING SHARE PRICES

Share prices in a publicly traded hotel are determined by market supply and demand, and thus depend upon the expectations of buyers and sellers. Among these are:

- The hotel's future and recent performance
- New product lines
- Prospects for companies of this type, the "market sector"
- Prevailing moods and fashions.

By dividing the price of one share in a hotel by the profits earned by the hotel per share, you arrive at the P/E ratio. If earnings move up in line with share prices (or vice versa) the ratio stays the same. But if stock prices gain in value and earnings remain the same or go down, the P/E rises. For example, if a stock price was $70 per share and it got $2 in earnings, the P/E is 35, historically high.

The price used to calculate a P/E ratio is usually the most recent price. The earnings figure used is the most recently available, but this figure is often a year old and does not necessarily reflect the current position of the hotel. Many times, you will hear this referred to as a trailing P/E, because it involves taking earnings from the last four quarters. It is possible, however, to use the earnings estimate for the next four quarters. When doing so, the ratio is referred to as a projected or forward P/E.

Interpretation

The average U.S. equity P/E ratio from 1900 to 2005 is 14 (or 16, depending on whether the geometric mean or the arithmetic mean is used to average), meaning it takes about 14 years for a hotel you purchase to earn back your full purchase price for you. Normally, stocks with high earning growth are traded at higher P/E values. Say, stock A may earn $6 per share the next year. Then the future P/E ratio is $24/6 = 4. So, you are paying $4 for every one dollar of earnings, which makes the stock more attractive than it was the previous year.

Various interpretations of a particular P/E ratio are possible, and the historical table below is just indicative and cannot be a guide, as current P/E ratios have, obviously, to be compared to current - inflation-corrected - interest rates :

N/A	A hotel with no earnings has an undefined P/E ratio.
0-10	Either the stock is undervalued or the hotel's earnings are thought to be in decline.
10-17	For many companies a P/E ratio in this range may be considered fair value.
17-25	Either the stock is overvalued or the hotel's earnings have increased since the last earnings figure was published.
25+	A hotel whose shares have a very high P/E either really does have an exceptionally rosy future or the stock may be the subject of a speculative bubble.

It is usually not enough to look at the P/E ratio of one hotel and determine its status. Usually, an analyst will look at a hotel's P/E ratio compared to the industry the hotel is in, the sector the hotel is in, as well as the overall market (usually the S&P 500). Sites such as Reuters offer these comparisons in one table. Example of RHAT Oftentimes, comparisons will also be made between quarterly and annual data. Only after a comparison with the industry, sector, and market can an analyst determine whether a P/E ratio is high or low with the above mentioned distinctions (i.e., undervaluation, over valuation, fair valuation, etc).

The Market P/E

To calculate the P/E ratio of a market index such as the S&P500, it is not accurate to take the "simple average" of the P/Es of all stock constituents. The preferred and accurate method is to calculate the weighted average. In this case, each stock's underlying market cap (price multiplied by number of shares in issue) is summed to give the total value in terms of market capitalization for the whole market index. The same method is computed for each stock's underlying net earnings (earnings per share multiplied by number of shares in issue). In this case the total of all net earnings is computed and this gives the total earnings for the whole market index. The final stage is to divide the total market capitalization by the total earnings to give the market P/E ratio. The reason for using the weighted average method rather than 'simple' average can best be described by considering a recessionary period of the economic cycle, where a number of stocks would be reporting a loss. For example, a hotel with a share price of $100, may have made a slight loss of say 10 cents giving a P/E ratio of –1000 (100/0.1). In another case, a hotel with a share price of $1 may have made a serious loss of 50 cents giving a P/E ratio of – 2 (1/0.5). This mathematical anomaly would create a misrepresentation of the underlying hotel losses on the overall market index.

The P/E and Inflation

There is evidence that the P/E of the market has more to do with changes in consumer prices than any other factor. From 1900 to 2005, the highest average P/E occurred when the average change in consumer prices was 2.6%. In general, the P/E ratio is inversely proportional to the absolute value of the change in prices, in other words, the higher the price change, the lower the P/E.

Some claim that the P/E ratio is mostly dictated by interest rates, but the level of correlation of P/E ratios to interest rates is much lower versus that to the magnitude of price change.

An example An easy and perhaps intuitive way to understand the concept is with an analogy:

Let's say, I offer you a privilege to collect a dollar every year from me forever. How much are you willing to pay for that privilege now? Let's say, you are only willing to pay me 50 cents, because you may think that paying for that privilege coming from me could be risky. On the other hand, suppose that the offer came from Bill Gates, how much would you be willing to pay him? Perhaps, your answer would be at least more than 50 cents, let's say, $20. Well, the price earnings ratio or sometimes known as earnings multiple is nothing more than the number of dollars the market is willing to pay for a privilege to be able to earn a dollar forever in perpetuity. Bill Gates's P/E ratio is 20 and my P/E ratio is 0.5.

Now view it this way: The P/E ratio also tells you how long it will take before you can recover your investment (ignoring of course the time value of money). Had you invested in Bill Gates, it would have taken you at least 20 years, while investing in me could have taken you less than a year, i.e. only 6 months.

If a stock has a relatively high P/E ratio, let's say, 100 (which Google exceeded during the summer of 2005), what does this tell you? The answer is that it depends. A few reasons a stock might have a high P/E ratio are:

The market expects the earnings to rise rapidly in the future. For example a gold mining hotel which has just begun to mine may not have made any money yet but next quarter it will most likely find the gold and make a lot of money. The same applies to pharmaceutical companies — often a large amount of their revenue comes from their best few patented products, so when a promising new product is approved, investors may buy up the stock.

The hotel was previously making a lot of money, but in the last year or quarter it had a special one time expense (called a "charge"), which lowered the earnings significantly. Stockholders, understanding (possibly incorrectly) that this was a one time issue, will still buy stock at the same price as before, and only sell at at least that same price.

Hype for the stock has caused people to buy the stock for a higher price than they normally would. This is called a bubble. One of the most important uses for the P/E metric is to decide whether a stock is undergoing a bubble or an anti-bubble by comparing its P/E to other similar companies. Historically, bubbles have been followed by crashes. As such, prudent investors try to stay out of them.

The hotel has some sort of business advantage which seems to ensure that it will continue making money for a long time with very little risk. Thus investors are willing to buy the stock even at a high price for the peace of mind that they will not lose their money.

A large amount of money has been inserted into the stock market, out of proportion with the growth of companies across the same time period. Since there are only a limited amount of stocks to buy, supply and demand dictate that the prices of stocks must go up. This factor can make comparing P/E ratios over time difficult.

Likewise, a specific stock may have a temporarily high price when, for whatever reason, there has been high demand for it. This demand may have nothing to do with the hotel itself, but may rather relate to, for example, an institutional investor trying to diversify out risk.

Inputs

Accuracy and context

In practice, decisions must be made as to exactly how to specify the inputs used in the calculations.

Does the current market price accurately value the organization?

How is income to be calculated and for what periods? How do we calculate total capitalization?

Can these values be trusted?

What are the revenue and earnings growth prospects over the time frame one is investing in?

Was there special one time charges which artificially lowered (or artificially raised) the earnings used in the calculation, and did those charges cause a drop in stock price or were they ignored?

Were these charges truly one-time, or is the hotel trying to manipulate us into thinking so?

What kind of P/E ratios is the market giving to similar companies, and also the P/E ratio of the entire market?

Historical vs Projected Earnings

A distinction has to be made between the *fundamental (or intrinsic) P/E* and the way we actually compute P/Es. The fundamental or intrinsic P/E examines earnings forecasts. That is what was done in the analogy above. In reality, we actually compute P/Es using the latest 12 month corporate earnings. Using past earnings introduces a temporal mismatch, but it is felt that having this mismatch is better than using future earnings, since future earnings estimates are notoriously inaccurate and susceptible to deliberate manipulation.

On the other hand, merely because a stock is trading at a low fundamental P/E is not an indicator that the stock is undervalued. A stock may be trading at a low P/E because the investors are less optimistic about the future earnings from the stock. Thus, one way to get a fair comparison between stocks is to use their *primary P/E*. This primary P/E is based on the earnings projections made for the next years to which a discount calculation is applied.

THE P/E CONCEPT IN BUSINESS CULTURE

The P/E ratio of a hotel is a significant focus for management in many companies and industries. This is because management is primarily paid with their hotel's stock (a form of payment that is supposed to align the interests of management with the interests of other stock holders), in order to increase the stock price. The stock price can increase in one of two ways: either through improved earnings or through an improved multiple that the market assigns to those earnings. As mentioned earlier, a higher P/E ratio is the result of a sustainable advantage that allows a hotel to grow earnings over time (ie, investors are paying for their peace of mind). Efforts by management to convince investors that their companies do have a sustainable advantage have had profound effects on business:

- The primary motivation for building conglomerates is to diversify earnings so that they go up steadily over time.
- The choice of businesses which are enhanced or closed down or sold within these conglomerates is often made based on their perceived volatility, regardless of the absolute level of profits or profit margins.

3. One of the main genres of financial fraud, "slush fund accounting" (hiding excess earnings in good years to cover for losses in lean years), is designed to create the image that the hotel always slowly but steadily increases profits, with the goal to increase the P/E ratio.
4. These and many other actions used by companies to structure themselves to be perceived as commanding a higher P/E ratio can seem counterintuitive to some, because while they may decrease the absolute level of profits they are designed to increase the stock price. Thus in this situation maximizing the stock price acts as a perverse incentive.

DIVIDEND

When a hotel earns a profit, some of it is reinvested in the business and called retained earnings, and some of it can be paid to its shareholders as a dividend. The frequency of these varies by country. In the United States dividends are usually declared quarterly by the board of directors. In some other countries dividends are paid biannually, as an interim dividend shortly after the hotel announces its interim results and a final dividend typically following its annual general meeting. In other countries, the board of directors will propose the payment of a dividend to shareholders at the annual meeting who will then vote on the proposal.

In the United States, decisions regarding the amount and frequency of dividends is solely at the discretion of the board of directors. Shareholders are explicitly forbidden from introducing shareholder resolutions involving specific amounts of dividends. Where a hotel makes a loss during a year, it may opt to continue paying dividends from the retained earnings from previous years or to suspend the dividend. Where a hotel receives a one-off gain, e.g. from the sale of some assets, and has no plans to reinvest the proceeds, the money is often returned to shareholders in the form of a *special* dividend.

DIVIDEND YIELD

Publicly traded companies often make periodic quarterly or yearly cash payments to their owners, the shareholders, in direct proportion to the number of shares held. According to US law, such payments can only be made out of current earnings or out of reserves (earnings retained from previous years). The hotel decides on the total payment and this is divided by the number of shares. The resulting dividend is an amount of cash per share. The dividend yield is the dividend paid in the last accounting year divided by the current share price.

If a stock paid out $5 per share in cash dividends to its shareholders last year and its price is currently $50, then it has a dividend yield of 10%. Historically, at severely high P/E ratios (such as over 100x), a stock has NO

(0.0%) or negligible dividend yield. With a P/E ratio over 100x, and supposing a portion of earnings is paid as dividend, it would take *over a century* to earn back the purchase price. Such stocks are extremely overvalued, unless a huge growth of earnings in the next years is expected.

The P/E is calculated primarily for common shares, not for preferred shares. The appropriate calculation for preferreds is the preferred dividend coverage ratio. A related concept is the "PEG ratio". This is the P/E ratio adjusted by a growth coefficient. It is sometimes used in high growth industries and new ventures. Its use is controversial.

Another practice, which is not mainstream, based on behavioral finance, is to take market behaviour parameters, among which the stock image, as factors playing a part in the level and evolution of the P/E. The P/E can be applied not only to shares, but to other assets also. Thus the P/E, comparing Price to Rental Incoming for housing, is an important measure in determining the existence or absence of Property bubbles.

Forms of Payment

Cash

Cash dividends (most common) are those paid out in form of "real cash". Such dividends are a form of investment interest/income and are taxable to the recipient in the year they are paid. This is the most common method of sharing corporate profits.

Stock

Stock or scrip dividends (common) are those paid out in form of additional stock shares of the issuing corporation, or other corporation (e.g., its subsidiary corporation). They are usually issued in proportion to shares owned (e.g., for every 100 shares of stock owned, 5% stock dividend will yield 5 extra shares). This is very similar to a stock split in that it increases the total number of shares while lowering the price of each share and does not change the market capitalization or the total value of the shares held.

Property

Property dividends or dividends *in specie* (Latin for "in kind") (rare) are those paid out in form of assets from the issuing corporation or another corporation, such as a subsidiary corporation. Property dividends are usually paid in the form of products or services provided by the corporation. When paying property dividends, the corporation will often use securities of other companies owned by the issuer.

Dates

Dividends must be "declared" (approved) by a hotel's Board of Directors each time they are paid. There are four important dates to remember regarding dividends.

Declaration date

The declaration date is the day the Board of Director's announces their intention to pay a dividend. On this day, the hotel creates a liability on its books; it now owes the money to the stockholders. On the declaration date, the Board will also announce a date of record and a payment date.

Date of record

Shareholders who properly registered their ownership on or before the date of record will receive the dividend. Shareholders who are not registered as of this date will not receive the dividend. Registration in most countries is essentially automatic for shares purchased before the ex-dividend date.

Ex dividend date

The "ex dividend" date is set by the exchange where the stock is traded, several days (usually two) before the date of record, so that all trades made on previous dates can be properly settled and the shareholder list on the date of record will accurately reflect the current owners. Purchasers buying before the ex-dividend date will receive the dividend. The stock is said to trade "cum dividend" (meaning "with dividend") on these dates. Purchasers buying on or after the ex-dividend date will not receive the dividend. The stock trades ex-dividend on these dates.

Payment date

The payment date is the day when the dividend cheques will actually be mailed to the shareholders of a hotel or credited to brokerage accounts.

Dividend-reinvestment plans

Some companies have dividend reinvestment plans, or DRIPs. These plans allow shareholders to use dividends to systematically buy small amounts of stock, usually with no commission and sometimes at a slight discount. In some cases the shareholder might not need to pay taxes on these re-invested dividends, but in most cases they do.

Shareholders like dividends because...

- Shareholders have their own personal cash needs and self-select the companies whose dividends satisfy these.
- Preferred shareholders like common share dividends because it creates a cushion that must be cut before their own dividends are.
- Shareholders feel the risk of returns from reinvested earnings at a later date, is higher than the risk of cash received today.

- Benjamin Graham and David Dodd, in the 1934 book Security Analysis, suggest that retaining earnings is, in effect, management dictating to owners how to invest their money.

Reasons Companies don't pay Dividends

- Management and the board may believe that the money is best re-invested into the hotel: research and development, capital investment, expansion, etc. Proponents suggest that a management eager to return profits to shareholders may have run out of good ideas for the future of the hotel.
- When dividends are paid, shareholders in many countries suffer from double taxation of those dividends: the hotel pays income tax to the government when it earns any income, and then when the dividend is paid, the individual shareholder pays income tax on the dividend payment. This is often used as justification for retaining earnings, or for performing a stock buyback, in which the hotel buys back stock, thereby increasing the value of the stock left outstanding. The shareholder will pay a tax on capital gains (which is often taxed at a lower rate than ordinary income) only when the shareholder chooses to sell the stock. If a holder of the stock chooses to not participate in the buyback, the price of the holder's shares should rise, but the tax on these gains is delayed until the actual sale of the shares. Certain types of specialized investment companies (such as a REIT in the U.S.) allow the shareholder to partially or fully avoid double taxation of dividends.
- Shareholders in companies which pay little or no cash dividends can reap the benefit of the hotel's profits when they sell their shareholding, or when a hotel is wound down and all assets liquidated and distributed amongst shareholders.

Franking Credits

In Australia and New Zealand, companies also forward franking credits to shareholders along with dividends. These franking credits represent the tax paid by the hotel upon its pre-tax profits. One dollar of hotel tax paid generates one franking credit. Companies can forward any proportion of franking up to a maximum amount that is calculated from the prevailing hotel tax rate: for each dollar of dividend paid, the maximum level of franking is the hotel tax rate divided by (1 - hotel tax rate). At the current 30% rate, this works out at 0.30 of a credit per 70 cents of dividend, or 42.857 cents per dollar of dividend. The shareholders who are able to use them offset these credits against their income tax bills at a rate of a dollar per credit, thereby effectively eliminating the double taxation of hotel profits. This system is called dividend imputation. The UK's taxation system operates along similar lines: dividends come with an attached tax credit which ensures that double taxation does not take place.

Dividends from trusts

In real estate investment trusts and royalty trusts, the distributions paid often will be consistently greater than the hotel earnings. This can be sustainable because the accounting earnings do not recognize any increasing value of real estate holdings and resource reserves. If there is no economic increase in the value of the hotel's assets then the excess distribution (or dividend) will be a return of capital and the book value of the hotel will have shrunk by an equal amount. This may result in capital gains which may be taxed differently than dividends representing distribution of earnings.

Reliability of Dividends

To determine the long run reliability of dividends, use either of two metrics that show the hotel's ability to pay.

Dividend Cover

Divide the hotel's Earnings per share by the Dividend. A Dividend Cover of less than 1 means the hotel is paying out more in dividends for the year than it earned.

Payout Ratio

Divide the hotel's Cash Flow from Operations by the Dividend. This ratio is used by analysts of Income Trusts in Canada.

Etymology

The word "dividend" ultimately comes from the Latin word "*dividendum*" meaning "the thing which is to be divided".

In the United States, credit unions generally use the term "dividends" to refer to interest payments they make to depositors. These are not dividends in the normal sense and are not taxed as such; they are just interest payments. Credit unions call them dividends since, as credit unions are owned by their members, interest payments are effectively payments to owners. Consumer co-operative societies use the term "dividend" for profit-sharing payments to their members. Unlike joint stock hotel dividends, these payments are made in proportion to a members' spending with the co-operative society, not the number of shares they hold in it.

BOOK VALUE

Book Value is the shareholders' equity of a business (assets - liabilities) as measured by the accounting 'books'. The term is used in the context where the speaker is trying to distinguish between the accounting measures (usually historical cost) and the market value. While it can be used to refer to the business' total equity, it is most used

- As a 'per share' value': The balance sheet Equity value is divided by the number of shares outstanding at the date of the balance sheet (not the average o/s in the period).
- As a 'diluted per share value': The Equity is bumped up by the exercise price of the options, warrants or preferred shares. Then it is divided by the number of shares that has been increased by those added.

Uses

- Book value is used in the financial ratio price/book. It is a valuation metric that sets the floor for stock prices under a worst-case scenario. When a business is liquidated, the book value is what may be left over for the owners after all the debts are paid. Paying only a price/ book – 1 means the investor will get all his investment back. Share of capital intensive industries trade at lower price/book ratios because they generate lower earnings per dollar of assets. Business depending on human capital will generate higher earnings per dollar of assets, so will trade at higher price/book ratios.
- Book value per share can be used to generate a measure of comprehensive earnings, when the opening and closing values are reconciled.

Bk/s, beg.of year – Dividends + Sh issue Premium + Comprehensive EPS = Bk/s, end of year

Changes are caused by

The sale of shares/units by the business increases the total book value. Book/sh will increase if the additional shares are issued at a price higher than the pre-existing book/sh. The purchase of its own shares by the business will decrease total book value. Book/sh will decrease if more is paid for them than was received when originally issued (pre-existing book/sh). Dividends paid out will decrease book value and book/sh.

Comprehensive earnings/losses will increase/decrease book value and book/sh. Comprehensive earnings, in this case, includes net income from the Income Statement, foreign exchange translation changes to Balance Sheet items, accounting changes applied retroactively, and the opportunity cost of options exercised.

New share Issues do not Dilute Shareholder value

It is a common misperception that the issue of more shares will decrease the value of the current owner. While it is correct that when the number of shares is doubled the EPS will be cut in half, it is too simple to be the full story. It all depends on how much was paid for the new shares and what return the new captital earns once invested.

Net book value of Long term Assets

Book value is often used interchangeably with "net book value", which is the original acquisition cost less accumulated depreciation, depletion or amortization.

6

Bonds, Leases and Mortgages

OPTION (FINANCE)

An option contract is an agreement in which the buyer (*holder*) has the right (but not the obligation) to exercise by buying or selling an asset at a set price (strike price) on or before a future date (the exercise date or expiration); and the seller (*writer*) has the obligation to honor the terms of the contract. Since the option gives the buyer a right and the writer an obligation, the buyer pays the option premium to the writer. The buyer is considered to have a long position, and the seller a short position.

Because the contract's value is determined by an underlying asset and other variables, it is classified as a derivative. For every open contract there is a buyer and a seller. Traders in exchange-traded options do not usually interact directly, but through a clearing house such as, in the U.S., the Options Clearing Corporation (OCC). The OCC guarantees that an assigned writer will fulfill his obligation if the option is exercised.

The Contract Specifies

Whether it is a put option or call option. Put options give the holder the right to sell the asset at the strike price. Call options give the holder the right to purchase the asset at the strike price. The underlying security (e.g. XYZ Co.) The strike price or exercise price. It can be specified, or based on a reference rate, or measured at agreed-upon intervals during the life of the contract. The date that will be either the last possible date for exercise (American options) , or the only date for exercise (European options). This date is commonly known as the expiration date.

The quantity of the security included in each contract. This is standard and predetermined by the exchanges for traded options, e.g. common share options have 100 shares in 1 contract. The ratio of actual settlement price to the price quoted in the market, also known as the 'multiplier'.

Types of Options

Real option (real option) is a choice that an investor has when investing in the real economy (i.e. in the production of goods or services, rather than in financial contracts). This option may be something as simple as the opportunity to expand production, or to change production inputs. Real options are an increasingly influential tool in corporate finance. They are typically difficult or impossible to trade, and lack the liquidity of exchange-traded options.

Traded options (also called "Exchange-Traded Options" or "Listed Options") is a class of Exchange traded derivatives. As for other classes of exchange traded derivatives, trade options have standardized contracts, quick systematic pricing, and are settled through a clearing house (ensuring fulfillment). Trade options include:

Stock options,

Commodity options,

Bond options,

Interest rate options

Index (equity) options,

Currency cross rate options, and

Swaption.

Vanilla options are 'simple', well understood, and traded options; Exotic options are more complex, or less easily understood. Asian options, lookback options, barrier options are considered to be exotic, especially if the underlying instrument is more complex than simple equity or debt.

Employee stock options (employee stock option) are issued by a hotel to its employees as compensation.

BOND

In finance, a bond is a debt security, in which the issuer owes the holders a debt and is obliged to repay the principal and interest (the coupon) at a later date, termed maturity. Other stipulations may also be attached to the bond issue, such as the obligation for the issuer to provide certain information to the bond holder, or limitations on the behaviour of the issuer. Bonds are generally issued for a fixed term (the maturity) longer than ten year. U.S Treasury securities issued debt with life of ten years or more is a bond. New debt between one year and ten years is a note, and new debt less than a year-bill. A bond is mostly just a loan, but in the form of a security, although terminology used is rather different. The *issuer* is equivalent to the *borrower*, the *bond holder* to the *lender*, and the *coupon* to the *interest*. Bonds enable the issuer to finance long-term investments with external funds. Debt securities with a maturity shorter than one year are typically *bills*. Certificates of deposit (CDs) or commercial paper are considered money market instruments.

Traditionally, the U.S. Treasury uses the word *bond* only for their issues with a maturity longer than ten years, and calls issues between one and ten year notes. Elsewhere in the market this distinction has disappeared, and both *bonds* and *notes* are used irrespective of the maturity. Market participants normally use *bonds* for large issues offered to a wide public, and *notes* rather for smaller issues originally sold to a limited number of investors. There are no clear demarcations. There are also "bills" which usually denote fixed income securities with three years or less, from the issue date, to maturity. Bonds have the highest risk, notes are the second highest risk, and bills have the least risk. This is due to a statistical measure called duration, where lower durations have less risk, and are associated with shorter term obligations.

Bonds and stocks are both securities, but the difference is that stock holders own a part of the issuing hotel (have an equity stake), whereas bond holders are in essence lenders to the issuer. Also bonds usually have a defined term, or maturity, after which the bond is redeemed whereas stocks may be outstanding indefinitely. An exception is a consol bond, which is a perpetuity, a bond with no maturity.

Issuers

The range of issuers of bonds is very large. Almost any organization could issue bonds, but the underwriting and legal costs can be prohibitive. Regulations to issue bonds are very strict. Issuers are often classified as follows:

Supranational agencies, such as the European Investment Bank or the Asian Development Bank issue supranational bonds. National Governments issue government bonds in their own currency. They also issue sovereign bonds in foreign currencies. Sub-sovereign, provincial, state or local authorities (municipalities). In the U.S. state and local government bonds are known as municipal bonds.

Government sponsored entities. In the U.S., examples include the Federal Home Loan Mortgage Corporation (Freddie Mac), the Federal National Mortgage Association (Fannie Mae), and the Federal Home Loan Banks. The bonds of these entities are known as agency bonds, or agencies. Companies (corporates) issue corporate bonds. Special purpose vehicles are companies set up for the sole purpose of containing assets against which bonds are issued, often called asset-backed securities.

Issuing Bonds

Bonds are issued by public authorities, credit institutions, companies and supranational institutions in the primary markets. The most common process of issuing bonds is through underwriting. In underwriting, one or more securities firms or banks, forming a syndicate, buy an entire issue of bonds from an issuer and re-sell them to investors. Government bonds are typically auctioned. The pictured bond was issued for the construction of the building now known as New York City Centre. The elaborate engraving is typical of certificated bonds, in this case using the fraternal organization's logo, rather than neoclassical human figures, idealized versions of the corporation's business, or architectural elements, all common decorations on bonds.

Coupons from this bond can be seen under Coupon. The bond and the coupons have no economic value today because the corporation became insolvent within a few years after the Wall Street Crash of 1929. The bond was purchased from a dealer of worthless securities, sometimes called wallpaper.

Features of bonds

The most important features of a bond are:

1. *Nominal, principal or face amount*—the amount over which the issuer pays interest, and which has to be repaid at the end.
2. *Issue price*—the price at which investors buy the bonds when they are first issued. The net proceeds that the issuer receives are calculated as the issue price, less issuance fees, times the nominal amount.
3. *Maturity date*—the date on which the issuer has to repay the nominal amount. As long as all payments have been made, the issuer has no more obligations to the bond holders after the maturity date. The length of time until the maturity date is often referred to as the term or maturity of a bond. The maturity can be any length of time, although debt securities with a term of less than one year are generally designated money market instruments rather than bonds. Most bonds have a term of up to thirty years. Some bonds have been issued with maturities of up to one hundred years, and some even do not mature at all. In early 2005, a market developed in euros for bonds with a maturity of fifty years. In the market for U.S. Treasury securities, there are three groups of bond maturities:
4. *Short term (bills)*: maturities up to one year;
5. *Medium term (notes)*: maturities between one and ten years;
6. *Long term (bonds)*: maturities greater than ten years.
7. *Coupon*—the interest rate that the issuer pays to the bond holders. Usually this rate is fixed throughout the life of the bond. It can also vary with a money market index, such as LIBOR, or it can be even more exotic. The name coupon originates from the fact that in the past, physical bonds were issued which had coupons attached to them. On coupon dates the bond holder would give the coupon to a bank in exchange for the interest payment.
8. *Coupon dates*—the dates on which the issuer pays the coupon to the bond holders. In the U.S., most bonds are semi-annual, which means that they pay a coupon every six months. In Europe, most bonds are annual and pay only one coupon a year.
9. *Indenture or covenants*—a document specifying the rights of bond holders. In the U.S., federal and state securities and commercial laws

apply to the enforcement of those documents, which are construed by courts as contracts. The terms may be changed only with great difficulty while the bonds are outstanding, with amendments to the governing document generally requiring approval by a majority (or super-majority) vote of the bond holders.

10. *Optionality*: a bond may contain an embedded option; that is, it grants option like features to the buyer or issuer:
11. *Callability*—Some bonds give the issuer the right to repay the bond before the maturity date on the call dates; see call option. These bonds are referred to as callable bonds. Most callable bonds allow the issuer to repay the bond at par. With some bonds, the issuer has to pay a premium, the so called call premium. This is mainly the case for high-yield bonds. These have very strict covenants, restricting the issuer in its operations. To be free from these covenants, the issuer can repay the bonds early, but only at a high cost.
12. *puttability*—Some bonds give the bond holder the right to force the issuer to repay the bond before the maturity date on the put dates; see put option.
13. *Call dates and put dates*—the dates on which callable and puttable bonds can be redeemed early. There are four main categories.
    - A Bermudan callable has several call dates, usually coinciding with coupon dates.
    - A European callable has only one call date. This is a special case of a Bermudan callable.
    - An American callable can be called at any time until the maturity date.
    - A death put is an optional redemption feature on a debt instrument allowing the beneficiary of the estate of the deceased to put (sell) the bond (back to the issuer) in the event of the beneficiary's death or legal incapacitation. Also known as a "survivor's option".
    - An IMRU callable can only be purchased by buyers of the highest quality (in financial terms) and remains the highest quality and hardest to obtain bond on the market. Originally conceived by financial guru M. Last with the help of A. Thein and T. Gardner.
14. Sinking fund provision of the corporate bond indenture requires that a certain portion of the issue to be retired periodically. The entire bond issue can be liquidated by the maturity date. If that is not the case, then the remainder is called balloon maturity. Issuers may either pay to trustees, which in turn call randomly selected

bonds in the issue, or, alternatively, purchase bonds in open market, then return them to trustees.

15. Convertible bond lets a bondholder to exchange a bond to a number of shares of issuer's common stock.
16. Exchangeable bond allows for exchange to shares of a corporations other than the issuer.

Types of bond

- Fixed rate bonds have a coupon that remains constant throughout the life of the bond.
- Floating rate notes (FRN's) have a coupon that is linked to a money market index, such as LIBOR or EURIBOR, for example three months USD LIBOR +0.20%. The coupon is then reset periodically, normally every three months.
- High yield bonds are bonds that are rated below investment grade by the credit rating agencies. As these bonds are relatively risky, investors expect to earn a higher yield. These bonds are also called junk bonds.
- Zero coupon bonds do not pay any interest. They trade at a substantial discount from par value. The bond holder receives the full principal amount as well as value that has accrued on the redemption date. An example of zero coupon bonds are Series E savings bonds issued by the U.S. government. Zero coupon bonds may be created from fixed rate bonds by financial institutions by "stripping off" the coupons. In other words, the coupons are separated from the final principal payment of the bond and traded independently.
- Inflation linked bonds, in which the principal amount is indexed to inflation. The interest rate is lower than for fixed rate bonds with a comparable maturity. However, as the principal amount grows, the payments increase with inflation. The government of the United Kingdom was the first to issue inflation linked Gilts in the 1980s. Treasury Inflation-Protected Securities (TIPS) and I-bonds are examples of inflation linked bonds issued by the U.S. government.
- Other indexed bonds, for example Equity Linked Notes and bonds indexed on a business indicator (income, added value) or on a country GDP...
- Asset-backed securities are bonds whose interest and principal payments are backed by underlying cash flows from other assets. Examples of asset-backed securities are mortgage-backed securities (MBS's), collateralized mortgage obligations (CMOs) and collateralized debt obligations (CDOs).

- Subordinated bonds are those that have a lower priority than other bonds of the issuer in case of liquidation. In case of bankruptcy, there is a hierarchy of creditors. First the liquidator is paid, then government taxes, etc. The first bond holders in line to be paid are those holding what is called senior bonds. After they have been paid, the subordinated bond holders are paid. As a result, the risk is higher. Therefore, subordinated bonds usually have a lower credit rating than senior bonds. The main examples of subordinated bonds can be found in bonds issued by banks, and asset-backed securities. The latter are often issued in tranches. The senior tranches get paid back first, the subordinated tranches later.
- Perpetual bonds are also often called perpetuities. They have no maturity date. The most famous of these are the UK Consols, which are also known as Treasury Annuities or Undated Treasuries. Some of these were issued back in 1888 and still trade today. Some ultra long-term bonds (sometimes a bond can last centuries: West Shore Railroad issued a bond which matures in 2361 (i.e. 24th century)) are sometimes viewed as perpetuities from a financial point of view, with the current value of principal near zero.
- Bearer bond is an official certificate issued without a named holder. In other words, the person who has the paper certificate can claim the value of the bond. Often they are registered by a number to prevent counterfeiting, but may be traded like cash. Bearer bonds are very risky because they can be lost or stolen. Especially after federal income tax began in the United States, bearer bonds were seen as an opportunity to conceal income or assets. U.S. corporations stopped issuing bearer bonds in the 1960's, the U.S. Treasury stopped in 1982, and state and local tax-exempt bearer bonds were prohibited in 1983.
- Registered bond is a bond whose ownership (and any subsequent purchaser) is recorded by the issuer, or by a transfer agent. It is the alternative to a Bearer bond. Interest payments, and the principal upon maturity, are sent to the registered owner.
- Municipal bond is a bond issued by a state, U.S. Territory, city, local government, or their agencies. Interest income received by holders of municipal bonds is often exempt from the federal income tax and from the income tax of the state in which they are issued, although municipal bonds issued for certain purposes may not be tax exempt.
- Book-entry bond is a bond that does not have a paper certificate. As physically processing paper bonds and interest coupons became more expensive, issuers (and banks that used to collect coupon interest for

depositors) have tried to discourage their use. Some book-entry bond issues do not offer the option of a paper certificate, even to investors who prefer them.

Bonds issued by foreign entities

Some companies, banks, governments, and other soverign entities may decide to issue bonds in foreign currencies as it may appear to be more stable and predictable than their domestic currency. Some foreign issuer bonds are called by their nicknames, such as the "Samurai bond", but this is ironic in that the issuer is neither a samurai nor even Japanese.

- Eurodollar bond is a bond issued by a non-European entity in the European market in Euro-dollar denominations.
- Samurai bond is a bond issued by a non-Japanese entity in the Japanese market in Japanese Yen denominations.
- Yankee bond is a bond issued by a non-US entity in the US market in US Dollar denominations.

Trading and Valuing bonds

The interest rate that the issuer of a bond must pay is influenced by a variety of factors, such as current market interest rates, the length of the term and the credit worthiness of the issuer. These factors are likely to change over time, so the market value of a bond can vary after it is issued. Because of these differences in market value, bonds are priced in terms of percentage of par value. Bonds are not necessarily issued at par (100% of face value, corresponding to a price of 100), but all bond prices converge to par at the moment before they reach maturity. At other times, prices can either rise (bond is priced at greater than 100), which is called trading at a premium, or fall (bond is priced at less than 100), which is called trading at a discount. Most government bonds are denominated in units of $1000, if in the United States, or in units of £100, if in the United Kingdom. Hence, a deep discount US bond, selling at a price of 75.26, indicates a selling price of $752.60 per bond sold. (Often, bond prices are quoted in points and thirty-seconds of a point, rather than in decimal form.) Some short-term bonds, such as the U.S. T-Bill, are always issued at a discount, and pay par amount at maturity rather than paying coupons. This is called a discount bond.

The market price of a bond is the present value of all future interest and principal payments of the bond discounted at the bond's yield, or rate of return. The yield represents the current market interest rate for bonds with similar characteristics. The yield and price of a bond are inversely related so that when market interest rates rise, bond prices generally fall and vice versa. The market price of a bond may include the accrued interest since the last coupon date. (Some bond markets include accrued interest in the trading price and others add it on explicitly after trading.) The price including accrued interest is known as the "flat" or "dirty price". The price excluding accrued interest is sometimes known as the Clean price.

The interest rate adjusted for the current price of the bond is called the "current yield" or "earnings yield" (this is the nominal yield multiplied by the par value and divided by the price). Taking into account the expected capital gain or loss (the difference between the current price and the redemption value) gives the "redemption yield": roughly the current yield plus the capital gain (negative for loss) per year until redemption. The relationship between yield and maturity for otherwise identical bonds is called a yield curve.

Bonds markets, unlike stock or share markets, often do not have a centralized exchange or trading system. Rather, in most developed bond markets such as the U.S., Japan and western Europe, bonds trade in decentralized, dealer-based over-the-counter markets. In such a market, market liquidity is provided by dealers and other market participants committing risk capital to trading activity. In the bond market, when an investor buys or sells a bond, the counterparty to the trade is almost always a bank or securities firm acting as a dealer. In some cases, when a dealer buys a bond from an investor, the dealer carries the bond "in inventory." The dealer's position is then subject to risks of price fluctuation. In other cases, the dealer immediately resells the bond to another investor.

Bond markets also differ from stock markets in that investors generally do not pay brokerage commissions to dealers with whom they buy or sell bonds. Rather, dealers earn revenue for trading with their investor customers by means of the spread, or difference, between the price at which the dealer buys a bond from one investor—the "bid" price—and the price at which he or she sells the same bond to another investor—the "ask" or "offer" price. The bid/offer spread represents the total transaction cost associated with transferring a bond from one investor to another.

Investing in bonds

Bonds are bought and traded mostly by institutions like pension funds, insurance companies and banks. Most individuals who want to own bonds do so through bond funds. Still, in the U.S., nearly ten percent of all bonds outstanding are held directly by households. As a rule, bond markets rise (while yields fall) when stock markets fall. Thus bonds are generally viewed as safer investments than stocks, but this perception is only partially correct. Bonds do suffer from less day-to-day volatility than stocks, and bonds' interest payments are higher than dividend payments that the same hotel would generally choose to pay to its stockholders. Bonds are liquid — it is fairly easy to sell one's bond investments, though not nearly as easy as it is to sell stocks — and the certainty of a fixed interest payment twice per year is attractive. Bondholders also enjoy a measure of legal protection: under the law of most countries, if a hotel goes bankrupt, its bondholders will often receive some money back, whereas the hotel's stock often ends up valueless. However, bonds can be risky:

- Fixed rate bonds are subject to *interest rate risk,* meaning their market price will decrease in value when the generally prevailing interest rate rises. Since the payments are fixed, a decrease in the market price of the bond means an increase in its yield. When the market's interest rates rise, then the market price for bonds will fall, reflecting investors' improved ability to get a good interest rate for their money elsewhere — perhaps by purchasing a newly issued bond that already features the newly higher interest rate. This drop in the bond's market price does not affect the interest payments to the bondholder at all, so long-term investors need not worry about price swings in their bonds.

  However, price changes in a bond immediately affect mutual funds that hold these bonds. Many institutional investors have to "mark to market" their trading books at the end of every day. If the value of the bonds held in a trading portfolio has fallen over the day, the "mark to market" value of the portfolio may also have fallen. This can be damaging for professional investors such as banks, insurance companies, pension funds and asset managers. If there is any chance a holder of individual bonds may need to sell his bonds and "cash out" for some reason, interest rate risk could become a real problem. (Conversely, bonds' market prices would increase if the prevailing interest rate were to drop, as it did from 2001 through 2003.) One way to quantify the interest rate risk on a bond is in terms of its duration. Efforts to control this risk are called immunization or hedging.
- Bond prices can become volatile if one of the credit rating agencies like Standard and Poor's or Moody's upgrades or downgrades the credit rating of the issuer. A downgrade can cause the market price of the bond to fall. As with interest rate risk, this risk does not affect the bond's interest payments, but puts at risk the market price, which affects mutual funds holding these bonds, and holders of individual bonds who may have to sell them.
- A hotel's bondholders may lose much or all their money if the hotel goes bankrupt. Under the laws of the United States and many other countries, bondholders are in line to receive the proceeds of the sale of the assets of a liquidated hotel ahead of some other creditors. Bank lenders, deposit holders (in the case of a deposit taking institution such as a bank) and trade creditors may take precedence.

There is no guarantee of how much money will remain to repay bondholders. As an example, after an accounting scandal and a Chapter 11 bankruptcy at the giant telecommunications hotel Worldcom, in 2004 its bondholders ended up being paid 35.7 cents on the dollar. In a bankruptcy involving reorganization or recapitalization, as opposed to liquidation, bondholders may end up having the value of their bonds reduced, often through an exchange for a smaller number of newly issued bonds.

- Some bonds are callable, meaning that even though the hotel has agreed to make payments plus interest towards the debt for a certain period of time, the hotel can choose to pay off the bond early. This creates reinvestment risk, meaning the investor is forced to find a new place for his money, and the investor might not be able to find as good a deal, especially because this usually happens when interest rates are falling.

Bond indices

A number of bond indices exist for the purposes of managing portfolios and measuring performance, similar to the SandP 500 or Russell Indexes for stocks. The most common American benchmarks are the Lehman Aggregate, Citigroup BIG and Merrill Lynch Domestic Master. Most indices are parts of families of broader indices that can be used to measure global bond portfolios, or may be further subdivided by maturity and/or sector for managing specialized portfolios.

MORTGAGE

A mortgage is a method of using property (real or personal) as security for the payment of a debt. The term mortgage (from Law French, lit. *death vow*) refers to the legal device used in securing the property, but it is also commonly used to refer to the debt secured by the mortgage. In most jurisdictions mortgages are strongly associated with loans secured on real estate rather than other property (such as ships) and in some cases only land may be mortgaged. Arranging a mortgage is seen as the standard method by which individuals or businesses can purchase residential or commercial real estate without the need to pay the full value immediately. In many countries it is normal for home purchase to be funded by a mortgage. In countries where the demand for home ownership is highest, strong domestic markets have developed, notably in Spain, the United Kingdom and the United States.

Participants and Variant Terminology

Each legal system tends to share certain concepts but vary in the terminology and jargon they use. In general terms the main participants in a mortgage are:

Creditor

The creditor has legal rights to the debt secured by the mortgage and often makes a loan to the debtor of the purchase money for the property. Typically, creditors are banks, insurers or other financial institutions who make loans available for the purpose of real estate purchase. A creditor is sometimes referred to as the *mortgagee* or *lender*.

Debtor

The debtor[s] must meet the requirements of the mortgage conditions (and often the loan conditions) imposed by the creditor in order to avoid the creditor enacting provisions of the mortgage to recover the debt. Typically the debtors will be the individual home-owners, landlords or businesses who are purchasing their property by way of a loan. A debtor is sometimes referred to as the *mortgagor, borrower,* or *obligor*.

Other participants

Due to the complicated legal exchange, or *conveyance,* of the property, one or both of the main participants are likely to require legal representation. The terminology varies with legal jurisdiction; see lawyer, solicitor and conveyancer. Because of the complex nature of many markets the *debtor* may approach a mortgage broker or financial adviser to help them source an appropriate *creditor* typically by finding the most competitive loan. Recently, many consumers (particularly higher income borrowers) are choosing to work with Certified Mortgage Planners, industry experts that work closely with Certified Financial Planners to align the home finance position(s) of homeowners with their larger financial portfolio(s).

The debt is sometimes referred to as the *hypothecation,* which may make use of the services of a *hypothecary* to assist in the hypothecation. In addition to Borrowers, Lenders, Government Sponsored Agencies (FNMA, GNMA, etc), Private agencies; there is also a fifth class of participants who are the source of funds - the Life Insurers, Pension Funds, etc.

Other Terminologies

Like any other legal system, mortgage has several jargons that may confuse some people. Below are several mortgage terminologies explained in brief for better understanding.

Advance: This is the money you have borrowed plus all the additional fees.

Base Rate: In UK, this is the base interest rate set by the Bank of England.

Bridging Loan: This is a temporary loan that enables you to purchase your new property before you are able to sell your old property.

Conveyance: This is the legal document that transfers ownership of unregistered land to you.

Disbursements: These are all the fees of your solicitors, such as stamp duty, land registry, search fees, etc.

Early Redemption Charge / Pre-Payment Penalty / Redemption Penalty: This is the amount of money you have to pay if you pay your mortgage in full before the time finished.

Equity: This is the amount of your property in the market minus all loans that it has.

Freehold: This means the ownership of a property and the land.

Land Registration: This is a legal document that records the ownership of a property and land.

Legal Charge: This is a legal document that records the data of the rightful owner of a property or land.

Mortgage Deed: This is a legal document that stated that the lender has a legal charge over your property.

Mortgage Payment Protection Insurance: This is the insurance that insures your mortgage payment arrives on time in case you are unable to pay your mortgage.

Sealing Fee: This is a fee made when the lender releases the legal charge over your property.

Subject To Contract: This is an agreement between seller and buyer before the actual contract is made.

LEGAL ASPECTS

There are essentially two types of legal mortgage.

Mortgage by demise

In a mortgage by demise, the creditor becomes the owner of the mortgaged property until the loan is repaid in full (known as "redemption"). This kind of mortgage takes the form of a conveyance of the property to the creditor, with a condition that the property will be returned on redemption. This is an older form of legal mortgage and is less common than a mortgage by legal charge. It is no longer available in the UK, by virtue of the Land Registration Act 2002.

Mortgage by legal charge

In a mortgage by legal charge, the debtor remains the legal owner of the property, but the creditor gains sufficient rights over it to enable them to enforce their security, such as a right to take possession of the property or sell it. To protect the lender, a mortgage by legal charge is usually recorded in a public register. Since mortgage debt is often the largest debt owed by the debtor, banks and other mortgage lenders run title searches of the real property to make certain that there are no mortgages already registered on the debtor's property which might have higher priority.

Tax liens, in some cases, will come ahead of mortgages. For this reason, if a borrower has delinquent property taxes, the bank will often pay them to prevent the lienholder from foreclosing and wiping out the mortgage. This type of mortgage is common in the United States and, since 1925, it has been the usual form of mortgage in England and Wales. In Scotland, the mortgage by legal charge is also known as standard security.

History

At common law, a mortgage was a conveyance of land that on its face was absolute and conveyed a fee simple estate, but which was in fact conditional, and would be of no effect if certain conditions were not met — usually, but not necessarily, the repayment of a debt to the original landowner. Hence the word "mortgage," Law French for "dead pledge;" that is, it was absolute in form, and unlike a "live gage", was not conditionally dependent on its repayment solely from raising and selling crops or livestock, or of simply giving the fruits of crops and livestock coming from the land that was mortgaged. The mortgage debt remained in effect whether or not the land could successfully produce enough income to repay the debt. In theory, a mortgage required no further steps to be taken by the creditor, such as acceptance of crops and livestock, for repayment.

The difficulty with this arrangement was that the lender was absolute owner of the property and could sell it, or refuse to reconvey it to the borrower, who was in a weak position. Increasingly the courts of equity began to protect the borrower's interests, so that a borrower came to have an absolute right to insist on reconveyance on redemption. This right of the borrower is known as the "equity of redemption".

This arrangement, whereby the mortgagee (the lender) was on theory the absolute owner, but in practice had few of the practical rights of ownership, was seen in many jurisdictions as being awkwardly artificial. By statute the common law position was altered so that the mortgagor would retain ownership, but the mortgagee's rights, such as foreclosure, the power of sale and the right to take possession would be protected. In the United States, those states that have reformed the nature of mortgages in this way are known as lien states. A similar effect was achieved in England and Wales by the Law of Property Act 1925, which abolished mortgages by the conveyance of a fee simple.

In the United States, mortgages became widely used starting in 1934. In that year, the Federal Housing Administration (FHA) lowered the down payment requirements by offering 80% loan-to-value loans. Next, banks, insurance companies, and other lenders followed the example. The FHA also lengthened loan terms by first introducing 15-year loans to supplant 3, 5, and 7-years loans which ended with a balloon payment. Until the 1930s only 40% of U.S. households owned homes; the rate today is nearly 70%, though the percentage of equity belonging to owners is at a record low. In 2003, total U.S. residential mortgage production reached a record level of $3.8 trillion through record low interest rates (though these continue to vary according to credit rating.)

REPAYING THE CAPITAL

There are various ways to repay a mortgage loan; repayment depends on locality, tax laws and prevailing culture.

Capital and Interest

The most common way to repay a loan is to make regular payments of the capital (also called principal) and interest over a set term. This is commonly referred to as (self) amortization in the U.S. and as a repayment mortgage in the UK. Depending on the size of the loan and the prevailing practice in the country the term may be short (10 years) or long (50 years plus). In the UK and U.S., 25 to 30 years is typical (in the U.S. 15-year notes are also common). Mortgage repayments, which are typically made monthly, contain a capital element and an interest element. The amount of capital included in each repayment varies throughout the term of the mortgage. In the early years the repayments are largely interest and a small part capital. Towards the end of the mortgage the repayments are mostly capital and a small part interest. In this way the repayment amount determined at outset is calculated to ensure the loan is repaid at a specified period in the future. This gives borrowers assurance that by maintaining repayment the loan will definitely be cleared at a specified date, if the interest rate does not increase.

Interest only

The main alternative to capital and interest mortgage is an *interest only* mortgage, where the capital is not repaid throughout the term. This type of mortgage is common in the UK, especially when associated with a regular investment plan. With this arrangement regular contributions are made to a separate investment plan designed to build up a lump sum to repay the mortgage at maturity. This type of arrangement is called an *investment-backed mortgage* or is often related to the type of plan used: endowment mortgage if an endowment policy is used, similarly a Personal Equity Plan (PEP) mortgage, Individual Savings Account (ISA) mortgage or pension mortgage. Historically, investment-backed mortgages offered various tax advantages over repayment mortgages, although this is no longer the case in the UK. Investment-backed mortgages are seen as higher risk as they are dependent on the investment making sufficient return to clear the debt. It is not uncommon for interest only mortgages to be arranged without a repayment vehicle, with the borrower gambling that the property market will rise sufficiently for the loan to be repaid by trading down at retirement (or when rent on the property and inflation combine to surpass the interest rate).

No Capital or Interest

For older borrowers (typically in retirement), it is possible to arrange a mortgage where neither the capital nor interest is repaid. The interest is rolled up with the capital, increasing the debt each year. These arrangements are variously called reverse mortgages, lifetime mortgages or *equity release mortgages*, depending on the country. The loans are typically not repaid until the borrowers die, hence the age restriction. For further details.

Interest and partial capital

In the U.S. a partial amortization or balloon loan is one where the amount of monthly payments due are calculated (amortized) over a certain term, but the outstanding capital balance is due at some point short of that term. In the UK, a part repayment mortgage is quite common, especially where the original mortgage was investment-backed and on moving house further borrowing is arranged on a capital and interest (repayment) basis.

Mortgages in the United States

Types of Mortgage Instruments

Two types of mortgage instruments are used in the United States: the mortgage (sometimes called a mortgage deed) and the deed of trust.

The Mortgage

In all but a few states, a mortgage creates a lien on the mortgaged property. Foreclosure of that lien almost always requires a judicial proceeding declaring the debt to be due and in default and ordering a sale of the land to pay the debt.

The Deed of Trust

The deed of trust is a deed by the borrower to a trustee for the purposes of securing a debt. In most states, it also merely creates a lien and not a title transfer, regardless of its terms. It differs from a mortgage in that, in many states, it can be foreclosed by a non-judicial sale held by the trustee. It is also possible to foreclose them through a judicial proceeding. Most "mortgages" in California are actually deeds of trust. The effective difference is that the foreclosure process can be much faster for a deed of trust than for a mortgage, on the order of 3 months rather than a year.

Deeds of trust to secure a debts should not be confused with deeds to trustees to create trusts for other purposes, such as estate planning. Though there are superficial similarities in the form, many states hold deeds of trust to secure repayment of debts do not create true trust arrangements.

Mortgage Loan types

There are many types of mortgage loans. The two basic types of amortized loans are the fixed rate mortgage (FRM) and adjustable rate mortgage (ARM).

In a FRM, the interest rate, and hence monthly payment, remains fixed for the life (or term) of the loan. In the U.S., the term is usually for 10, 15, 20, or 30 years (15 and 30 being the most common). However recently lenders have introduced terms that are amoritized over 40 and 50 year terms. The only increase a consumer might see in their monthly payments would result from an increase in their property taxes or insurance rates (paid using an escrow account, if they've opted to use an escrow). But payments for principal and interest will be consistent throughout the life of the loan using an FRM.

In an ARM, the interest rate is fixed for a period of time, after which it will periodically (annually or monthly) adjust up or down to some market index. Common indices in the U.S. include the Prime Rate, the London Interbank Offered Rate (LIBOR), and the Treasury Index ("T-Bill"). Other indexes like 11th District Cost of Funds Index, COSI, and MTA, are also available but are less popular.

Adjustable rates transfer part of the interest rate risk from the lender to the borrower, and thus are widely used where unpredictable interest rates make fixed rate loans difficult to obtain. Since the risk is transferred, lenders will usually make the initial interest rate of the ARM's note anywhere from 0.5% to 2% lower than the average 30-year fixed rate.

Additionally, lenders rely on credit reports and credit scores derived from them. The higher the score, the more creditworthy the borrower is assumed to be. Favorable interest rates are offered to buyers with high scores. Lower scores indicate higher risk to the lender, and lenders require higher interest rates in such scenarios to compensate for increased risk.

A partial amortization or balloon loan is one where the amount of monthly payments due are calculated (amortized) over a certain term, but the outstanding principal balance is due at some point short of that term. This payment is sometimes referred to as a "balloon payment". A balloon loan can be either a Fixed or Adjustable in terms of the Interest Rate. Many Second Trust mortgages use this feature. The most common way of describing a *balloon loan* uses the terminology X due in Y, where X is the number of years over which the loan is amortized, and Y is the year in which the principal balance is due. A contract could be written up so there would be more than one "balloon payment" required to be paid during the life of the loan.

Other loan types:

- Assumed mortgage
- Balloon mortgage

- Blanket loan
- Bridge loan
- Budget loan
- Buydown mortgage
- Commercial loan
- Equity loan
- Foreign National mortgage
- Graduated payment mortgage loan
- Hard money loan
- Jumbo mortgages
- Package loan
- Participation mortgage
- Reverse mortgage
- Repayment mortgage
- Seasoned mortgage
- Term loan or Interest-only loan
- Wraparound mortgage
- Negative amortization loan
- Non-Conforming Mortgage

United States Mortgage Process

In the U.S., the process by which a mortgage is secured by a borrower is called origination. This involves the borrower submitting an application and documentation related to his/her financial history and/or credit history to the underwriter. Many banks now offer "no-doc" or "low-doc" loans in which the borrower is required to submit only minimal financial information. These loans carry a slightly higher interest rate (perhaps 0.25% to 0.50% higher) and are available only to borrowers with excellent credit.

Sometimes, a third party is involved, such as a mortgage broker. This entity takes the borrower's information and reviews a number of lenders, selecting the ones that will best meet the needs of the consumer. Loans are often sold on the open market to larger investors by the originating mortgage hotel. Many of the guidelines that they follow are suited to satisfy investors. Some companies, called correspondent lenders, sell all or most of their closed loans to these investors, accepting some risks for issuing them. They often offer niche loans at higher prices that the investor does not wish to originate.

If the underwriter is not satisfied with the documentation provided by the borrower, additional documentation and conditions may be imposed, called stipulations. The meeting of such conditions can be a daunting experience for the consumer, but it is crucial for the lending institution to ensure the information being submitted is accurate and meets specific guidelines. This is done to give the lender a reasonable guarantee that the borrower can and will repay the loan. If a third party is involved in the loan, it will help the borrower to clear such conditions.

The following documents are typically required for traditional underwriter review. Over the past several years, use of "automated underwriting" statistical models has reduced the amount of documentation required from many borrowers. Such automated underwriting engines include Freddie Mac's "Loan Prospector" and Fannie Mae's "Desktop Underwriter". For borrowers who have excellent credit and very acceptable debt positions, there may be virtually no documentation of income or assets required at all. Many of these documents are also not required for no-doc and low-doc loans.

- Credit Report
- 1003 — Uniform Residential Loan Application
- 1004 — Uniform Residential Appraisal Report
- 1005 — Verification Of Employment (VOE)
- 1006 — Verification Of Deposit (VOD)
- 1007 — Single Family Comparable Rent Schedule
- 1008 — Transmittal Summary
- Copy of deed of current home
- Federal income tax records for last two years
- Verification of Mortgage (VOM) or Verification of Payment (VOP)
- Borrower's Authorization
- Purchase Sales Agreement
- 1084A and 1084B (Self-Employed Income Analysis) and 1088 (Comparative Income Analysis) - used if borrower is self-employed

Predatory Mortgage Lending

There is concern in the U.S. that consumers are often victims of predatory mortgage lending. The main concern is that mortgage brokers and lenders, operating legally, are finding loopholes in the law to obtain additional profit. The typical scenario is that terms of the loan are beyond the means of the borrower. The borrower makes a number of interest and principle payments, and then defaults. The lender then takes the property and recovers the amount of the loan, and also keeps the interest and principle payments, as well as loan origination fees.

Option ARM

An option ARM allows you the option to pay as little as a 1% interest rate. As a result, the difference between your payment and the interest on your loan that month becomes negative. The option ARM gives you four payment choices each month (1%, interest only, 30 year fixed rate, 15 year fixed rate). The interest rate will adjust every month, depending on which index the loan is tied to. These loans are useful for people who have a lot of equity in their home and don't want to pay higher monthly costs, as well as investors, allowing them the flexibility to choose which payment to make every month.

One of the important feature of this type of loan is that the minimum payments are often fixed for each year for an initial term of up to 5 years. The minimum payment may rise each year a little (payment size increases of 7.5% are common) but remain the same for another year. For example, a minimum payment for year 1 may be $1,000 per month each month all year long. In year 2 the minimum payment for each month is $1,075 each month. This is a gradual increase in the minimum payment. The interest rate may fluctuate each month, which means you can't predict your negative amortization ahead of time.

Costs

Lenders may charge various fees when giving a mortgage to a mortgagor. These include entry fees, exit fees, administration fees and lenders mortgage insurance. There are also settlement fees (closing costs) the settlement hotel will charge. In addition, if a third party handles the loan, it may charge other fees as well.

The United States Mortgage Finance Industry

Mortgage lending is a major category of the business of finance in the United States. Mortgages are commercial paper and can be conveyed and assigned freely to other holders. In the U.S., Federal government created several programs, or government sponsored entities, to foster mortgage lending, construction and encourage home ownership. These programs include the Government National Mortgage Association (known as Ginnie Mae), the Federal National Mortgage Association (known as Fannie Mae) and the Federal Home Loan Mortgage Corporation (known as Freddie Mac). These programs work by buying a large number of mortgages from banks and issuing (at a slightly lower interest rate) "mortgage-backed bonds" to investors, which are known as Mortgage Backed Securities (MBS).

This allows the banks to quickly relend the money to other borrowers (including in the form of mortgages) and thereby to create more mortgages than the banks could with the amount they have on deposit. This in turn allows the public to use these mortgages to purchase homes, something the government wishes to encourage. The investors, meanwhile, gain low-risk income at a higher interest rate (essentially the mortgage rate, minus the cuts of the bank and GSE) than they could gain from most other bonds.

Securitization is a momentous change in the way that mortgage bond markets function which has grown rapidly in the last 10 years as a result of the wider dissemination of technology in the mortgage lending world. For borrowers with superior credit, government loans and ideal profiles, this securitization keeps rates almost artificially low, since the pools of funds used to create new loans can be refreshed more quickly than in years past, allowing for more rapid outflow of capital from investors to borrowers without as many personal business ties as the past.

Mortgage in the UK

The UK mortgage market is one of the most innovative and competitive in the world. Unlike other countries there is no intervention in the market by the state or state funded entities and virtually all borrowing is funded by either mutual organisations (building societies and credit unions) or proprietary lenders (typically banks). Since 1982, when the market was substantially deregulated, there has been substantial innovation and diversification of strategies employed by lenders to attract borrowers. This has led to a wide range of mortgage types.

As lenders derive their funds either from the money markets or from deposits, most mortgages revert to a variable rate, either the lenders standard variable rate or a tracker rate, which will tend to be linked to the underlying Bank of England (BoE) repo rate (or sometimes LIBOR). Initially they will tend to offer an *incentive deal* to attract new borrowers. This may be:

- A fixed rate; where the interest rate remains constant for a set period; typically for 2, 3, 4, 5 or 10 years. Longer term fixed rates (over 5 years) whilst available, tend to be more expensive and therefore less popular than shorter term fixed rates.
- A capped rate; where similar to a fixed rate, the interest rate cannot rise above the *cap* but can vary beneath the cap. Sometimes there is a collar associated with this type of rate which imposes a minimum rate. Capped rate are often offered over periods similar to fixed rates, e.g. 2, 3, 4 or 5 years.
- A discount rate; where there is set margin reduction in the standard variable rate (e.g. a 2% discount) for a set period; typically 1 to 5 years. Sometimes the discount is expressed as a margin over the base rate (e.g. BoE base rate plus 0.5% for 2 years) and sometimes the rate is stepped (e.g. 3% in year 1, 2% in year 2, 1% in year three).
- A cashback mortgage; where a lump sum is provided (typically) as a percentage of the advance e.g. 5% of the loan.

To make matters more confusing these rates are often combined: For example, 4.5% 2 year fixed then a 3 year tracker at BoE rate plus 0.89%. With each incentive the lender may be offering a rate at less than the market cost of the borrowing. Therefore, they typically impose a penalty if the borrower repays the loan; this used to be called a *redemption penalty* or *tie-in*, however since the onset of Financial Services Authority regulation they are referred to as an early repayment charge.

Self Cert Mortgage

Mortgage lenders usually use salaries declared on wage slips to work out a borrower's annual income and will usually lend up to a fixed multiple of the borrower's annual income. Self Certification Mortgages, informally known as "self cert" mortgages, are available to employed and self employed people who have a deposit to buy a house but lack the sufficient documentation to prove their income. This type of mortgage can be beneficial to people whose income comes from multiple sources, whose salary consists largely or exclusively of commissions or bonuses, or whose accounts may not show a true reflection of their earnings. Self cert mortgages have two disadvantages: the interest rates charged are usually higher than for normal mortgages and the loan to value ratio is usually lower. Normally when a bank lends a customer money they want to protect their money as much as possible, they do this by asking the borrower to pay a certain percentage of the loan in the form of a deposit. 100% mortgages are mortgages that require no deposit (100% loan to value). These are sometimes offered to first time buyers, but almost always carry a higher interest rate on the loan.

UK Mortgage Process

UK lenders usually charge a valuation fee, which pays for a chartered surveyor to visit the property and ensure it is worth enough to cover the mortgage amount. This is not a full survey so it may not identify all the defects that a house buyer needs to know about. Also, it does not usually form a contract between the surveyor and the buyer, so the buyer has no right to sue if the survey fails to detect a major problem. For an extra fee, the surveyor can usually carry out a building survey or a (cheaper) "homebuyers survey" at the same time.

Islamic Mortgages

The Sharia law of Islam prohibits the payment or receipt of interest, which means that practising Muslims cannot use conventional mortgages. However, real estate is far too expensive for most people to buy outright using cash: Islamic mortgages solve this problem by having the property change hands twice. In one variation, the bank will buy the house outright and then act as a landlord. The homebuyer, in addition to paying rent, will pay a contribution towards the purchase of the property. When the last payment is made, the property changes hands.

Typically, this may lead to a higher final price for the buyers. This is because in some countries (such as the United Kingdom and India) there is a Stamp Duty which is a tax charged by the government on a change of ownership. Because ownership changes twice in an Islamic mortgage, a stamp tax is charged twice. An alternative scheme involves the bank reselling the property according to an installment plan, at a price higher than the original price. All of these methods are still compensating the lender as if they were charging interest, but the loans are structured in a way that in name they are not, but they share the financial risks involved in the transaction with the homebuyer.

ANNUITY

The term *annuity* is used in finance theory to refer to any terminating stream of fixed payments over a specified period of time. This usage is most commonly seen in academic discussions of finance, usually in connection with the valuation of the stream of payments, taking into account time value of money concepts.

Ordinary Annuity

An ordinary annuity (also referred as annuity-immediate) is an annuity whose payments are made at the end of each period (e.g. a month, a year). The present value of an ordinary annuity can be calculated through the formula

$$PV = A \bullet \frac{1 - \frac{1}{(1+r)^n}}{r}$$

In the limit as n increases,

$$\lim_{n \to \infty} PV = \frac{A}{r}$$

Thus even an infinite series of payments with a non-zero discount rate has a finite Present Value.

The future value of an ordinary annuity can be calculated through the formula

$$FV = A \bullet \frac{(1+r)^n - 1}{r}$$

In each of these formulae, A is the periodic amount of the annuity, r is the period interest rate, and n is the number of periods.

Annuity Due

An annuity-due is an annuity whose payments are made at the beginning of each period.

Because each annuity payment is allowed to compound for one extra period, the value of an annuity-due is equal to the value of the corresponding ordinary annuity multiplied by (1+r). Thus, the present value of an annuity-due can be calculated through the formula

$$PV = A \bullet \frac{1-\frac{1}{(1+r)^n}}{r} \bullet (1+r)$$

The future value of an of annuity-due can be calculated through the formula

$$FV = A \bullet \frac{(1+r)^n - 1}{r} \bullet (1+r)$$

Another intuitive way to interpret an annuity-due is as the sum of one annuity payment now (at time = 0) and an ordinary annuity without an annuity payment at the end of the last period (e.g. n-1).

Finding Annuity Values with a Financial Calculator

To calculate present value of an ordinary annuity, with an annual payment of $2000 for 10 years and an interest rate of 5%

To	*Press*	*Display*
Set all variables to defaults	[2nd] [RESET] [ENTER]	RST 0.00
Enter number of payments	*10* [N]	N= 10.00<
Enter interest rate per payment period	*5* [I/Y]	I/Y= 5.00<
Enter payment	*2000* [PMT]	PMT= 2,000.00<
Compute present value	[CPT] [PV]	PV= 15443.47

Note: Press [CPT] [FV] in the last step instead of [CPT] [PV] to calculate the future value

To calculate present value of an annuity due, with an annual payment of $2000 for 10 years and an interest rate of 5%

To	*Press*	*Display*
Set all variables to defaults	[2nd] [RESET] [ENTER]	RST 0.00
Enter number of payments	*10* [N]	N= 10.00<
Enter interest rate per payment period	*5* [I/Y]	I/Y= 5.00<
Enter payment	*2000* [PMT]	PMT= 2,000.00<
Set beginning-of-period payments	[2nd] [BGN] [2nd] [SET]	BGN
Return to calculator mode	[2nd] [QUIT]	0.00
Compute present value	[CPT] [PV]	PV= 16215.64

Note: Press [CPT] [FV] in the last step instead of [CPT] [PV] to calculate the future value(1)

Annuity (financial contracts)

Annuity contracts are offered by organizations and individuals that may accumulate value and take a current value and pay it out over a period of years. These contracts are regulated by various jurisdictions. Variable annuities are used for many different objectives. One common objective is tax deferral. Your money grows tax deferred meaning you do not pay taxes on gains until a withdrawal is made. Annuities offer a variety of subaccounts from various money managers. This gives investors the ability to move between subaccounts without incurring fees or loads.

Annuity contracts in the United States are defined by the Internal Revenue Code and regulated by the individual states. Annuities have features of life insurance and investment products. In the US, annuity contracts are only allowed to be sold by insurance companies, although private annuity contracts may be arranged between donors to non-profits to reduce taxes. Insurance companies are regulated by the states, so contracts or options that may be available in some states may not be available in others. However, their tax treatment is dictated by the Internal Revenue Code. There are two possible phases for an annuity, one phase where the customer deposits and accumulates money into the account, and the annuity phase where the insurance hotel pays income until the death of the customers named in the contract. The first phase has come to be named a "deferred annuity" as if it was a distinct product, while the second phase has been called an "immediate annuity", even though any annuity by definition must have the option for both phases.

Immediate Annuity

The term annuity in financial theory is most closely related to what is today called an *immediate annuity*. This is an insurance policy which in exchange for a sum of money, makes a series of payments. These payments may be either level or increasing periodic payments for a fixed term of years or until the ending of a life or two lives, or even whichever is longer. An immediate annuity is an annuity for which the income stream begins at a time after the initial payment which is less than the payment frequency. A common use for an immediate annuity is to provide a pension to a retired person or persons.

It is a financial contract which makes a series of payments with certain characteristics:

Rither level or fluctuating periodical payments

Made annually, or at more frequent intervals

Either for a fixed term of years (Annuity certain) or during the lifetime or one or more persons.

In advance or arrears

Reducing after the death of an annuitant

With a guaranteed period so the payment continues after the death of an annuitant. The overarching characteristic of the immediate annuity is that it is a vehicle for distributing savings with a tax deferred growth factor. A common use for an immediate annuity might be to provide a pension income.

In the US, the tax treatment of an immediate annuity is that every payment is a combination of a return of principal (not taxed) and income (taxed at normal income rates, not capital gain rates.) When a deferred annuity is annuitized, it works like an immediate annuity from that point on, but with a lower cost basis and thus more of the payment is taxed.

Annuity with Period Certain

This type of Immediate Annuity pays the annuitant for a designated number of years, and is used to fund a need that will end when the period is up (an example of this might be a life insurance policy). Thus this option is not necessarily suitable for an individuals retirement income, as the person may outlive the number of years the annuity will pay.

Life annuities

A life or lifetime immediate annuity is used to provide an income for the life of the annuitant similar to a defined benefit or pension plan. A life annuity works somewhat like a loan that is made by the purchaser (contract owner) to the issuing (insurance) hotel, who then pays back the original capital or principal (which isn't taxed) with interest and/or gains (which is taxed as ordinary income) to the *annuitant* on whose life the annuity is based. The assumed period of the loan is based on the life expectancy of the annuitant. In order to guarantee that the income continues for life, the insurance hotel relies on a concept called *cross-subsidy* or the "law of large numbers". Because an *annuity population* can be expected to have a distribution of lifespans around the population's mean (average) age, those dying earlier will give up income to support those living longer whose money may otherwise run out.

A life annuity, ideally, can reduce the 'problem' faced by a wealthy person that he/she doesn't know how long he/she will live, so doesn't know how fast to spend. Life annuities with payments indexed to the Consumer Price Index could be a good solution to this problem, but there is only a thin market for them in North America. Often life annuities are sold with a 'guarantee period' so that payments continue to designated beneficiaries, or are paid as a lump sum, if the annuitant dies within the guarantee period.

At a cost to the payments, an annuity can be purchased with addition of another life such as a spouse on whose life the annuity is wholly or partly guaranteed. For example, it is common to buy an annuity which will continue to pay out to the spouse of the annuitant after death, for as long as the spouse survives. The annuity paid to the spouse is called a reversionary annuity or survivorship annuity. However, if the annuitant is in good health, it may be more beneficial to select the higher payout option on their life only and purchase a life insurance policy that would pay income to the survivor. Other features such as a minimum guaranteed payment period irrespective of death, known as life with period certain, or *escalation* where the payment rises by inflation or a fixed rate annually can also be purchased.

Annuities with guaranteed periods are available from most providers. In such a product, if death takes place within the guaranteed period, payments continue top be made to a nominated beneficiary. Impaired life annuities for smokers or those with a particular illness are also available from some insurance companies. Since the life expectancy is reduced, the annuity rate is better (i.e. a higher annuity for the same initial payment).

Life annuities are priced based on the probability of the nominee surviving to receive the payments. Longevity insurance is a form of annuity that defers commencement of the payments until very late in life. A common longevity contract would be purchased at or before retirement but would not commence payments until 20 years after retirement. If the nominee dies before payments commence there is no payable benefit. This drastically reduces the cost of the annuity while still providing protection against outliving one's resources.

Life Annuity Variants

For an additional expense, (either by an increase in payments (premium) or decrease in benefits) an annuity or benefit rider can be purchased on another life such as a spouse, family member or friend whose life the annuity is wholly or partly guaranteed. For example, it is common to buy an annuity which will continue to pay out to the spouse of the annuitant after death, for as long as the spouse survives. The annuity paid to the spouse is called a reversionary annuity or survivorship annuity. However, if the annuitant is in good health, it may be more beneficial to select the higher payout option on their life only and purchase a life insurance policy that would pay income to the survivor. Other features such as a minimum guaranteed payment period irrespective of death, known as life with period certain, or *escalation* where the payment rises by inflation or a fixed rate annually can also be purchased.

Life with period certain annuities are more palatable to people who have accumulated money and would not like to lose all of it if they were to die soon after annuitization. At least the period certain payments will be made to their beneficiary. However, a viable alternative is to purchase a single premium life policy that would cover the lost premium in the annuity. Impaired life annuities for smokers or those with a particular illness are also available from some insurance companies. Since the life expectancy is reduced, the annual payment to the purchaser is raised.

Life annuities are priced based on the probability of the nominee surviving to receive the payments. Longevity insurance is a form of annuity that defers commencement of the payments until very late in life. A common longevity contract would be purchased at or before retirement but would not commence payments until 20 years after retirement. If the nominee dies before payments commence there is no payable benefit. This drastically reduces the cost of the annuity while still providing protection against outliving one's resources.

Deferred Annuity

The second usage for the term *annuity* came into being during the 1970s. This contract is more correctly referred to as a *deferred annuity* and is chiefly a vehicle for accumulating savings, and eventually distributing them either in the manner of an immediate annuity or as a lump-sum payment.

All varieties of deferred annuities owned by individuals have one thing in common: any increase in account values is *not* taxed until those gains are withdrawn. This is also known as tax-deferred growth. A deferred annuity which grows by interest rate earnings alone is correctly called a *fixed deferred annuity* (FAs). A deferred annuity that permits allocations to stock or bond funds and for which the account value is not guaranteed to stay above the initial amount invested is correctly called a *variable annuity* (VAs).

A new category of deferred annuities has emerged in 1995, called *equity indexed annuity* (EIA). Equity indexed annuities may have features of both deferred annuities just described. The insurance hotel typically guarantees a minimum return for EIA. An investor can still lose money if he or she cancels (or surrenders) the policy early, before a "break even" period. An over simplified EIA rate of return is equal to the "participation rate" multiplied by a target stock market index's performance excluding dividends. Interest rate caps, or administrative fee may be applicable.

There are two phases to a deferred annuity. The accumulation phase is the time between initial purchase and annuitization. The annuitization phase starts when the annuity is turned into a stream of payments. Before annuitization, the deferred annuity contract may allow the purchase of additional (premium) payments to the contract, increasing the contract's value. It should be noted that less than 1% of deferred annuinties are annuitized by annuitants.

Deferred annuities in the United States have an advantage that all capital gains and income are tax deferred until withdrawn. In theory, this allows more money to be put to work while the savings are accumulating, leading to higher returns. A disadvantage, however, is that when a variable annuity is withdrawn or inherited the interest/gains are treated as ordinary income and are taxed as such.

Features

A wide variety of features and guarantees have been developed by insurance companies in order to make annuity products more attractive. These include death and living benefit options, extra credit options, account balance guarantees, spousal continuation benefits, reduced CDSC (Contingent Deferred Sales Charge) or surrender charges and combinations thereof. Each feature or benefit added to a contract will typically be accompanied by an additional expense either directly (billed to client) or indirectly (inside product).

Deferred annuities are usually divided into two different kinds:

- Fixed Annuities offer some sort of guaranteed rate of return over the life of the contract. In general these are often positioned to be somewhat like bank CDs, and offer a rate of return competitive to CD's of similar time frames (with different tax treatments as previously mentioned). However, many fixed annuities do not have a completely fixed rate of return over the life of the contract, but rather a guaranteed minimum rate and a first year "teaser rate". The rate after the first year is often any amount that the insurance hotel wants to pay, but at least the minimum amount (typically 3%). Unlike most CD's, there are usually some clauses in the contract to allow a percentage of the interest and/or principal to be withdrawn early and without penalty (usually the interest earned in a 12 month period or 10%). Normally, fixed annuities become fully liquid upon death. Most Equity Index Annuities (EIA) also fall into this fixed category (aka Fixed Indexed Annuities - FIA) and their performance is typically tied to a stock market index (usually the SandP 500 or DOW). These products are guaranteed but are not as easy to understand as many think since there are usually caps, spreads, margains and crediting methods that can hender returns. These products also don't pay any of the participating market indices dividends, however the trade-off is you can never earn less than 0% in a negative year.

- Variable Annuities allow money to be invested in separate accounts (similar to mutual funds) in a tax deferred manner. Overall their primary use is to allow someone to engage in tax deferred investing for retirement at amounts greater than permitted by individual retirement or 401(k) plans. In addition, many variable annuity contracts offer a guaranteed minimum rate of return (either for a future withdrawal and/or in the case of the owners death), even if the underlying separate account investments perform poorly. This can be attractive to people uncomfortable investing in the equity markets without the guarantees. However, an investor will pay for each benefit provided by a variable annuity, since insurance companies in general do not write money losing contracts; look at the charges carefully. These products are often heavily criticized as being sold to the wrong persons, who could have done better doing something else, since the commissions paid by this product are often very high relative to other investment products.

There are several types of these performance guarantees, and many times one can choose them a la carte, with higher charges for guarantees that are riskier for the insurance companies. There are guaranteed minimum death benefits (GMDBs), which can be received only if the owner of the annuity contract, or the covered annuitant, dies.

These GMDBs come in various flavors, in order of increasing risk to the insurance hotel:

1. Return of premium (a guarantee that you will not have a negative return)
2. Roll-up of premium at a particular rate (a guarantee that you will achieve a minimum rate of return, greater than 0)
3. Maximum anniversary value (looks back at account value on the anniversaries, and guarantees you will get at least as much as the highest values upon death)
4. Greater of maximum anniversary value or particular roll-up

Even riskier for insurance companies are the guaranteed living benefits, which tend to be elective. Unlike death benefits, which the contractholder generally can't time, living benefits have significant risk for the insurance companies as contractholders will likely exercise these benefits when they are worth the most. Annuities with guaranteed living benefits (GLBs) tend to have very high fees.

Some GLB examples, in no particular order:

1. Guaranteed minimum income benefit (a guarantee that one will get a minimum income stream upon annuitization at a particular point in the future.)
2. Guaranteed minimum accumulation benefit (a guarantee that the account value will be at a certain amount at a certain point in the future)
3. Guaranteed minimum withdrawal benefit (a guarantee similar to the income benefit, but one that doesn't require annuitizing)
4. Guaranteed for-life income benefit (a guarantee similar to a withdrawal benefit, but will pay you for as long as you live and does not require annuitization)

Criticisms of Deferred Annuities

Deferred annuities are, generally, sold by financial professionals some might work directly for an insurance hotel. The financial professional who sells annuities do collect a commission from the insurance hotel. This commission will be a percentage of the total premium paid by the investor. This percentage can be as little as 1% and as high as 12%, the commission is usually 6% on average. Since these commissions, on the surface, seem high and there are deferred sales charges on annuities many financial gurus have criticized annuity products.

The investor will, generally, not pay any of this commission directly to the financial professional; the commission is paid by the insurance hotel to the financial professional up front. The insurance hotel will recapture the commission paid to the financial professional through the fees charged to the customer (in a variable or equity index annuity) or the spread in the interest rate market (for a fixed annuity). There are also deferred backend charges that will be applied if the investor closes out their contract before the agreed upon time frame, usually 8 years. These charges can be as little as 1 year or as many as 20 years. These backend charges are of concern to many financial professionals and financial gurus. There are annuities available that do not have any deferred surrender charges and they do not pay the financial professional commissions. These contracts are called "no-load" variable annuity products and are available, usually, from a fee-based financial planner or a no-load mutual fund hotel. There are, however, still fees that are imposed on these contracts, but they are less than those sold by commissioned brokers.

Variable Annuities are contraversial because many believe the extra fees involved with them will almost certainly reduce the rate of return compared to what the investor could make by investing directly in the market. A big selling point for variable annuities are the guaruntees many have, such as the guaruntee that the customer will not lose their principal. Critics say that these guaruntees are not necessary because over the long term the market has always been positive, while others say that many unsophisticated investors simply will not invest without the guaruntees.

A controversial practice of insurance sales is the selling of insurance contracts within an IRA or 401(k) plan in the US. Since these investment vehicles are already tax deferred, investors do not receive additional tax shelters from the annuities. The benefit of the annuity contract is the guaranteed lifetime income that all annuity contracts must have by state law. However, over 90% of annuitants do not take the life annuity upon retirement but take a lump sum cash out. If you do not intend to take the life income option from an annuity contract at retirement, then consider a low cost deferred annuity. On the other hand, if you need to take lifetime income at retirement, try to buy it when you retire or select a 401(k) plan with an option to buy the annuity just before retirement. Only if you want the security of having a lifetime option guaranteed for you should you take the annuity during the deferral (or savings phase) of your 401(k) planning.

ACTUARIAL CONSIDERATIONS

Actuarial Formulae are used to model annuities and determine their price.

Payment options for Immediate Annuities

In technical language an annuity is said to be payable for an assigned *status*, this being a general word chosen in preference to such words as "time", "term" or "period," because it may include more readily either a term of years certain, or a life or combination of lives. The *magnitude* of the annuity is the sum to be paid (and received) in the course of each year. Thus, if £100 is to be received each year by a person, he is said to have *"an annuity of £100."* If the payments are made half-yearly, it is sometimes said that he has *"a half-yearly annuity of £100"*; but to avoid ambiguity, it is more commonly said he has *an annuity of £100, payable by half-yearly instalments*. An annuity is considered as accruing during each instant of the status for which it is enjoyed, although it is only payable at fixed intervals. If the enjoyment of an annuity is postponed until after the lapse of a certain number of years, the annuity is said to be *deferred*. If an annuity, instead of being payable at the end of each year, half-year, andc., is payable in advance, it is called an *annuity-due*. The holder of an annuity is called an *annuitant*, and the person on whose life the annuity depends is called the *nominee*.

Upon immediate annuitization, a wide variety of options are available in the way the stream of payments is paid. If the annuity is paid over a fixed period independent of any contingency, it is known as an *"annuity with period certain"*, or just *annuity certain*; if it is to continue for ever, it is called a *perpetuity*; and if in the latter case it is not to commence until after a term of years, it is called a *deferred perpetuity*. An annuity depending on the continuance of an assigned life or lives would commonly be called a *life annuity*, but also known as a *life-contingent annuity* or simply *lifetime annuity*; but more commonly the simple term "annuity" is understood to mean a life annuity, unless the contrary is stated. The payments can also be paid over the lifetime of the nominee(s) or for a fixed period, whichever is longer. This is known as *"life with period certain"*.

A hybrid of these is when the payments stop at death, but also after a predetermined number of payments, if this is earlier: known as a *temporary life annuity*. The difference with the period certain annuity is that the period certain annuity will keep paying after the death of the nominee until the period is completed. If not otherwise stated, it is always understood that an annuity is payable yearly, and that the annual payment (or rent, as it is sometimes called) is a single currency unit.

Instances of perpetuities are the dividends upon the public stocks in England, France and some other countries. Thus, although it is usual to speak of £100 consols, the reality is the yearly dividend which the government pays by quarterly instalments. The practice of the French in this is arguably more logical. In speaking of their public funds (*rentes*) they do not mention the ideal capital sum, but speak of the annuity or annual payment that is received by the public creditor. Other instances of perpetuities are the incomes derived from the debenture stocks of railway companies, also the feu-duties commonly payable on house property in Scotland. The number of years' purchase which the perpetual annuities granted by a government or a railway hotel realize in the open market, forms a very simple test of the credit of the various governments or railways.

In the United Kingdom, the income from *Compulsory Purchase Annuities* purchased with pension funds or by an employer immediately on retirement (a *Hancock* annuity) is treated as taxable income. The income from *Purchased Life Annuities*, bought by any other means, has an element which is considered return of capital, and only the excess over this is considered a gain that is subject to income tax. The element considered capital return is based on life expectancy and will therefore increase with age.

Government Incentives

Because of cross-subsidy and the guarantees an annuity can give against running out of income and becoming dependent on state welfare in old age, annuities often have a favourable tax treatment, which may affect how attractive they are relative to other investments.

Immediate annuities are a compulsory feature of certain pension saving schemes in some countries, where the government grants tax deductions, provided that savings are paid into a fund which can only (or mainly) be withdrawn as an annuity. The United Kingdom and the Netherlands have such schemes. From 2003 the tax deduction in the Netherlands is only allowed if, without additional savings, the old age income would be less than 70% of the current income.

In the UK and the Republic of Ireland contributions into pension savings are generally nett of income tax (i.e tax relief is available), up to certain limits. Although a number of different regimes exist, personal pension funds taken out since 1988 must use at least 75% of the fund to purchase an annuity by the 75th birthday of the annuitant. If an annuity is not immediately purchased retirement income up until this age can be drawn from the fund by using *Pension Income Withdrawal* commonly known as *Income Drawdown*. This operates under a strict code of rules and limits according to age and figures said by the Government Actuarial Department to prevent the fund being eroded too fast. Individuals may vary withdrawals between 35% and 100% of a maximum limit, that is reset every three years - known as the *triennial review*. Income Drawdown carries both the investment risk of the invested pension fund and mortality drag that occurs from the loss of cross subsidy and advancing average age expectancy that occurs in the time over which annuity purchase is delayed.

Terminable Annuities

Terminable annuities are employed in the system of British public finance as a means of reducing the National Debt. This result is attained by substituting for a perpetual annual charge (or one lasting until the capital which it represents can be paid off *en bloc*), an annual charge of a larger amount, but lasting for a short term. The latter is so calculated as to pay off, during its existence, the capital which it replaces, with interest at an assumed or agreed rate, and under specified conditions. The practical effect of the substitution of a terminable annuity for an obligation of longer currency is to bind the present generation of citizens to increase its own obligations in the present and near future in order to diminish those of its successors. This end might be attained in other ways; for instance, by setting aside out of revenue a fixed annual sum for the purchase and cancellation of debt (Pitt's method, in intention), or by fixing the annual debt charge at a figure sufficient to provide a margin for reduction of the principal of the debt beyond the amount required for interest (Sir Stafford Northcote's method), or by providing an annual surplus of revenue over expenditure (the "Old Sinking Fund"), available for the same purpose. All these methods have been tried in the course of British financial history, and the second and third of them are still employed; but on the whole the method of terminable annuities has been the one preferred by chancellors of the exchequer and by parliament.

Terminable annuities, as employed by the British government, fall under two heads:—

Those issued to, or held by private persons;

Those held by government departments or by funds under government control.

The important difference between these two classes is that an annuity under (1), once created, cannot be modified except with the holder's consent, *i.e.* is practically unalterable without a breach of public faith; whereas an annuity under (2) can, if necessary, be altered by interdepartmental arrangement under the authority of parliament. Thus annuities of class (1) fulfil most perfectly the object of the system as explained above; while those of class (2) have the advantage that in times of emergency their operation can be suspended without any inconvenience or breach of faith, with the result that the resources of government can on such occasions be materially increased, apart from any additional taxation. For this purpose it is only necessary to retain as a charge on the income of the year a sum equal to the (smaller) perpetual charge which was originally replaced by the (larger) terminable charge, whereupon the difference between the two amounts is temporarily released, while ultimately the increased charge is extended for a period equal to that for which it is suspended.

Annuities of class (1) were first instituted in 1808, but were later regulated by an act of 1829. They may be granted either for a specified life, or two lives, or for an arbitrary term of years; and the consideration for them may take the form either of cash or of government stock, the latter being cancelled when the annuity is set up. Annuities (2) held by government departments date from 1863. They were created in exchange for permanent debt surrendered for cancellation, the principal operations having been effected in 1863, 1867,

1870, 1874, 1883 and 1899. Annuities of this class do not affect the public at all, except of course in their effect on the market for government securities. They are merely financial operations between the government, in its capacity as the banker of savings banks and other funds, and itself, in the capacity of custodian of the national finances. Savings bank depositors are not concerned with the manner in which government invests their money, their rights being confined to the receipt of interest and the repayment of deposits upon specified conditions. The case is, however, different as regards forty millions of consols (included in the above figures), belonging to suitors in chancery, which were cancelled and replaced by a terminable annuity in 1883. As the liability to the suitors in that case was for a specified amount of stock, special arrangements were made to ensure the ultimate replacement of the precise amount of stock cancelled.

ANNUITY CALCULATIONS

The mathematical theory of life annuities is based upon a knowledge of the rate of mortality among mankind in general, or among the particular class of persons on whose lives the annuities depend. It involves a mathematical treatment too complicated to be dealt with fully in this place, and in practice it has been reduced to the form of tables, which vary in different places, but which are easily accessible.

Abraham Demoivre, in his *Annuities on Lives*, put forth a very simple law of mortality which is to the effect that, out of 86 children born alive, 1 will die every year until the last dies between the ages of 85 and 86. This law agreed sufficiently well at the middle ages of life with the mortality deduced from the best observations of his time; but, as observations became more exact, the approximation was found to be not sufficiently close. This was particularly the case when it was desired to obtain the value of joint life, contingent or other complicated benefits. Therefore Demoivre's law is entirely devoid of practical utility. No simple formula has yet been discovered that will represent the rate of mortality with sufficient accuracy. The rate of mortality at each age is, therefore, in practice usually determined by a series of figures deduced from observation; and the value of an annuity at any age is found from these numbers by means of a series of arithmetical calculations.

DE WITT'S PRINCIPLE

The first writer who is known to have attempted to obtain, on correct mathematical principles, the value of a life annuity, was Jan De Witt, grand pensionary of Holland and West Friesland. Our knowledge of his writings on the subject is derived from two papers contributed by Frederick Hendriks to the *Assurance Magazine*, vol. ii. p. 222, and vol. in. p. 93. The former of these contains a translation of De Witt's report upon the value of life annuities, which was prepared in consequence of the resolution passed by the states-general, on the 25th of April 1671, to negotiate funds by life annuities, and which was distributed to the members on the 30th of July 1671. The latter contains the translation of a number of letters addressed by De Witt to Burgomaster Johan Hudde, bearing dates from September 1670 to October 1671. The existence of De Witt's report was well known among his contemporaries, and Hendriks collected a number of extracts from various authors referring to it; but the report is not contained in any collection of his works extant, and had been entirely lost for 180 years, until Hendriks discovered it among the state archives of Holland in hotel with the letters to Hudde. It is a document of extreme interest, and (notwithstanding some inaccuracies in the reasoning) of very great merit, more especially considering that it was the very first document on the subject that was ever written.

It appears that it had long been the practice in Holland for life annuities to be granted to nominees of any age, in the constant proportion of double the rate of interest allowed on stock; that is to say, if the towns were borrowing money at 6%, they would be willing to grant a life annuity at 12%, and so on. De Witt states that "annuities have been sold, even in the present century, first at six years' purchase, then at seven and eight; and that the majority of all life annuities now current at the country's expense were obtained at nine years' purchase"; but that the price had been increased in the course of a few years from eleven years' purchase to twelve, and from twelve to fourteen. He also states that the rate of interest had been successively reduced from 6–¼% to 5%, and then to 4%. The principal object of his report is to prove that, taking interest at 4%, a life annuity was worth at least sixteen years' purchase; and, in fact, that an annuitant purchasing an annuity for the life of a young and healthy nominee at sixteen years' purchase, made an excellent bargain.

It may be mentioned that he argues that it is more to the advantage, both of the country and of the private investor, that the public loans should be raised by way of grant of life annuities rather than perpetual annuities. It appears conclusively from De Witt's correspondence with Hudde, that the rate of mortality assumed as the basis of his calculations was deduced from careful examination of the mortality that had actually prevailed among the nominees on whose lives annuities had been granted in former years. De Witt appears to have come to the conclusion that the probability of death is the same in any half-year from the age of 3 to 53 inclusive; that in the next ten years, from 53 to 63, the probability is greater in the ratio of 3 to 2; that in the next ten years, from 63 to 73, it is greater in the ratio of 2 to 1; and in the next seven years, from 73 to 80, it is greater in the ratio of 3 to 1; and he places the limit of human life at 80. If a mortality table of the usual form is deduced from these suppositions, out of 212 persons alive at the age of 3, 2 will die every year up to 53, 3 in each of the ten years from 53 to 63, 4 in each of the next ten years from 63 to 73, and 6 in each of the next seven years from 73 to 80, when all will be dead.

De Witt calculates the value of an annuity in the following way. Assume that annuities on 10,000 lives each ten years of age, which satisfy the Hm mortality table, have been purchased. Of these nominees 79 will die before attaining the age of 11, and no annuity payment will be made in respect of them; none will die between the ages of 11 and 12, so that annuities will be paid for one year on 9921 lives; 40 attain the age of 12 and die before 13, so that two payments will be made with respect to these lives. Reasoning in this way we see that the annuities on 35 of the nominees will be payable for three years; on 40 for four years, and so on. Proceeding thus to the end of the table, 15 nominees attain the age of 95, 5 of whom die before the age of 96, so that 85 payments will be paid in respect of these 5 lives. Of the survivors all die before attaining the age of 97, so that the annuities on these lives will be payable for 86 years. Having previously calculated a table of the values of annuities certain for every number of years up to 86, the value of all the annuities on the 10,000 nominees will be found by taking 40 times the value of an annuity for 2 years, 35 times the value of an annuity for 3 years, and so on—the last term being the value of 10 annuities for 86 years—and adding them together; and the value of an annuity on one of the nominees will then be found by dividing by 10,000.

De Witt's report being thus of the nature of an unpublished state paper, although it contributed to its author's reputation, did not contribute to advance the exact knowledge of the subject; and the author to whom the credit must be given of first showing how to calculate the value of an annuity on correct principles is Edmund Halley. He gave the first approximately correct mortality table (deduced from the records of the numbers of deaths and baptisms in the city of Breslau), and showed how it might be employed to calculate the value of an annuity on the life of a nominee of any age.

Previously to Halley's time, and apparently for many years subsequently, all dealings with life annuities were based upon mere conjectural estimates. The earliest known reference to any estimate of the value of life annuities rose out of the requirements of the Falcidian law, which (40 B.C.) was adopted in the Roman empire, and which declared that a testator should not give more than three-fourths of his property in legacies, so that at least one-fourth must go to his legal representatives. It is easy to see how it would occasionally become necessary, while this law was in force, to value life annuities charged upon a testator's estate. Aemilius Macer (A.D. 230) states that the method which had been in common use at that time was as follows:—From the earliest age until 30 take 30 years' purchase, and for each age after 30 deduct 1 year. It is obvious that no consideration of compound interest can have entered into this estimate; and it is easy to see that it is equivalent to assuming that all persons who attain the age of 30 will certainly live to the age of 60, and then certainly die. Compared with this estimate, that which was propounded by the praetorian prefect Ulpian was a great improvement. His table is as follows:—

Age	Years' Purchase	Age	Years' Purchase
Birth – 20	30	45 – 46	14
20 – 25	28	46 – 47	13
25 – 30	25	47 – 48	12
30 – 35	22	48 – 49	11
35 – 40	20	49 – 50	10
40 – 41	19	50 – 55	9
41 – 42	18	55 – 60	7
42 – 43	17	60 and upwards	
43 – 44	16		
44 – 45	15		

Here also we have no reason to suppose that the element of interest was taken into consideration; and the assumption, that between the ages of 40 and 50 each addition of a year to the nominee's age diminishes the value of the annuity by one year's purchase, is equivalent to assuming that there is no probability of the nominee dying between the ages of 40 and 50. Considered, however, simply as a table of the average duration of life, the values are fairly accurate. At all events, no more correct estimate appears to have been arrived at until the close of the 17th century.

The first author who fully developed the powers of the table was John Nicholas Tetens, a native of Schleswig, who in 1785, while professor of philosophy and mathematics at Kiel, published in the German language an *Introduction to the Calculation of Life Annuities and Assurances*. This work appears to have been quite unknown in England until F. Hendriks gave, in the first number of the *Assurance Magazine,* an account of it, with a translation of the passages describing the construction and use of the commutation table, and a sketch of the author's life and writings, to which we refer the reader who desires fuller information. It may be mentioned here that Tetens also gave only a specimen table, apparently not imagining that persons using his work would find it extremely useful to have a series of commutation tables, calculated and printed ready for use.

The use of the commutation table was independently developed in England-apparently between the years 1788 and 1811— by George Barrett, of Petworth, Sussex, who was the son of a yeoman farmer, and was himself a village schoolmaster, and afterwards farm steward or bailiff. It has been usual to consider Barrett as the originator in England of the method of calculating the values of annuities by means of a commutation table, and this method is accordingly sometimes called Barrett's method. (It is also called the commutation method and the columnar method.) Barrett's method of calculating annuities was explained by him to Francis Baily in the year 1811, and was first made known to the world in a paper written by the latter and read before the Royal Society in 1812.

By what has been universally considered an unfortunate error of judgment, this paper was not recommended by the council of the Royal Society to be printed, but it was given by Baily as an appendix to the second issue (in 1813) of his work on life annuities and assurances. Barrett had calculated extensive tables, and with Baily's aid attempted to get them published by subscription, but without success; and the only printed tables calculated according to his manner, besides the specimen tables given by Baily, are the tables contained in Babbage's *Comparative View of the various Institutions for the Assurance of Lives*, 1826.

The theory of annuities may be further studied in the discussions in the English *Journal of the Institute of Actuaries*. The institute was founded in the year 1848, the first sessional meeting being held in January 1849. Its establishment has contributed in various ways to promote the study of the theory of life contingencies. Among these may be specified the following:— Before it was formed, students of the subject worked for the most part alone, and without any concert; and when any person had made an improvement in the theory, it had little chance of becoming publicly known unless he wrote a formal treatise on the whole subject. But the formation of the institute led to much greater interchange of opinion among actuaries, and afforded them a ready means of making known to their professional associates any improvements, real or supposed, that they thought they had made. Again, the discussions which follow the reading of papers before the institute have often served, first, to bring out into bold relief differences of opinion that were previously unsuspected, and afterwards to soften down those differences,— to correct extreme opinions in every direction, and to bring about a greater agreement of opinion on many important subjects. In no way, probably, have the objects of the institute been so effectually advanced as by the publication of its *Journal*.

The first number of this work, which was originally called the *Assurance Magazine*, appeared in September 1850, and it has been continued quarterly down to the present time. It was originated by the public spirit of two well-known actuaries (Mr Charles Jellicoe and Mr Samuel Brown), and was adopted as the organ of the Institute of Actuaries in the year 1852, and called the *Assurance Magazine and Journal of the Institute of Actuaries*, Mr Jellicoe continuing to be the editor,—a post he held until the year 1867, when he was succeeded by Mr T. B. Sprague (who contributed to the 9th edition of this Encyclopaedia an elaborate article on "Annuities," on which the above account is based). The name was again changed in 1866, the words "Assurance Magazine" being dropped; but in the following year it was considered desirable to resume these, for the purpose of showing the continuity of the publication, and it is now called the *Journal of the Institute of Actuaries and Assurance Magazine*.

This work contains not only the papers read before the institute (to which have been appended of late years short abstracts of the discussions on them), and many original papers which were unsuitable for reading, together with correspondence, but also reprints of many papers published elsewhere, which from various causes had become difficult of access to the ordinary reader, among which may be specified various papers which originally appeared in the *Philosophical Transactions*, the *Philosophical Magazine*, the *Mechanics' Magazine*, and the *Companion to the Almanac*; also translations of various papers from the French, German, and Danish. Among the useful objects which the continuous publication of the *Journal* of the institute has served, we may specify in particular two:—that any supposed improvement in the theory was effectually submitted to the criticisms of the whole actuarial profession, and its real value speedily discovered; and that any real improvement, whether great or small, being placed on record, successive writers have been able, one after the other, to take it up and develop it, each commencing where the previous one had left off.

VALUATION

The premium for an option contract is ultimately determined by supply and demand, but is influenced by five principal factors:

- The price of the underlying security in relation to...
- The strike price. Options will be in-the-money when there is a positive intrinsic value; when the strike price is above/below (put/call) the security's current price. They will be at-the-money when the strike price equals the security's current price. They will be out-of-the-money when the strike price is below/above (put/call) the security's current price. Options at-the-money or out-of-the-money have an intrinsic value of zero.
- The cumulative cost required to hold a position in the security (including interest + dividends).
- The time to expiration. The time value decreases to zero at its expiration date. The option style determines when the buyer may exercise the option. Generally the contract will either be American style - which allows exercise up to the expiration date - or European style - where exercise is only allowed on the expiration date - or Bermudan style - where exercise is allowed on several, specific dates up to the expiration date. European contracts are easier to value. Due to the *"American"* style option having the advantage of an early exercise day (*i.e.* at any time on or before the options expiry date), they are always at least as valuable as the *"European"* style option (only exercisable at the expiration date).
- The estimate of the future volatility of the security's price. This is perhaps the least-known input into any pricing model for options, therefore traders often look to the marketplace to see what the implied volatility of an option is — meaning that given the price of an option and all the other inputs except volatility you can solve for that value.

Pricing models include the binomial options model for American options and the Black-Scholes model for European options. Even though there are pricing models, the value of an option is a personal decision, requiring multiple trade offs and depending on the investment objective.

Because options are derivatives, they can be combined with different combinations of

- Other options
- Risk free T-bills
- The underlying security, and
- Futures contracts on that security to create a risk neutral portfolio (zero risk, zero cost, zero return). In a liquid market, arbitrageurs ensure that the values of all these assets are 'self-leveling', i.e. they incorporate the same assumptions of risk/reward. In theory traders could buy cheap options and sell expensive options (relative to their theoretical prices), in quantities such that the overall delta is zero, and expect to make a profit. Nevertheless, implementing this in practice may be difficult because of "stale" stock prices, large bid/ ask spreads, market closures and other symptoms of stock market illiquidity. If stock market prices do not follow a random walk (due, for example, to insider trading) this delta neutral strategy or other model-based strategies may encounter further difficulties. Even for veteran traders using very sophisticated models, option trading is not an easy game to play.

History of Valuation

Models of option pricing were very simple and incomplete until 1973 when Fischer Black and Myron Scholes published the Black-Scholes pricing model. Scholes received the 1997 Bank of Sweden Prize in Economic Sciences (Nobel Prize of Economics) for this work, along with Robert C. Merton. In a departure from tradition, Fischer Black was specifically mentioned in the award, even though he had died and was therefore not eligible.

The Black-Scholes model gives theoretical values for European put and call options on non-dividend paying stocks. The key argument is that traders could risklessly hedge a long options position with a short position in the stock and continuously adjust the hedge ratio (the delta value — one of the option sensitivities known as "greeks") as needed. Assuming that the stock price follows a random walk, and using the methods of stochastic calculus, a price for the option can be calculated where there is no arbitrage profit. This price depends only on 5 factors: the current stock price, the exercise price, the risk-free interest rate, the time until expiration, and the volatility of the stock price. Eventually, the model was adapted to be able to price options on dividend paying stocks as well.

The availability of a good estimate of an option's theoretical price contributed to the explosion of trading in options. Other option pricing models have since been developed for other markets and situations using similar arguments, assumptions, and tools, including the Black model for options on futures, Monte Carlo methods, Path Integrals, and Binomial options models.

Market interest rates

There are markets for investments which include the money market, bond market, as well as retail financial institutions like banks, which set interest rates. Each specific debt takes into account the following factors in determining its interest rate:

Inflation: Since the lender is deferring his consumption, he will at a bare minimum, want to recover enough to pay the increased cost of goods due to inflation. Because future inflation is unknown, there are three tactics.

- Charge X% interest 'plus inflation'. Many governments issue 'real-return' or 'inflation indexed' bonds. The principal amount and the interest payments are continually increased by the rate of inflations.
- Decide on the 'expected' inflation rate. This still leaves both parties exposed to the risk of 'unexpected' inflation.
- Allow the interest rate to be periodically changed. While a 'fixed interest rate' remains the same throughout the life of the debt, 'variable' or 'floating' rates can be reset. There are derivative products that allow for hedging and swaps between the two.

Default: There is always the risk the borrower will become bankrupt, abscond or otherwise default on the loan. The risk premium attempts to measure the integrity of the borrower, the risk of his enterprise succeeding and the security of any collateral pledged. Loans to developing countries have higher risk premiums than those to the US government. An operating line of credit to a business will have a higher rate than a mortgage.

The credit worthiness of businesses is measured by bond rating services and individual's credit scores by credit bureaus. The risks of an individual debt may have a large standard deviation of possibilities. The lender may want to cover his maximum risk. But lenders with portfolios of debt can lower the risk premium to cover just the most probable outcome.

Deferred consumption: Charging interest equal only to inflation will leave the lender with the same purchasing power, but he would prefer his own consumption NOW rather than later. There will be an interest premium of the delay. He may not want to consume, but instead would invest in another product. The possible return he could realize in competing investments will determine what interest he charges.

Length of time: Time has two effects.

- Shorter terms have less risk of default and inflation because the near future is easier to predict than events 20 year off.

- Longer terms allow for investments in larger projects with higher eventual returns. Contrast this to the lender's preference for readily available cash for contingencies. This is why banks pay higher interest on non-redeemable GICs than on chequing account balances.

Other: Borowers and lenders may face individual tax rates, transaction costs and foreign exchange rate risks. In a liquid market they cannot exert their personal preferences. It is the sum total of the participants who determine rates. The market for financial instruments has moved from the local, to the national, and is now international.

INTEREST RATES

Output and unemployment

Interest rates are the main determinant of investment on a macroeconomic scale. Broadly speaking, if interest rates increase across the board, then investment decreases, causing a fall in national income. Note that if interest rates are high, that means the broad economy is doing well and thus people will be willing to borrow money at higher interest rates.

Interest rates are generally determined by the market, but government intervention - usually by a central bank- may strongly influence short-term interest rates, and is used as the main tool of monetary policy. The central bank offers to buy or sell money at the desired rate and, because of their immense size, they are able to influence in. By altering in the central bank is able to affect the interest rates faced by everyone who wants to borrow money for economic investment. Investment can change rapidly to changes in interest rates, affecting national income. Through Okun's Law changes in output affect unemployment. Open Market Operations in the United States

The Federal Reserve (often referred to as 'The Fed') implements monetary policy largely by targeting the federal funds rate. This is the rate that banks charge each other for overnight loans of federal funds, which are the reserves held by banks at the Fed.

Open market operations are one tool within monetary policy implemented by the Federal Reserve to steer short-term interest rates. Using the power to buy and sell treasury securities, the Open Market Desk at the Federal Reserve Bank of New York can supply the market with dollars by purchasing T-notes, hence increasing the nation's money supply. By increasing the money supply or Aggregate Supply of Funding (ASF), interest rates will fall due to the excess of dollars banks will end up with in their reserves. Excess reserves may be lent in the Fed funds market to other banks, thus driving down rates.

Money and Inflation

Loans, bonds, and shares have some of the characteristics of money and are included in the broad money supply. By setting, the government institution can affect the markets to alter the total of loans, bonds and shares issued. Generally speaking, a higher real interest rate reduces the broad money supply.

Through the quantity theory of money, increases in the money supply lead to inflation. This means that interest rates can affect inflation in the future.

Historical documents dating back to the Sumerian civilization, circa 3000 B.C., reveal that the ancient world had developed a formalized system of credit based on two major commodities, grain and silver. Before there were coins, metal loans were based on weight. Archaeologists have uncovered pieces of metal that were used in trade in Troy, Minoan and Mycenaean civilizations, Babylonia, Assyria, Egypt and Persia. Before money loans came into existence, loans of grain and silver served to facilitate trade. Silver was used in town economies, while grain was used in the country.

The collection of interest was restricted by Jewish, Christian, Islam and other religions under laws of usury (essentially a derogatory term for interest). This is still the case with Islam, which mandates no-interest Islamic finance.

Irving Fisher is largely responsible for shaping the modern concept of interest with his 1930 work, *The Theory of Interest*.

INVESTMENT

Investment or investing is a term with several closely-related meanings in business management, finance and economics, related to saving or deferring consumption. An asset is usually purchased, or equivalently a deposit is made in a bank, in hopes of getting a future return or interest from it. Literally, the word means the "action of putting something in to somewhere else" (perhaps originally related to a person's garment or 'vestment').

Types of Investment

The major difference in the use of the term investment between the economics field and the finance field is that economists refer to a real investment (such as a machine or a house), while financial economists refer to a financial asset, such as money that is put into a bank or the market, which may then be used to buy a real asset.

Business Management

The investment decision (also known as capital budgeting) is one of the fundamental decisions of business management: managers determine the assets that the business enterprise obtains; these assets may be physical (e.g. buildings or machinery), intangible (e.g. patents, software, goodwill), or financial. Whatever the type of asset, the manager must assess whether the net present value of the investment to the enterprise is positive; the net present value is calculated using the enterprise's marginal cost of capital.

Economics

In Economics, investment means the purchase (and thus the production) and/or stock of capital goods and/or technology - goods which are not consumed but instead used in future production. Examples include building a railroad, or a factory, clearing land, or putting oneself through college. In measures of national income and output, investment is also a component of GDP given in the formula GDP = C + I + G + NX. The investment function in that aspect is divided into non-residential investment (such as factories, machinery etc) and residential investment (new houses). Investment is often modeled as a function of income and interest rates, given by the relation I = (Y, i). An increase in income will encourage higher investment, whereas a higher interest rate may discourage investment as it becomes costlier to borrow money. Even if a firm chooses to use its own funds in an investment, the interest rate represents an opportunity cost of investing those funds rather than loaning them out for interest.

Finance

In finance, investment means buying securities or other monetary or paper (financial) assets in the money markets or capital markets, or in fairly liquid real assets, such as gold as an investment, real estate, or collectibles. Valuation is the method for assessing whether a potential investment is worth its price.

Types of financial investments include shares or other equity investment, and bonds (including bonds denominated in foreign currencies). These investments assets are then expected to provide income or positive future cash flows, but may increase or decrease in value giving the investor capital gains or losses.

Trades in contingent claims or *derivative securities* do not necessarily have future positive expected cash flows - so are not considered to be assets, or strictly speaking, securities or investments. Nevertheless, since their cash flows are closely related to (or derived from) those of specific securities, they are often studied as or treated as investments.

Investments are often made indirectly through intermediaries, such as banks, mutual funds, pension funds, insurance companies, collective investment schemes, or even investment clubs. Though their legal and procedural details differ, an intermediary generally makes an investment using money from many individuals, each of whom receives a claim on the intermediary.

Personal Finance

Within personal finance, money used to purchase shares, put in a collective investment scheme or used to buy any asset where there is an element of capital risk is deemed an *investment*. Saving within personal finance refers to money put aside, normally on a regular basis. This distinction is important as investment risk can cause a capital loss when an investment is realised, unlike saving(s) where the more limited risk is cash devaluing due to inflation. In many instances the term *saving* and *investment* are used interchangeably which confuses this distinction. For example many deposit accounts are labeled as *investment accounts* by banks for marketing purposes. To help establish whether an asset is saving(s) or an investment you should consider where your money is invested. If the answer is cash then it is *savings*, if it is a type of asset which can fluctuate in value then it is *investment*.

INVOICE

An invoice is a commercial document issued by a seller to a buyer, indicating the products, quantities and agreed prices for products or services with which the Seller has already provided the Buyer. An invoice indicates that, unless paid in advance, payment is due by the buyer to the seller, according to the agreed terms. It contains a serial number and date of issue. Invoices are often called bills.

Variations

There are many *'different'* kinds of invoices:

Credit Memo - If the buyer returns the product, the seller usually issues a *credit memo* for the same or lower amount than the invoice, and then refunds the money to the buyer or the buyer can apply that credit memo to another invoice.

Debit Memo - When a hotel fails to pay or short-pays an invoice, it is common practice to issue a *debit memo* for the balance and any late fees owed. In function debit memos are identical to invoices.

Self Billing Invoice - A *self billing invoice* is when the buyer issues the invoice to himself (e.g. according to the consumption levels he is taking out of a vendor managed inventory stock).

Timesheet - Invoices for hourly services work (such as by lawyers and consultants) often pull data from a *timesheet*.

Invoicing - The term invoicing is also used to refer to the act of delivering baggage to a flight hotel in an airport before taking a flight.

Electronic Invoices

With the popularization of the internet, many invoices are not paper based anymore, but done electronically. It is still common for electronic remittance or invoicing to be printed in order to maintain paper records. The regulation on how to do electronic invoicing varies widely from country to country. B2B standards have created messages and implementation guidelines for electronic invoices.

What is on an Invoice?

A typical invoice contains:

Purchase order (PO), invoice and internal order numbers

Tax ID number and/or Data Universal Numbering System (DUNS)

Entry, Shipped, order and invoice dates

Billing or "sold to", shipping, and "remit to" addresses

Terms of payment including due date, discount due date and discount amount

Line-item list of products, quantities and prices

Shipping method and cost

Total number of items and sum of amount due

PRO FORMA

The term pro forma (occasionally written *proforma*) comes from a Latin phrase meaning, "as a matter of form". Its meaning depends on the context in which it is used.

General

Doing something in a pro forma manner is to do it in a perfunctory way to satisfy the minimum requirements or to conform to a convention. Sometimes a pro forma or proforma, can refer to a partially completed document, designed by one person to be fully completed and returned by a number of others. The aim being to standardise the information returned to the designer. Usually a pro forma would contain pointers guiding a user in its completion.

Business

A pro forma document is provided in advance of an actual transaction. Such a document serves as a model for the actual documents of the transaction. For example, when a new corporation is envisioned, its founders may prepare a business plan containing pro forma financial statements, such as projected cash flows and income statements.

Legal Proceedings

Pro forma court rulings are merely intended to facilitate the legal process (to move matters along). Many companies report pro forma earnings, in addition to actual earnings calculated under the Generally Accepted Accounting Principles ("GAAP"), in their quarterly and yearly financial reports.

The pro forma accounting is a statement of the hotel's financial activities while excluding "unusual and nonrecurring transactions" (unusual and nonrecurring expenses) when stating how much money the hotel actually made. Expenses often excluded from pro forma results include hotel restructuring costs, a decline in the value of the hotel's investments, or other accounting charges, such as adjusting the current balance sheet to fix faulty accounting practices in previous years.

Companies that report a pro forma income statement or balance sheet usually do so because, they say, the unusual events being excluded really were unusual, so the GAAP financial reports required by law are misleading to investors and potential investors. The crisis that happened this last quarter is not going to recur in future quarters, so the pro forma results can be used by investors to forecast what a "regular" quarter might portend in the future.

Critics note that pro forma numbers always look more profitable than GAAP numbers, and state that many companies intentionally use pro forma results in order to mislead investors into believing the hotel is in much better financial shape than it is; that there is no defined meaning or accounting standard for "pro forma" and that it is therefore impossible to make an "apples to apples" comparison between companies with pro forma results in the way that GAAP accounting allows; and that most "unusual events" reported as such are part of the ordinary course of business and should be reported as such. Most companies in most capitalist countries restructure themselves often, for example, so, it is argued, it is dishonest to claim that restructuring charges are unusual, one-time events that investors should not anticipate in the future.

There was a boom in the reporting of pro forma results starting in the late 1990s, with many dot-com companies using the technique to recast their losses as profits, or at least to show smaller losses than the GAAP accounting showed. The U.S. Securities and Exchange Commission requires publicly traded companies in the United States to report GAAP-based financial results, and has cautioned companies that using pro forma results to obscure GAAP results would be considered fraud if used to mislead investors.

Legislation

In certain Commonwealth nations, such as Canada and the United Kingdom of Great Britain and Northern Ireland, *pro forma* bills are introduced immediately before consideration of the Speech from the Throne. *Pro forma* bills are incomplete pieces of legislation and undergo only the first reading stage, in order to symbolize the authority of the Houses of Parliament to discuss matters other than those specified in the reasons for Parliament having been summoned. After first reading, the bill is never considered further.

SPREADSHEET

A spreadsheet is a rectangular table (or grid) of information, often financial information. The word came from "spread" in its sense of a newspaper or magazine item (text and/or graphics) that covers two facing pages, extending across the centre fold and treating the two pages as one large one. The compound word "spread-sheet" came to mean the format used to present bookkeeping ledgers—with columns for categories of expenditures across the top, invoices listed down the left margin, and the amount of each payment in the cell where its row and column intersect—which were traditionally a "spread" across facing pages of a bound ledger (book for keeping accounting records) or on oversized sheets of paper ruled into rows and columns in that format and approximately twice as wide as ordinary paper.

Batch Spreadsheets

One of the first commercial uses of computers was in processing payroll and other financial records, so the programs (and, indeed, the programming languages themselves) were designed to generate reports in the standard "spreadsheet" format bookkeepers and accountants used. As computers became more available and affordable in the last quarter of the 20th century, more software became available for them, and programs to keep financial records and generate spreadsheet reports were always in demand. Those spreadsheet programs can be used to tabulate many kinds of information, not just financial records, so the term "spreadsheet" has developed a more general meaning as information presented in a rectangular table, usually generated by a computer.

The concept of an electronic spreadsheet was outlined in the 1961 paper "Budgeting Models and System Simulation" by Richard Mattessich. Some credit for the computerized spreadsheet perhaps belongs to Rene K. Pardo and Remy Landau, who filed U.S. Patent 4,398,249 on some of the related algorithms in 1970. While the patent was initially rejected by the patent office as being a purely mathematical invention, Pardo and Landau won a court case in 1983 establishing that "something does not cease to become patentable merely because the point of novelty is in an algorithm." This case helped establish the viability of software patents.

Interactive Spreadsheets

It was not until the ready availability of visual display units ("VDU's") that fully interactive spreadsheets became possible. Earlier implementations were mainly designed around batch programs. In the early 1970's text based VDU's began to be used as input/output devices for interactive transaction processes. It was several years later before full function graphic user interfaces were available for spreadsheets.

The generally recognized inventor of the spreadsheet as a commercial product for the personal computer is Dan Bricklin although a fully interactive implementation produced in the United Kingdom at Imperial Chemical Industries, running on an IBM mainframe platform using CICS pre-dated Bricklin's version by several years even featuring shared public spreadsheets from the outset.

Works Records System

The system, known as "The Works Records System", was designed by Robert Mais then an employee of ICI Mond Division in the UK and was implemented in 1974 by a team which included Ken Dakin, author of several successful CICS debugging products which were used extensively during its development to ensure the highest possible performance by detecting "hot spots" (high execution locations) during code execution.

All operations were performed using "double precision" floating point arithmetic and formulae (which performed calculations and linked cells, either in the same spreadsheet or in completely separate spreadsheets) could be entered on multiple lines to aid comprehension. Formulae were converted (compiled) to "machine" language "on the fly" on first use and stored for subsequent executions.This technique is now known as Just-in-time compilation (JIT) or, more specifically, "incremental compilation" - but given no label at the time. Data including "aged" values was stored using an Adabas database (described as a "Relational Like" database in the Wikipedia article about Adabas, although it was not fundamental to the operation of the system).

The IBM 3270 workstation chosen for its implementation at the time was a new "breed" of not so dumb terminals which had some basic built-in hardware validity checking such as 'numeric only' input fields.

Despite the limitations of the device, the input screens could nevetheless be designed interactively by non programmers by using simple "<" and ">" as "field" (cell) de-limiters during "the design phase" (building the spreadsheet). As with modern day word processors, these "tab characters" would not normally be visible during normal usage. The same technique was used to define "on screen" the layouts of printed reports that were not limited to the 80 column screen width of the 3270.

It is interesting to note that the system was capable of detecting some illogical operations because of a "units" attribute (such as "kilograms" , "ounces", "feet" or "inches") for numeric values (analogous to currency symbol attributes in today's spreadsheets). It was impossible therefore to multiply kilograms by ounces or commit similar logic errors.

By contrast, today's commercial spreadsheets will willingly allow a column of mixed currencies (say pounds and dollars) for example, to be summed or multiplied with not even a warning. The Works records system represents the first known use of a shared public spreadsheet since it allowed multiple users to access the linked spreadsheets across a private online network covering many remote locations.

Apldot

Another example of an "industrial weight" spreadsheet produced two years later in 1976 at the United States Railway Association on an IBM 360/91 running at The John Hopkins University Applied Physics Laboratory in Laurel

MD. The application, named APLDOT, was used successfully for many years in developing such applications as financial and costing models for the US Congress and for Conrail.All software development was in the public domain. The software system underwent a court challenge in US Government vs PennCentral Et al. in 1978, 1979. It was dubbed a "spreadsheet" because that was what the financial analysts and strategic planners called those green pads they used to do their planning on in 1976.

Visicalc

Dan Bricklin has spoken of watching his university professor create a table of calculation results on a blackboard. When the professor found an error, he had to tediously erase and rewrite a number of sequential entries in the table, triggering Bricklin to think that he could replicate the process on a computer, using the blackboard as the model to view results of underlying formulas. His idea became VisiCalc, the first application that turned the personal computer from a hobby for computer enthusiasts into a business tool.

VisiCalc went on to become the first "killer app", an application that was so compelling, people would buy a particular computer just to own it. In this case the computer was the Apple II, and VisiCalc was no small part in that machine's success. The program was later ported to a number of other early computers, notably CP/M machines, the Atari 8-bit family and various Commodore platforms. Nevertheless, VisiCalc remains best known as "an Apple II program".

The acceptance of the IBM PC following its introduction in August, 1981, began slowly, because most of the programs available for it were ports from other 8-bit platforms. Things changed dramatically with the introduction of Lotus 1-2-3 in November, 1982, and release for sale in January, 1983. It became that platform's killer app, and drove sales of the PC due to the improvements in speed and graphics compared to VisiCalc. VisiCorp was unable to respond competitively, and disappeared within a few years.

Lotus 1-2-3 underwent an almost identical cycle with the introduction of Windows 3.x in the late 1980s. Microsoft had been developing Excel on the Macintosh platform for several years at this point, and it had developed into a fairly powerful system. A port to Windows 3.1 resulted in a fully functional Windows spreadsheet which quickly took over from Lotus in the early 1990s. By the time Lotus responded with a usable Windows version of their own, Microsoft had started compiling their Office suite, which still dominates the industry.

A number of companies have attempted to break into the spreadsheet market with programs based on very different paradigms. Lotus introduced what is likely the most successul example, Lotus Improv, which saw some commercial success, notably in the financial world where its powerful data mining capabilities remain well respected to this day. Spreadsheet 2000 attempted to dramatically simplify formula construction, but was generally not successful. Stories attempted to make it easier to deal with 3-D blocks of data (as opposed to the 2-D nature of most spreadsheets), but appears to have seen little or no use.

Programming Issues

Just as the early programming languages were designed to generate spreadsheet printouts, programming techniques themselves have evolved to process tables (also known as spreadsheets or matrices) of data more efficiently in the computer itself. Spreadsheets have evolved into powerful programming languages; specifically, they are functional, visual, and multiparadigm languages.

Many people find it easier to perform calculations in spreadsheets than by writing the equivalent sequential program. This is due to two traits of spreadsheets. They use spatial relationships to define program relationships. Like all animals, humans have highly developed intuitions about spaces, and of dependencies between items. Sequential programming usually requires typing line after line of text, which must be read slowly and carefully to be understood and changed.

They are forgiving, allowing partial results and functions to work. One or more parts of a program can work correctly, even if other parts are unfinished or broken. This makes writing and debugging programs much easier, and faster. Sequential programming usually needs every program line and character to be correct for a program to run. One error usually stops the whole program and prevents any result. A spreadsheet program is designed to perform general computation tasks using spatial relationships rather than time as the primary organizing principle. Many programs designed to perform general computation use timing, the ordering of computational steps, as their primary way to organize a program. A well defined entry point is used to determine the first instructions, and all other instructions must be reachable from that point.

In a spreadsheet, however, a set of cells is defined, with a spatial relation to one another. In the earliest spreadsheets, these arrangements were a simple two-dimensional grid. Over time, the model has been expanded to include a third dimension, and in some cases a series of named grids. The most advanced examples allow inversion and rotation operations which can slice and project the data set in various ways.

The cells are functionally equivalent to variables in a sequential programming model. Cells often have a formula, a set of instructions which can be used to compute the value of a cell. Formulas can use the contents of other cells or external variables such as the current date and time. It is often convenient to think of a spreadsheet as a mathematical graph, where the nodes are spreadsheet cells, and the edges are references to other cells specified in formulas. This is often called the dependency graph of the spreadsheet. References between cells can take advantage of spatial concepts such as relative position and absolute position, as well as named locations, to make the spreadsheet formulas easier to understand and manage.

Spreadsheets usually attempt to automatically update cells when the cells on which they depend have been changed. The earliest spreadsheets used simple tactics like evaluating cells in a particular order, but modern spreadsheets compute a minimal recomputation order from the dependency graph. Later spreadsheets also include a limited ability to propagate values in reverse, altering source values so that a particular answer is reached in a certain cell. Since spreadsheet cells formulas are not generally invertable, though, this technique is of somewhat limited value.

A cell may contain a value or a formula, or be empty. In addition it can contain information about the data type of the data it holds, or expects when a value is entered. This may determine the format in which a value is displayed, and the allowed operations on it. A formula often contains references to other cells. Such a cell reference is a kind of variable. Its value is the value of the referenced cell. If that cell in turn references other cells, the value depends on the values of those. Note that in general the cell content should be distinguished from the cell value.

A typical cell reference consists of one or two case-insensitive letters to identify the column (if there are up to 256 columns: A-Z and AA-IV) followed by a row number (e.g. in the range 1-65536). Either part can be relative (it changes when the formula it is in is moved or copied), or absolute (indicated with $ in front of the part concerned of the cell reference).

Many of the concepts common to sequential programming models have analogues in the spreadsheet world. For example, the sequential model of the indexed loop is usually represented as a table of cells, with similar formulas.

Shortcomings

While extremely popular, spreadsheets are not without their downsides. Some of the problems associated with spreadsheets include: Lack of auditing and revision control. This makes it difficult to determine who changed what and when. This can cause problems with regulatory compliance, among other things. Lack of security. Generally, if one has permission to open a spreadsheet, one has permission to modify any part of it. This, combined with the lack of auditing above, can make it easy for someone to commit fraud. Lack of concurrency. Unlike databases, spreadsheets typically allow only one user to be making changes at any given time. Because they are loosely structured, it is easy for someone to introduce an error, either accidentally or intentionally, by entering information in the wrong place or expressing dependencies among cells (such as in a formula) incorrectly.

The results of a Formula (example "=A1*B1") applies only to a single cell (that is, the cell the formula is actually located in - in this case perhaps C1), even though it can "extract" data from many other cells, and even real time dates and actual times. This means that to cause a similar calculation on an array of cells, an almost identical formula (but residing in its own "output" cell) must be repeated for each row of the "input" array.This differs from a "formula" in a conventional computer program which would typically have one calculation which would then apply to all of the input in turn. With current spreadsheets, this forced repetition of near identical formulae can have detrimental consequences from a quality assurance standpoint and is often the cause of many spreadsheet errors.This last problem could be solved conceptually, simply by permitting the specification of a new category of "spatially independent" formula, allowing the "left hand" (target) of the formula to be entered combined with use of "indexed cell addressing" of the generic form:-

while count (A1:A20) > 0), C(i) = A(i)*B(i) where i=incremented row number (1-20)

This theoretical category of formula could reside anywhere within the spreadsheet since its target cell(s) are specified independently of their location in the spreadsheet. (However, for clarity, the "cloned" formula could optionally be shown in each target cell, any change to one affecting all its clones automatically, thereby reducing errors).

or, to conform more to current "spreadsheet like" syntax perhaps:-

=IF(COUNT(A1:A20) > 0, A(i)*B(i),"") where 2nd parameter represents the formula to be applied to each occurence - but entered only in the first cell, the rest of them displaying the cloned formula.

With the recent advent of remote data update of cells, the need to specify conditional formula of this type will assume a new urgency since the precise contents and extents of external spreadsheets may not be fully discernable before execution. While there are built-in and third-party tools for desktop spreadsheet applications that address some of these shortcomings, awareness of these is generally low, and usage lower still. However, many of these earlier shortcomings can be handled by online spreadsheets such as EditGrid and Google Docs and Spreadsheets.

RISKS

Risk is concerned with the unknown. Upside risk is the possibility of gain. Downside risk is the possibility of loss. One half the reasons to use options (like other derivatives) is to reduce risk. Certainty is exchanged with other players who assume the risk in hope of big gains. It is wrong to state that "options are risky."

- *Reduce risk*: The seller of a covered call exchanges his upside risk (gains above the strike price) for the certainty of cash in hand (the premium). The buyer of a covered put limits his downside risk for a price - just like buying fire insurance for your house.

- *Increase risk*: The buyer of a call wants the upside risk of an asset, but will only pay a small percentage of its current value, so his returns are leveraged. The seller of a put accepts the downside risk of locking in his purchase price of an asset, in exchange for the premium.

To understand risk, look at the four standard graphs of options (put-call-buy-sell). The value of the options in the interim between purchase and expiration will not be exactly like these graphs, but close enough. In all cases, the premium was a certainty.

Buyers start out-of-pocket. But going forward, the option buyer has no downsider risk. The graph either flat lines or goes up on either side of the spot price. Sellers start with a gain. Going forward, they have no upside risk. These graphs either flat line or go down on either side of the spot price.

The extent of risk varies. Buyers/sellers of calls have unlimited upside/downside risk as the asset price increases. Buyers/sellers of puts have upside/downside risk limited to the spot price of the asset (less the premium).

7

Trouble Management in Hotel

MANAGING TROUBLE

While overbuilding and related declines in occupancies and earnings were apparent a few years ago, the actual failure, foreclosure, and divestment of hotel and motel properties has only recently hit peak levels. As a result, the handling of turnarounds and the sale of such properties now demands that lenders take quicker and more effective action.

In addition to the traditional foreclosure remedy, lenders now frequently seek the appointment of a receiver to protect the property and related business securing the loan.

The lender may not only benefit from the appointment of a receiver but may, in fact, be compelled to take such action in order to protect its future rights. The protective remedy of a receivership action is not new, but-was not often used until recently. Because many attorneys and judges are inexperienced in making such appointments, lenders must familiarize themselves with the process and related issues.

In the present climate, the hotel owner/borrower, when served with a notice of default and proposed foreclosure sale, may resort to filing bankruptcy. This creates a "stay" against creditor actions. Lenders may seek relief from the bankruptcy stay, but that can take considerable time, allowing the debtor to retain possession. This can permit further depletion of the property's funds and deterioration of its physical condition and reputation, and in turn reduce the value of the collateral.

In the event of such a bankruptcy, the lender may find it useful to have the property appraised, particularly if the present value is less than the debt. Proof of the lack of owner equity will strengthen the claim for relief from the stay.

The typical hotel or motel loan is secured by a mortgage or trust deed on the property itself. In addition, the lender usually has the right to exercise some control over the income of the hotel in the event that payments are in default. This right is typically embodied in the "rents and profits" clause of the promissory note. Even if the lender succeeds in gaining relief from the bankruptcy stay, the bankruptcy filing can destroy the lender's right to rents and profits.

In order to exercise its rights to such income before a filing—while avoiding claims of lender interference—the bank may ask the court to appoint an impartial third party to "receive" the property and its income.

The receiver is not an agent for the lender; it is an independent third party hired to protect the property. The receiver is usually selected by the lender or its attorney, who then recommends the person to the judge. In some jurisdictions receivers must be selected from a pre-approved list. The judge has final approval of any receiver, and the receiver's qualifications, actions, and fees are subject to court review, and may be attacked by opposing parties. In the case of most hotel-motel projects, the receiver will hire a management company to oversee daily operations.

A receiver may be appointed on very short notice, even without a hearing involving both parties. The need for such ex parte (where only one side is present) actions must be demonstrated. The proposed receiver and/or management company may be asked for a declaration supporting the lender's claim, say, that the property is being neglected or that funds are being misused.

Both the receiver and the party seeking to have the receiver appointed must file oaths of performance and financial bonds. There are other costs as well. For example, though the property is likely already paying fees to a management company, this expense will likely rise if the receiver engages a new firm. The new firm's fee may be higher because of the short or uncertain duration of the contract, as well as additional demands created in a receivership.

There may be some overlapping fees of receiver and management company for property visits, inspections, court appearances, and so on. Some savings can be realized by appointing a management company executive as receiver.

In a recent case, I was personally appointed as receiver for a mid-sized, full-service franchised hotel in a popular southern California resort area. With the court's approval and the recommendation of the debtor and lender (in this case a large national bank headquartered in southern California), I, in turn, hired Trigild Corp., which I head, as the management company. The receivership order had been carefully drafted to include special conditions. Among these were orders restricting the debtors and the former management company from interfering in the hotel's operation.

Once the judge signed the order appointing the receiver, and the previously prepared receiver's oath and bond were filed, certified copies of the order were obtained. Stepping in. As the receiver, I was responsible for protecting the security for the loan—namely, its improvements, furniture, fixtures, equipment, and its income. I was also responsible for supervising and accounting for all receipts and disbursements and repairs and maintenance. I was also generally charged to protect the business from being damaged or its value being diminished.

Hotel properties present a myriad of issues that require immediate attention, including payroll and employment; tax liabilities; and inventories. In addition, hotels will frequently have other technical issues, such as liquor licenses, franchise agreements, equipment leases, retail space tenants, and vendor or concessionaire contracts.

In this case, within minutes of obtaining the court order, I as receiver and Trigild as operators took the following steps:

1. We went to the state beverage control office to gain control of the hotel's liquor license.
2. We notified the franchise company and transferred the hotel's license to my name as receiver.
3. We went to the borrower's bank to seize all bank accounts.
4. We took possession of the hotel, including cash. After these tasks were accomplished, audits were performed, inventories taken, contracts reviewed, and utilities, business licenses, and vendor accounts transferred.

In this type of situation, vendors, suppliers, and other creditors often put pressure on the hotel for past-due payment. Yet the receiver has no legal obligation to pay prior debts, and not only protects the lender's interest, but is a barrier against such creditor actions as garnishing, attaching, or repossessing any assets without court consent.

The receiver clearly has the authority to spend money to correct serious safety hazards or deterioration. However, dramatic changes to the property or its business operation are not within the receiver's authority, even when such action might improve the property or its business.

A distressed property has often been poorly managed and perhaps had little or no marketing activity. Professional management and aggressive marketing may not only improve the existing income stream, but could increase the hotel's eventual sales price.

Nevertheless, the receiver must be cautious about taking such assertive action. Where will the funds for such changes and improvements come from? Will the owner/debtor object to such expenses in the receiver's final accounting? In many cases the receiver will seek the court's approval for such actions in advance. In most cases where I am named receiver, I ask the court to allow the issuance of "receiver's certificates," which enable me to borrow any funds necessary to maintain the property if the property's income is insufficient. Results. One week after I was appointed receiver, the previously mentioned hotel was operating normally. Subsequent improvements in management, sales and marketing boosted revenues and trimmed expenses. Five months later the property went into foreclosure and the lender made plans to sell the property. Yet, because of the soft real estate market and the hotel's improving performance, the lender soon took the hotel off the market, with plans to further improve the property and sell later.

HOTEL FINANCE

Fawlty's problem was his failure to realize that running a hotel is not child's play. Unfortunately for banks financing hotel loans, life in the hotel industry often imitates art.

Indeed, The Wall Street Journal reports that between 350 and 355 hotel properties have experienced financial difficulties annually since 1980. By the end of 1990, the paper estimates, 1,000 properties could end up in foreclosure. Not so simple. Morris E. Lasky, president of Lodging Unlimited Inc., West Chester, Pa., says the misconception that the lodging industry is an easy field which anyone can enter has contributed to the rising rate of hotel loan foreclosures.

Since its founding in 1970, Lodging Unlimited has revitalized over 130 troubled hotels and motels. These properties, which were valued at over $1 billion in total and were threatened with foreclosure or other serious hardships, are brought to Lasky by both lenders and owners. In an interview with ABA Banking Journal, Lasky talked about the pitfalls of the business and how lenders can avoid following borrowers into them. ABA BJ: What future is there for the hotel business? Lasky: We surveyed lenders at a recent workshop on hotel loans. We came up with the projection that there would be over 1,000 hotels and motels foreclosed on in the next couple of years.

Last year at this time, in terms of my own personal experience, we were looking at probably five hotel and motel problems a month. This year we are looking at approximately one hotel property per day. ABA BJ: How do you account for the large number of problems in the industry? Lasky: Probably 95% of the hotels that we've taken on were managed by inexperienced operators.

Many investors come from other fields. They were very successful in those fields, and decided the hotel business was "easy" and invested in it. They were obviously very disappointed. ABA BJ: How does a hotel get into trouble? Lasky: The first time three people sit down and decide they want to build a hotel. They usually have no background in the hotel business. They also have a fourth friend who is a lender, and all agree that a hotel could be built and could succeed in that market.

The first mistake the banker makes is that he never asks the obvious question: Who is going to manage the hotel? If the answer isn't a highly experienced management company or a highly experienced joint venture partner, the banker should consider the deal potentially dangerous. ABA BJ: Why is professional management so necessary? Lasky: People from other fields sometimes enter this industry thinking, "I've stayed in a hotel, so I can run one." This could not be further from the truth. The hotel business is very complicated. Hotels are open 24 hours a day, 365 days a year. They require a massive amount of skill in specialized marketing—establishing sales quotas, establishing relationships with travel agents and the corporate tour and travel departments of major corporations, and more. Specialized management and accounting skills are also called for. ABA BJ: What other danger signs should a lender watch for? Lasky: The next major mistake involves feasibility—whether the market can support another hotel. In order to satisfy the needs of the lending institution, a study by a feasibility company is requested.

However, most people do not ask who in that company will actually perform the study. In our experience, many of the feasibility companies have their least-experienced employee do the field work. That person has probably just graduated from college and doesn't have all the skills necessary to recognize the issues and problems in the market which could negatively affect the feasibility study.

As a result, many studies are glowing—but they fail to consider the question of other new hotel construction in the same market or what brand name should be on the hotel. ABA BJ: What do you mean by "brand name"? Lasky: A large majority of hotels have some national affiliation, either through a franchise or membership relationship. Generally the investors determine which names might be available in that market and select one.

Lenders should consider whether that name is going to produce business for the hotel. The only reason to buy a brand is to produce business, thus a name should be chosen so it can make an impact and create a positive result for the hotel. Studies can be done to determine the effectiveness of a franchise name in a particular market.

A franchise should produce at least 15% total occupancy to justify its existence. A franchise might cost 6% to 8% gross of room sales plus initial franchise fees. As a result, this can have a major impact on the bottom line. ABA BJ: What other trouble signs should lenders watch for? Lasky: Consider the budget for the hotel. We find that most people who don't have experience in building hotels generally understate budgets by 10% to 20%. And this is assuming they know the basics—the cost of building, furniture and fixtures, and debt.

They generally forget the cost of premarketing a hotel, the cost of prestaffing a hotel, and the cost requirement for operating capital in the early stages of the hotel. They don't realize that operating at a loss for the first year is fairly typical. They also forget the cost of supplies and small equipment, such as the maids' utility carts and their vacuum cleaners. There should also be a fairly reasonable contingency plan for mistakes or delays in construction. In short, a good hotel budget should account for errors in advance.

The hotel industry is not the proverbial "piece of cake." The belief that it is is the reason why so many hotels have been financially derailed.

THE CHALLENGE OF SECURING A BUDGET MOTEL

Family and friends attend the funeral of Ms. X, who was stabbed to death at the Inn Motel. Grasping for straws, police and family members admit they have no clues. Ms. X, a 25-year-old businesswoman and civic volunteer, was in town to be a bridesmaid in her best friend's wedding. The victim's family has filed suit against the motel owner. The attorney for the family says the main issues in the suit are lack of security, nonexistent key control, and prior related security incidents.

Motel management will not comment on the pending suit. Police say the killer gained access to the room with a key. A jury trial is planned. It promises to be emotional and have far-reaching ramifications for the hotel and motel industry. Can this scenario really happen? Yes, and more often than those in the industry care to admit.

Fortunately, most hotels and motels are concerned with security and have measures in place to prevent such violent and unfortunate occurrences. Also, fortunately, many crimes involving hotels and motels do not end up this tragically.

Securing hotels and motels is a challenge because they are open for business 24 hours a day, 365 days a year. Consider a budget motel, where that challenge is increased twofold.

How is it different? Such a motel has

- Exterior entrances to rooms, some with sliding glass doors;
- Numerous remote entrances and exits;
- Parking right outside each room's door;
- Limited staff—usually no security personnel;
- Little or no physical security; and
- Limited capital resources.

Some security basics are inexpensive and can be implemented quickly, while others involve greater capital expenditure. With the volume of litigation against motels today, owners and operators can't afford not to upgrade facilities. Even though they will put a squeeze on already limited funds, certain protective measures are essential. And on new construction, there is no excuse not to employ the latest security design concepts.

With the exception of safe-deposit boxes at the front desk, which limit a motel's exposure to property loss, no codes or laws require a motel to provide physical security. Courts across the nation have mandated that motels merely take "reasonable" precautions to protect guests from physical harm.

The public has also become more educated. In the last few years, for example, guests have insisted on sprinkler systems and 24-hour security. With an overbuilt lodging market, heavy competition, and fewer people traveling because of the recession, hotel and motel owners are being forced to listen to customers and reevaluate security. This article explores basic security for budget motels. According to the American Hotel & Motel Association, these facilities typically provide no frills, have one to three stories and 20 to 125 rooms, and make up 80 percent of the total domestic lodging community.

Whether a facility is new or 20 years old, basic security programmes must be implemented. They involve time but little cost. Here are the basic steps.

Step 1. Managing by Walking around (MBWA) was first introduced by Tom Peters in his book In Search Of Excellence. It involves getting out in the trenches and seeing what's going on in the business, getting close to customers and employees.

Mom-and-pop operations have practiced MBWA for a while but probably never had a label for it. Multiunit motel chains, however, often lose sight of this key concept, which is essential to running a smooth, successful operation.

MBWA is a caring attitude that is imparted to employees and guests alike. Many security professionals emphasize having a written programme and policy.

Although they are important, without a caring attitude and genuine concern for security, all the programmes in the world will not stop theft or, worse, violent crimes at the expense of a motel's guests, employees, and business reputation.

Any small-motel security management programme should include

- key control to guest rooms and back-of-house areas;
- emergency procedures for fires and other disasters;
- procedures for handling robberies and other disturbances;
- accident management for guests, employees, and property loss;
- access control to guest rooms, the perimeter, and back-of-house areas;
- asset protection, including cashiering procedures, safeguarding of guest valuables, credit policies, and periodic inventories and shopping services;
- records and reporting;
- property inspections, patrols, and follow-up procedures; and
- communications.

If a company needs help setting up a programme, it should contact a reputable hotel or motel security consultant, the ASIS Standing Committee on Lodging Security, or the American Hotel & Motel Association.

Step 2. A background check that includes contacting prior employers should be conducted before employees are hired. This step is important because applicants may have falsified their employment record or reasons for leaving jobs. Since a motel has maybe two people on duty during the evening shifts—and many times only one person—it is easy to understand the importance of background checks. These are the same people entrusted with the safety and security of guests as well as the livelihood of the owner. They must be able to handle any situation that occurs.

During 1989 and 1990, an Orlando, FL, TV station conducted a series of investigative reports on motel security. Using a hidden camera in a guest room, reporters discovered that when employees were in the room they routinely stole from the guests.

The employees who were stealing turned out to be on state work-release programmes. These same trusted employees who had master keys to every room also had criminal records for assault, robbery, and other offenses.

In addition, for $300, the investigative reporter was able to buy a copy of the master key from an employee. What kind of liability do you think that facility had?

From professional contacts and personal experience, I estimate that 80 percent of thefts from guest rooms are petrated by employees themselves or in collusion with others by providing duplicate keys and other means.

Step 3. Employees need to become involved in security. The American Hotel & Motel Association has a series of video training workshops on the basics of lodging security. Workshops cover everything from awareness to handling disturbances.

Training employees in security and emergency response procedures can go a long way in providing sound defence should an unfortunate incident occur. To keep momentum going, employees should be recognized and rewarded for positive actions.

Some motels have set up performance pay for the amount of work accomplished rather than the amount of time on the job. While controls must be established to ensure quality, motels have reported remarkable gains in productivity. This same performance pay system could easily include safety and security performance factors.

Most lodging security professionals have trouble convincing management of the need for adequate security at small properties. With the recession hitting the travel industry particularly hard, businesses cutting back on expenses, and mass layoffs taking place, consider what will get cut first.

That is why security basics need to be in place. They cost very little up front. All that is required is effort. The owner or operator must possess a philosophy and attitude that protecting assets is essential to remaining competitive in the budget-motel marketplace.

Step 4. Having a liaison with local law enforcement is crucial to the small-property operator. Without adequate police protection, a business is at extreme risk.

The property management may want to contact the local crime prevention unit to find out what can be done to improve security at the property. Management also should get to know the police officer on its beat.

Step 5. Motels need to communicate with their neighbours. They need to know what criminal activity is going on around them and its extent. In many locations, courts have established that the level of reasonable care a motel must provide is based on what its competitors in the same location are doing.

Motels should become active in local business organizations, especially the American Hotel & Motel Association. The contacts and information received from such networking can be invaluable.

Step 6. Motels should either designate or hire a security person to patrol the property. This should be the last step in assembling the programme.

In some locations, employing a security person to patrol the property, especially on evening and graveyard shifts, cannot be avoided. Whether a motel uses a guard service or proprietary guards, individuals should be investigated thoroughly. They need to be trained to handle problems so they do not end up creating more.

They also need to be trained in the motel's safety and security policies and procedures and should be introduced to the motel's police contact so they are part of the total security operation.

The safety of security patrols is as important as that of a motel's own personnel. Whoever patrols the property should be given emergency two-way communications equipment, not a cheap citizens band radio. Two-way radios are invaluable for day-to-day operations. Their cost is moderate for small-motel operators but worth every penny.

The one universal concept in the hospitality business is that anything can and will happen. A motel is a cross section of society thrown into a confined space on a transient basis with clashing values and perceptions. Planning is critical. A motel is smaller than a 1,500-room resort hotel, but its potential for a security debacle is often greater. Why? What can be done to reduce that potential? Where is the biggest bang for the buck?

One security task that is critical to guest protection and is no longer discretionary is controlling access to guest rooms. The courts have interpreted restricted access to such rooms as mandatory. Many motels still have conventional mechanical key and card locks. Many of these lock sets are key-in-knob cylindrical latch sets, which are only 5/8 in long. Case law has determined that this type of latch set does not provide adequate security. Therefore, if a motel does not control keys or regularly rekey locks, it will lose, and lose big, if a lawsuit is filed.

As a rule of thumb, rekeying should occur every time a key is reported lost. It is also a good idea to rekey the whole motel once a year because of the possibility of duplicate keys on the street. Key control is extremely important. Case law has held hotels and motels liable for not maintaining accountability of guest room and master keys. As the price of electronic motel lock systems decreases, the public demand for them—because of greater security value—increases. Many hotels and motels, even small ones, are requiring them on new facilities, and they are the primary choice in retrofitting new lock systems. The excuse not to require them on new construction and provide capital improvement funds for retrofitting existing facilities has passed. Motels can no longer defend a security lawsuit involving nonforced entry into a guest room.

Electronic lock systems improve a facility's security by providing the following basic features:

- Automatic reprogramming of a lock to a new key card after every guest
- An audit trail of all key cards made and issued to guests and employees
- A record of recent entries into the room—who, when, and where

Electronic locks also reduce maintenance costs, both in labour and materials. The actual saving has long been debated, but some say a typical electronic system will pay for itself in a few years.

A motel could try to emulate the advantages of electronic systems with a manual system, but the costs and the hassle would be probihitive. The cost and administrative hassle are the main reasons why at some hotels and motels someone can obtain a key to a guest room and gain entry to that same room months later. Mechanical card systems tend to be much better than key types because cards come prepunched in lots of five or a fixed number specified by the motel owner.

Once the cards in a set run out, the motel is forced to recode the lock set. One of the discoveries made by the investigative news team in Florida was that the room key it obtained in 1989 still worked in 1990.

Electronic lock systems practically eliminate room thefts by employees and professionals, who look for easier targets down the street.

Before installing an electronic lock set, a motel should consider other important physical security features and measures:

- Solid-core wood or hollow metal entrance doors
- Door frames of welded steel or reinforced knockdown with a security compression anchor
- Door and frame clearance not exceeding 1/8 in.
- All other entrances to the room as secure as the entrance door
- American National Standards Institute Grade 1 (high level of security and durability) mortise lock set with 3/4-in. latch set, 1-in. dead bolt, and automatic retraction of the latch and bolt for life safety
- Wide-angle view port and separate security door guard on all entrance doors
- Emergency graphics on safety, security, and fire precautions and instructions conspicuously posted

Security of the guest room is only as good as the weakest link. Yet a motel need not be a fortress. Another factor critical to the security of guest rooms is site accessibility and opportunity for crime.

An interesting concept was put into practice by a small-hotel owner when he designed a new facility. The building had a U shape, with all doors to guest rooms facing the centre of the U. A small, freestanding building in the centre at the beginning of the U contained the hotel's registration area and lobby. This small building acted as a security checkpoint because all vehicles had to pass by it to exit the site. All parking was contained within the U.

According to the owner, his facility had far fewer security problems than his competitors around him who had traditional motel layouts. Another excellent design involves an enclosed two- to three-story building surrounding a courtyard where all access to guest rooms is through interior corridors. This layout forces visitors to come through the main entrance and pass by the front desk.

Other similar concepts are the traditional four-story or higher facility where all interior corridors, with access through a lobby, pass the front desk to elevators, and emergency fire exits cannot be entered from the outside.

Remote entrances and exits to a building should be minimized. Fire and life safety codes specify the number of exits a building must have. For the convenience of their guests, some hotels and motels permit guests to enter the building through these remote exits. However, they need not serve as entrances.

One way to add convenience and improve security at remote entrances is with readers that accept valid guestroom key cards. In some cases a perimeter door alarm system may alert staff to unauthorized entry or to a door that is propped open. Staff should be trained in how to respond, and the system should be kept in working condition and periodically tested. Although these designs improve guest room security, they do not secure parking lots and pathways.

The number-one deterrent to site crime and improved safety is lighting. Site lighting for a small motel should be a minimum of one footcandle, and the entire site should be uniformly lit. Entrances to the building should have higher illumination levels, around three to five footcandles, to draw attention to them. If a facility has outside entrances to guest rooms, lighting there should be brighter than lighting for walkways, but it does not need to be as bright as it is for the main entrance. Ramps, stairs, and elevator lobbies should be brightly lit.

Landscaping should be minimal and designed and maintained so hiding places and blind spots around the building are eliminated. Each state has some form of liability limits on loss of a guest's property. Laws require that motels provide guests with a safe or safe-deposit box for storing valuables. A motel should be sure to get enough safe-deposit boxes to meet the facility's needs.

The boxes should also be of good quality. Manufacturers usually provide two keys for each deposit box. This second key should be destroyed because some motels have been held liable for the missing contents when it was discovered a second key existed.

If a hotel or motel is in a resort area, room safes may be a worthwhile addition for both security and marketing appeal. In Hawaii in-room safes are a requirement of the innkeepers statutes. In-room safes, however, do not replace front-desk safes or safe-deposit boxes. Physical asset protection in a small hotel or motel begins with good perimeter protection. The more control over access to interior facilities, storage areas, and guest areas, the better.

Inexpensive access control devices can be placed on rear service entrances and high-value storage areas. As a minimum, a secure, restricted-keyway, removable-core commercial lock set with strict key control goes a long way in reducing theft in budget motels. Motels should also consider using an electronic stand-alone access device that provides an audit trail of entries. Some hotels and motels put these locks on storage rooms to control shortages. Armed robbery is a scary experience for roadside motel operators.

Many motels lock their lobbies after dark in the hopes of curtailing crime. Some innovative motel lobby designs have automated check-in equipment, where a guest inserts a credit card, registers, and receives a key card to the room without leaving his or her car. With this approach, however, the human element is lost.

Other facilities have installed bullet-resistive teller windows in the foyer leading to the lobby for after-hours check-in. The lobby should be well lit and open, giving wide visibility to personnel at the front desk. Frequent cash drops and trim safes help reduce dollar loss. Trim safes are small, locked boxes that are mounted under the counter so large bills or excess cash can be dropped inside during high-volume business.

Holdup alarms have pluses and minuses and should be used only after carefully considering all the facts.

Support has grown for CCTV with time-lapse video, both as a deterrent and in documenting events during a robbery. The camera is usually positioned to provide a front view of the assailant, but another good location is a wide-angle view of the front desk and lobby. The use of any of these tools is only as good as the training and instruction of the employees on the front line.

Access to the areas behind the front desk should always be secured with a door and some form of access control device, such as a push-button, reprogrammable lock. The combination should be changed frequently. Drop safes and safe-deposit boxes for employee banks should be contained in a secure workroom, usually behind the front desk. Here, again, key control is a paramount concern.

Often adjacent to this area is the property manager's office, which should have a high-security lock set on the entrance. The front desk acts as a physical barrier, separating the workroom and administrative areas from the lobby. All motels should have an emergency two-way radio system. The system also can be used for day-to-day staff communications.

For a modest investment, three radios with related equipment can be purchased with a somewhat private frequency established and licensed by the Federal Communications Commission. One radio should be placed at the front desk as a base station and the other two given to the property manager and maintenance person.

At night, radios become the primary security and emergency communications between staff on duty and the security officer, if there is one. This small communication system is worth its weight in gold in time saved, in fast response to day-to-day activities, and especially in an emergency.

As security professionals, we tend to notice the extravagant approaches to security at larger hotels and resorts and forget about the small hotel or motel. Being small and located off Highway 1 in Podunk does not denote having small problems. These facilities have just as many security problems as big facilities but with fewer resources to solve them.

As mentioned earlier, 80 percent of the lodging facilities in the United States have fewer than 125 guest rooms. That 80 percent will have the majority of problems. So if your company owns and operates small hotels and motels, make sure they receive a large measure of your expertise.

8

Motel and Hotel Taxes

ABOUT THE TAX

The use of hotel/motel taxes to fund cultural programmes and facilities in the United States now is widespread and considered a popular way of dedicating tax dollars to the arts. The arts programming supported with these funds boosts local tourism and has a significant impact on local economies. Nationally, the arts are a $36.8 billion industry, which supports 1.3 million full-time jobs and generates $790 million in local government revenue. Expenditures by arts audiences on restaurants, hotels, parking facilities, and retail uses spur even more economic activity.

There are tremendous differences in the ways in which hotel/motel taxes have been established, the levels of taxation that have been allocated to the arts, and the purposes for which funds have been disbursed. This article examines the emergence of the hotel/motel tax with a general overview and a series of case studies from across the country. Each of these cases is unique, yet common themes and experiences can provide insights and direction to agencies and local governments now considering the hotel/motel tax as a funding source for cultural development.

The hotel/motel tax (also sometimes called a bed tax) has emerged over the last 15 years as a means of financing activities that attract tourists and visitors. With the phenomenal growth of tourism in the 1980s and the declining fiscal situation in many regions, communities have soughtnew means by which to promote and develop their tourist industries, without placing an additional burden on residents.

American and foreign visitors now are spending close to $450 billion ear in the United States. At the same time, federal contributions to cities and counties have dropped by more than two-thirds since 1980. Not surprisingly, then, state and local governments around the country have created and/or raised taxes on meals, rental cars, alcoholic beverages, and hotel and motel rooms.

The hotel/motel tax is considered the major generator of tourism taxes. A 1'992 survey by the National Conference of State Legislatures (NCSL) shows that 42 states have a local-option accommodation tax, meaning that local governments in these states can elect to add a hotel tax. The local tax usually is collected and disbursed by that _jurisdiction. Ill a 1991 survey by NCSL, the hotel tax in 25 cities ranged from a low of 6 percent in Sioux Falls, South Dakota, to a high of 19.25 percent in New York City and averaged 11.1 percent (these rates include state taxes).

Hotel/motel taxes, together with other tourism taxes, historically have been used for a broad range of services and activities, from operating support for visitors' bureaus to funding for summer concerts and fireworks displays.

For the arts, hotel tax funding can be dedicated to a specific facility, to re-granting of programmes, or to events with some relation to local tourism. Funds also can be forwarded to the local arts agency or paid directly. to arts presenters and producers by a local commission, which manages fund distribution. The level of funding also can be fixed by statute or be left to the discretion of the taxing body. With these profound differences, it is best to consider specific examples.

"The arts are an important economic component in San Diego," says jack McGrory, city manager for the past five years. "They create an attraction in and of themselves. By supporting these organizations and helping them to grow, they in turn give something back to the city."

For many years, San Diego has had a transient occupancy tax. Starting in the 1980s, a portion of that tax revenue has been allocated to the San Diego Commission for the Arts and Culture for re-granting to local arts and cultural programmes. In 1988, in conjunction with the increase of the tax to 9 percent, the city council awarded the arts commission a more substantial portion of the tax revenue. From 1988 to 1993, annual allocations ranged from $4.5 million to $6 million.

In 1994, the arts commission received a one-cent dedication of the tax, which concurrently was increased to 10.5 percent. This amendment has taken effect recently and likely, will result in a 10 percent increase in local arts funding. The 1995 allocation was budgeted at $5.6 million.

The commission splits funding into four pots: I percent is a public art fund, which is in addition to capital improvement projects funded elsewhere; 2 percent goes to neighbourhood arts programmes; 7 percent goes to administration of the programmes; and the remaining 90 percent is re-granted to local arts organizations as organizational support ($5 million in 1995). Of thc 90 applicants for these funds in 1995, 84 will receive support.

According to the commission, the key to getting the increase and the dedicated income stream from the occupancy tax was a strong relationship with the convention and tourist bureau, which made a number of joint presentations with the commission to the council and has maintained a close relationship. The commission also maintains a standing committee on cultural tourism.

"Historically, our room tax has been spent principally on areas where the city could promote itself, particularly with respect to tourism," says McGrory. "We think the arts and cultural life in the city are key components to attracting people to it."

To receive room tax funds, local arts organizations and individuals must go through a rigorous evaluation process that involves an initial application, screening by a 15-member commission appointed by the mayor and council, and final council approval. Not only says McGrory, has this process brought the arts community together "but the council has a process they. can rely on. I think [the room tax] has helped our city. We're proud of the arts and cultural organizations that we have and the level of support that they get reflects that."

A 2 percent bed tax was established in 1978 by state enabling legislation, a local referendum, and a county ordinance. By ordinance, 20 percent of the annual proceeds from the tax are dedicated to the Dade County Cultural Affairs Council. Another 60 percent goes to the countywide convention and visitors' bureau, with the balance going to the city of Miami for renovations to the Orange Bowl.

Funds are delivered to the Cultural Affairs Council to support a full range of cultural activities. Bed tax revenues to the council in 1995 will total S1.5 million, roughly 35 percent of its annual budget. More than 700 individuals and organizations apply annually to the council's competitive grants programmes; on average, 350 applicants are awarded grants.

The council has managed the administration of this significant funding initiative successfully on behalf of the county, earning praise and support from county and community leaders. The arts council also has developed a strong relationship with the local tourism industry. The council and the industry have worked together to secure this funding stream, to pursue other dedicated revenues, and to build numerous programmes and services that link culture and tourism in Dade County. Representatives from the Cultural Affairs Council and the convention and visitors' bureau sit on each others' committees and boards.

Currently, these two groups have joined with economic development interests in Dade County to pursue the establishment of a food and beverage tax. This will provide an additional dedicated source of funding for the county's cultural activities, for its tourism advertising and promotion, and for economic development initiatives.

Finally, the county has committed proceeds from the convention development tax (an additional 3 percent bed tax) to plan, develop, and construct the new performing arts centre in downtown Miami. This revenue is anticipated to yield $140 million in bond proceeds.

Columbus began arts funding in 1973 through the Greater Columbus Arts Council (GCAC). In 1978, the source of these funds was changed from general funds to hotel/motel tax funds. In 1982, the city revised its tax code to increase the municipal room tax and to dedicate a 20 percent portion to the GCAC and its grants programme. These changes resulted from an intensive advocacy effort undertaken by the GCAC and its member organizations.

In 1985, the allocation to the arts was increased to 25 percent, and the total tax climbed from 4 to 6 percent. Funding for the arts has continued to rise since the beginning of the programme. The 1982 allocation to the GCAC vas $425,000. For 1995, that allocation has risen to S2.2 million, which represents some 50 percent of the total GCAC budget.

Funds are distributed to approximately 50 organizations each year. Grants are available for projects, management assistance, and operating support. Funds also help the GCAC deliver such services as technical assistance, training, information services, and residency programmes.

The GCAC maintains a close relationship with the tourism industry, in Columbus. Their premier annual event is the Columbus Arts Festival, which brings 500,000 people to the downtown. The industry and the GCAC also fund a number of downtown special events for residents and visitors. Arts council board members and staff also sit on boards of the convention and visitors' bureau and the chamber of commerce, acting as conduits between the arts and tourism industries.

Though there is no legislation that guarantees the arts allocation of the hotel/motel tax, the income stream is relatively secure, thanks to the benefits that this allocation provides to the arts, the tourism industry, and the community as a whole.

Creating, increasing, or dedicating a room tax to the arts has proven to be a popular means of funding the arts as a basic city or county service. These arts programmes increase tourism and have a significant economic impact on the community. Because the Source of these funds can be identified specifically and because the funds are dedicated to a particular purpose, the tax is politically attractive, as it is not collected from local residents/taxpayers/ voters but from renters of a city's local hotel rooms. This dedicated revenue stream is also less competitive than a city s general fund, which supports core services like policing, fire protection, and garbage collection.

For a local government official or an arts advocate to obtain a portion of a local hotel tax requires a strong argument that the arts contribute to local tourism, either through arts programmes or facilities. To make this argument, a close relationship between the arts and the tourism industry is mandatory. This is a real challenge, as the hotel operators who collect the tax must be convinced of its long-term benefit to their businesses.

The downside to a dedicated income stream is that funds can vary from year to year with the varying health of the local tourism industry. Yet, if properly, managed by a local arts agency, as one of several funding sources, room tax revenue can provide meaningful support for local arts groups, as well as capital and/or operating funds for arts facilities.

This article is based on a report by AMS Planning and Research for the National Assembly of Local Arts Agencies' (NALAA) Institute for Community Development and the Arts, of which ICMA is a partner. The purpose of NALAA's Institute is to educate local arts agencies, elected and appointed local government officials, and arts funders about the important role of the arts as community change agents for economic, social, and educational problem. NALAA's Institute also will identify innovative community arts programmes and nontraditional funding sources to enable local arts agencies and local civic officials to adapt these programmes to their own communities.

HOTEL LENDING

Banks are dipping their toes back into the hotel-lending business. But inexperienced owners and operators need not apply. Banks are interested in financing people who have proven track records. Financing for construction of new hotels and motels, however, is frequently difficult to obtain. And where credit is being extended, bankers are striking tougher deals, putting more of the onus of bad performance in the borrower's lap.

Yet to the hotel industry, this is good news. "Lenders are no longer hanging up when they hear the word 'hotel'," says Kyle Draggoo, director of hotel brokerage at Merimark Corp., Houston. "They'll at least listen to you."

Prices on the rise

Many banks are still smarting from the hotel overbuilding of the 1980s that turned lenders into landlords.

It wasn't long ago that experts were suggesting the best thing that could be done with hotels involved dynamite and a detonator. Though some banks still have a fair share of seized properties to unload, prices are beginning to firm for hotels, and demand is up.

In September, Hospitality Valuation Services, Inc., Mineola, N.Y., released its latest "Hotel Valuation Index." The lodging consulting firm's study found that U.S. hotel values increased an average of 15% across the country in 1993. This compares to an 8% increase in 1992 and a 14% decrease in 1991. The HVS index is based on analysis using occupancy and average daily room rate data to compute value.

The strongest comebacks were seen in Atlanta, which gained 39% in value; Phoenix, 31%; Denver, 28%; and Washington, D.C., 23%. On the other hand, Orlando, Honolulu, and Los Angeles saw values based on occupancies and room rates drop. Stephen Rushmore, president of HVS, sees the overall strengthening value of the business to be an indication that interested buyers should move now to obtain the properties still on lender's books.

"The beauty of lending to hotel operators today is that the downside risk has been taken away," says Rushmore. Besides the improvements in value, the consultant notes, "there is virtually no hotel building taking place." (The one exception in 1993 was the construction of three mega-hotels in Las Vegas. People in the hotel trade believe they were an anomoly. The Hotel & Motel Brokers of America estimates that if Las Vegas is subtracted from rooms opened in 1993, the total for that year comes to 23,500, which it says is a six-year low for new construction.) What contributed to this improving picture? Business is better. In 1993, U.S. hotels annual occupancy rates hit 64%, according to Hospitality Directions, a quarterly journal of the national hospitality group at Coopers & Lybrand. This was the highest occupancy rate reached by the industry since 1984, Coopers & Lybrand notes. The firm predicts steady improvement at least through 1996, when it expects occupancy rates to approach 70%. Average daily room rates and growth in demand for rooms have also been steadily improving, though the firm observed that they were still behind the rates of growth seen before the recession.

Small Banks More Active

"Financing for hotel real estate acquisitions and new construction was more attainable in 1993 than at any time since the late 1980s," stated a mid-1994 report by the Hotel & Motel Brokers of America. "Currently activity is not widespread, but there is sufficient volume to speculate that the credit logjam is breaking up, and the future holds more promise."

The report, Transactions by HMBA, is based on a survey of the activity of HMBA members. Brokers belonging to the organization account for about 25% of all hotels sold nationwide and about 35% of the middlemarket segment of the business. Thus the study is considered a good proxy for the industry's experiences. The HMBA survey indicates that the bulk of activity is actually centreed in the nation's community banks, rather than among the large banks. "For loans of $4 million and under, local community banks were primary resources in 1993," states the HMBA report. "These lenders, who have a stake in building their local economies, treat the financing as a business loan, requiring personal guarantees from owner/operators. Rates and terms are generally more favourable than those offered by credit companies. Lower debt coverage ratios often can be negotiated, especially if the loan carries a Small Business Administration guarantee."

LTV ratios are down

Generally speaking, however, bankers from institutions of all sizes are playing harder ball. "They're definitely trying to be more conservative in this recovery," says Merimark's Draggoo. He (and others) points out that underwriting has become much stricter than it had been during the 1980s. "We're finding that lenders are typically lending no more than 75%," says Patrick H. Ford, Sr., a principal with National Hotel Realty Advisors, Portsmouth, N.H. Others say they've heard of lenders going as low as a 60% loan-to-value ratio. By contrast, lenders were frequently willing to go to 90%

and beyond during the 1980s. "As lenders get back into business, they are being much more prudent," says Mark Woodworth, national hospitality industry chairman for Coopers & Lybrand. "They are basing decisions on current hotel earnings, rather than on prospective earnings."

As mentioned at the outset, this is a difficult time for newcomers to the lodging business to obtain financing. Lenders are much less likely to entertain a newcomer's application than someone who knows the business. In fact, says Woodworth, just knowing the hotel business isn't always considered sufficient.

Nowadays lenders look for expertise in the particular type of hotel being financed: luxury, upscale, mid-price, economy, and budget. In addition, lenders are paying more attention than ever to the track record of the particular brand name a hotel has decided to affiliate itself with, according to Woodworth. Most of the financing referred to thus far consists of making loans to purchase existing hotels from current operators or from lenders. Other credits include renovations to an aging hotel and refinancing of outstanding debt. Loans for construction of new hotels are scarce to nonexistent, except in some pockets of unusual growth. Las Vegas is one, Branson, Mo., is another.

This is as much a matter of market demand as lender willingness. Coopers & Lybrand's Mark Woodworth notes that while hotel values are rising again, it is only beginning to make as much sense to build a new hotel than to buy one that's already up. Woodworth doesn't expect to see any meaningful amount of construction in the mid-price range for another year or so, and generally expects little construction of luxury hotels for another three.

As more than one expert noted, large-bank lenders still have a ways to go before they finish unloading the big hotels they got stuck with after the debacle of the late 1980s. Thus, most of the big domestic banks remain on the sidelines. "A couple of them are talking about getting back into the market, but they haven't yet," says Tom Arasi, executive vicepresident of finance and development at Tishman Hotel Corp., a subsidiary of Tishman Realty & Construction. "There has been a great deal of equity trying to get into the hospitality business," says Arasi, "and it is way ahead of the debt side."

A particularly hot source of equity funding in recent times has been real estate investment trusts dedicated to hotel properties. Much of what debt financing is available has come from hotel mortgage conduits set up by major hotel companies to provide financing to their franchisees.

Among big commercial bank lenders, says Arasi, what activity there has been has chiefly come from European banks operating in the U.S. Even they are very selective, however. Roderick Rohrbach, vice-president at Credit Lyonnais, New York, points out that even fast-growing markets can be risky. A property in a market where hotels still sell out on many nights of the year has appeal, he says.

But a hot market will attract new development, which could lead to a glut that would upset the economics that make a loan appealing at first glance.

As a result, in some circumstances Credit Lyonnais would find the proposed acquisition of a high performer in a satisfactory market to be preferable to lending for acquisition in a roaring market. (In no event does it finance construction.)

While loans for big hotel projects remain elusive, the hospitality industry has begun going directly to the credit markets with the assistance of Wall Street investment banks.

These players are forming hotel mortgage conduits, similar in principle to the secondary mortgage market for residential loans. The Hotel & Motel Brokers of America report cited earlier makes these observations about the relatively new conduits:

"The terms are restrictive and the loans are for only the highest-performing hotels, but the availability of funds is most welcome. Total loan volume, however, is only a trickle of the traditional flow of funds that it is replacing. Nonetheless, these loans are an important and needed interim step prior to the expected return of conventional sources of financing over the next few years."

One example of the technique is Richfield Hotel Management, Inc.'s partnership with Lehman Brothers. In June the two companies introduced a programme that Richfield clients could use for acquisition, refinancing, and renovations. One advantage Richfield claims for its programme is that borrowers can operate their hotels as independent brands or under the national brand of their choice, whereas financing programmes offered by franchisors require that the borrower fly the franchisor's flag. Rates start at 290 basis points over the 20-year Treasury bill rate.

No deals had been closed in the Richfield programme as of mid-September, but several were in the pipeline, according to Roberta Griffin, senior director of corporate finance at Richfield. Industry observers reported that many conduits have yet to do a great deal of actual lending. Do conduits represent a threat to traditional lenders? Roderick Rohrbach of Credit Lyonnais doesn't see them as shutting banks out.

"Lenders such as ourselves will naturally cater to the borrower who seeks more of a customized approach than the conduits, which are less conducive to customized financing," says Rohrbach.

Richfield's Roberta Griffin acknowledges Rohrbach's point. "Right now, because the conduit programmes involve rated securities, there isn't a whole lot of room" for flexibility. However, she adds that investors' changing appetites might someday enable securitization programmes to become more adaptable. Adaptable or not, right now conduit financing is expensive. Stephen Rushmore of Hospitality Valuation Services points out that a typical loan rate today is 9.5%; by contrast, the conduits are charging in the neighbourhood of 11%. "Conduits are very expensive," says Rushmore, "and you'd only use them if you had a gun to your head."

9

Management of Pay and Performance

PAY AND REWARD SYSTEMS

Budget tourism is in and the Indian Government is planning to use the opportunity. A change in its policy of auctioning hotel sites, with sops for attracting big players of the Indian hotel industry, is on the anvil. A significant change will be a more liberalised payment-of-land-cost plan, with a focus on budget hotels. This will require resizing of hotel plots, as, so far, hotel sites are auctioned within set parametres of shop-cum-office sites.

At present, bidders at hotel-site auctions have to pay the land cost within three years from the date of auction. The change will mean this schedule extended to between 15 and 20 years. Several leading hotel groups have shown interest in setting up hotels, but back off everytime they are asked to pay the cost of land within three years of auction. Industry pundits have told the Administration that it took upto six years for a new hotel venture to break even, so, the payment should be staggered. The first two years are spent just in construction, which means no recovery.

The Administration, by extending the payment schedule, will end up getting more from increased number of bids and interest spread over more time. The idea of revenue sharing between the Administration and a chosen hotel chain has been dropped, as a similar system has not worked well in New Delhi, with major hotel groups defaulting on payment. The hotel industry wants to go in for budget tourism, for which, the want fresh sites and not disputed property.

This develops some of the issues introduced in surrounding one of the most important sets of employment rules - pay and pay determination - but in the reverse order because pay is the outcome of the process of pay determination. As Rubery observes, 'Payment systems are a mechanism or a medium through which the employment relationship is constituted and codified development of a new payment system may be seen as part of a reconstitution of power relations'. In particular we show how pay and reward systems constitute one of the central facets of a managerial cost-control approach, with a strong gender effect.

Pay defines a worker's status and standard of living, and can affect motivation and commitment to work, so low pay may be detrimental on a number of grounds. Pay may be used by employers to signal they are good employers, to attract the best workers, to maximize control, to motivate workers, to improve performance, and as part of a change management programme. While some of these objectives are allied to higher pay, we must not assume that employers will apply all, or any, of these principles to every occupational group within the same organization. We have already noted that more beneficial conditions may be applied to a privileged core, while the rest of the workforce is subjected to less favourable and more controlling conditions, including low pay.

The term 'total reward system' has traditionally been used to describe remuneration in the HI. Employees in hotels and restaurants, but not necessarily in other sub-sectors, are assumed to receive all or most of the following variable reward system:

basic pay + subsidized lodging + subsidized food + tips or service charge + 'fiddles' and 'knock-offs'.

The wider application of this package may well have been overstated in an attempt by employers to justify that employees are not really low-paid. The stark reality is that the HCTS is low-paid, regardless of how pay is measured. Most of the elements of the total reward system can be applied to workers in other sectors, who may benefit from other more favourable monetary and non-monetary benefits. Hence shop workers can 'fiddle' by short-changing customers, while there are a host of occupations where workers can readily pilfer small items from their employer such as pens, sellotape and stationery. Tipping is common practice in hairdressing.

The unpredictable and variable nature of the total reward system says a great deal about the nature of the employment relationship in the HI. In spite of the legal and institutional framework, managers are able to exert strong control through individual contract making, and unilateral management determination of pay. Informal practices are not the preserve of any particular type of workplace or activity. In fast food stores practices involve the distribution of rewards and favours according to informal systems of individual bargaining, including access to days off and favourable rosters. An informal deal may bind a worker to a tacit understanding that may later be used as a sanction against her/him. The lack of transparency about reward systems reduces workers' bargaining power by isolating individuals. It is not surprising that the HI sustains high quit rates in these circumstances. Reward is not seen as a component part of culture change.

Apart from keeping pay low, there are other circumstances and conditions under which managerial control may be intensified. For example, control on wage costs and employee performanc e is achieved through high reliance on tips, particularly in pubs and bars. Work intensity is maximized by the provision of live-in facilities, enabling staff to be summoned to work at short notice. Tightening up on a 'blind eye' approach to 'fiddles' and pilfering when business slackens and dismissing the miscreants can be used to control employee numbers, e.g. strawberries at the Wimbledon lawn tennis championships. On the other hand managerial control has been weakened by the poor economic situation in Russia. The lack of funds to pay employees has led to demands for copious time off.

Regulation and Determination

Global commitment to a minimum wage and the equalization of pay between men and women provide the central foundation to the regulation of the pay of many HCTS workers. Both principles have been given legal effect in many countries throughout the world. While law-abiding employers will pay at least the minimum rate, and uprate it as required, the issue of narrowing the gender pay gap is far more problematic. We also consider how far collective bargaining has served the interests of employers and workers, although that its application and effects can be patchy and largely ineffectual. Hence the primary actor in pay determination is management.

Minimum Wages

By 1980 the ILO's minimum wage Convention had been ratified by 194 countries to the benefit of many hospitality and tourism workers. Large swathes of the British HI were within scope of wages councils system between the mid-1940s and mid-1990s. Abolition of the system in 1993 led to the deterioration in pay in the HI.

Although the objectives of a minimum wage can vary, one purpose is to provide a pay floor. However, the level at which the wage is set affects its 'bite'; a wage set very low and sporadically up rated will be largely symbolic. Three-quarters of minimum wage workers in the US work in the HI, and industry leaders are renowned in their fight to hold down the wage. Lower-level jobs in the HI in the US are paid at the same level as other industries, ostensibly because of minimum wage laws. In Australia and Singapore one-third and two-thirds of hotel workers respectively are paid above the minimum.

Favourable differential rates may apply to casuals and young workers, reinforcing their importance as integral to cost-minimization. Under the award system in Australia casuals receive a loading (about 20 per cent) above standard rates and a minimum pay guarantee (2-3 hours) in lieu of annual and sick leave, but are not entitled to premium payments for weekends. It is alleged that McDonald's dismiss workers when they reach the age of 20 to avoid paying full adult rates. Most other studies have found no evidence to support the employment of young workers as a means to evade the minimum wage.

The Minimum Wage

The introduction of a NMW in the UK has caused a pay spike at the minimum rate, showing that workers actually benefited from its introduction. The arrival of the NMW has not been a discrete event in a stable world. Individual firms do have scope for discretion, and to take random, opportunistic decisions. However, there has been a tendency for hospitality firms to take a 'low road' approach. Hotels have tended to adopt a cost-minimization strategy rather than pursue a quality enhancement route.

Case Study: Introducing the UK National Minimum Wage in Hospitality

The NMW was introduced in April 1999. Two rates were set - a full adult rate of £3.60, and a lower development rate for young workers aged 18-21 and adult trainees in the first six months of a new job. By October 2003 the full rate was £4.50 and the development rate £3.80. Rates of £4.85 and £4.10 have been provisionally accepted to apply from October 2004, subject to the LPC's advice in light of economic circumstances.

The NMW has been introduced successfully, with employers given plenty of warning about forthcoming increases. The HI has been disproportionately affected because it has the highest proportion of low-paid jobs, particularly among females, and employs large proportions of young people, the group most likely to suffer unemployment effects. Twenty-three per cent of hospitality jobs, 300,000 in total, benefited from a major hike in the NMW of 40p in 2001. Waiting and bar staff are among the occupational groups most affected. The impact on the wage bill of 0.7 per cent is less than at the time the NMW was introduced.

Employment has increased by 200,000 since 1999. Many firms have deployed a wide variety of coping strategies, including increased cost control, adjusting hours, employment restructuring, increasing prices and reducing profits. A pay spike at the level of the full adult rate has developed, with a mezzanine floor some 30-40p higher, reflecting tight labour market conditions in some parts of the country. Small firms have been more affected, because large companies' pay was already at or above the NMW rates.

The youth development rate is below the market rate and most employers pay the full rate at age 18. Most employers are likely to welcome the introduction of a lower rate for 16- and 17-year-olds in 2004, subject to the LPC's recommendations. There has been little take-up of the adult development rate, mainly because firms find it hard to recruit at this rate, recruits already have the skills and it is unfair/divisive.

In the UK three aspects of the NMW have particular resonance within the HI: tips and gratuities, an accommodation offset and the differential treatment of young workers. Employers may use tips or a service charge collected through the payroll to 'top up' hourly pay to the NMW, whereas cash tips paid to and kept by workers do not count. As there was a limited call to the LPC's suggestion that the rules for treatment of tips and gratuities be reconsidered, this remains unchanged.

An accommodation offset of £24.40 per week can be deducted from the NMW to pay for accommodation. Where accommodation is for less than a full week, the offset must be a corresponding reduction, which replaces specified hourly and daily rates. Employers can charge more provided the deduction does not bring the hourly rate to below the NMW. The BHA estimates that the average cost of accommodation is £42 per week, and that employers typically charge between £40 and £50. Other sources suggest wider weekly variations of between £20 and £95 and £35 and £65.

While youth pay is generally lower than adult pay (LPC, 2003), many employers have been uneasy about the exclusion of 16- and 17-year-olds from any form of minimum wage protection. Some believe that the absence of regulation will lead to a vulnerable group being exploited by ruthless employers, while others consider exclusion is discriminatory or not justified on grounds of equity. The government's decision to ask the LPC to consider the case for introducing a minimum wage rate for workers of these ages is likely to be uncontroversial. Some 25 per cent of students in employment aged 16 and 17 work in the HI, and a number of major fast food employers, including Burger King, already apply the full NMW rate from age 16.

The government's continued rejection of the LPC's advice to apply the full NMW rate at age 21, rather than 22, remains an anomaly and irrelevance for most firms. Yet there are still pockets in the economy where employers use the lower youth rate, including rural North Wales. The method of job evaluation, which can be used to determine equal value claims for equal pay, offers one way to establish the reasons for the differences in adult and youth pay and to assess whether differences can be objectively justified. This approach, based on job content and employee attribute analysis, has been used in North Wales, as Case study illustrates.

Case Study: Small Hospitality Firms in North Wales

Employers perceive a positive relationship between age and employee attributes, rating under 18s' attributes consistently lower than the rest of the workforce. Some attributes such as solving problems, making decisions, and interpersonal skills are developed through experience, hence lower pay. In most cases work also involves fewer tasks and responsibilities. The exception is fast food, where workers of all ages receive the same starter rate, as they are subject to the same tasks, responsibilities and working conditions.

Workers aged 18-21 are to an extent disadvantaged on lower pay, because they appear to be performing the same tasks as older workers. Employers appear to place more emphasis on the possession of higher personal attributes by older workers. The LPC was placed on a permanent footing in 2001, with a view to monitoring the impact of the NMW and making uprating recommendations. The pattern has been to recommend increases on a two-year basis from October, with the proviso that the second stage increases are reviewed nearer the time. Although the initial NMW rate was set 'prudently' because of the unknown effects, subsequent increases have been above average earnings. These have been of most benefit to workers on lowest docile earnings who are less likely to get incentive or overtime pay. Assuming the 2004 increase is implemented; estimates suggest that the NMW will have increased from 88.7 per cent to 94.5 per cent of half median male earnings in its first five years.

The principle of equal pay for equal work regardless of gender is more recent than a minimum wage, emerging from 1951 ILO Convention on Equal Pay. Equal pay was integral to the Treaty of Rome 1957 and has been addressed in subsequent EU Directives. In Britain the Equal Pay Act 1970 enabled equal pay claims to be made between men and women on the basis of like work or work rated as equivalent under a job evaluation scheme. The Act was amended in 1983 to allow women to claim equal pay for work of equal value, even where no job evaluation scheme was in place. Hence a female canteen worker could claim her job was of equal value to a male painter and decorator. Same sex claims between part time and full-time workers were not possible until the Part-time Employees (Prevention of Less Favourable Treatment) Regulations were introduced in 2000. However, minimum wage and equal pay legislation have had a limited effect on pay relativities.

In 2003 implementation of a provision of the Employment Act 2002 introduced an equal pay questionnaire in equal pay cases at employment tribunal, to make it easier for applicants to request key information from the employer when deciding whether to bring a case. Completion is not compulsory but failure to reply may lead to inferences from the tribunal.

Institutional Constraints

Men earn more than women, because every labour market in the EU is gender segregated. Full-timers earn more than part-timers, although the differential is smaller among women than among men. Strong collective bargaining and minimum wage regimes reduce the percentage of low-paid workers, but the benefits of regulation do not extend to women, especially parttimers, as much as to men. There is also a strong sectoral effect whether or not national arrangements are in place.

'It is extremely unlikely that both differences in systems of wage determination between countries and changes to wage structures would not have consequences for the relative pay of women and men'. Hence in the US, Canada and UK where pay determination systems are decentralized and fragmented, between 19 and 25 per cent of the full-time female labour force is low-paid compared to 6 per cent in Scandinavia where solidaristic bargaining prevails. That said, women executives in the US have lower starting salaries than their male counterparts, and pay inequality persists where directors are believed to be able to 'get more for less'. Whitehouse et al. (2001) conclude that the prosecution of pay equity cases has been limited by progressive decentralization in Australia and Britain, although in different ways.

The failure of minimum wage systems to deliver gender equity in the EU arises from strong political pressure not to increase minimum wages as a symbol of wage restraint and to promote a more flexible labour market. Unusually, a stated objective of the UK's NMW was to promote gender equality; over 70 per cent of beneficiaries were women, and around two-thirds of jobs below minimum wage levels were part-time. The gap between male and female hourly pay has narrowed, particularly among part-timers, but still remains at 82 per cent for full-timers and 89 per cent for part-timers.

In Western Europe collective agreements reached at multi-employer (sectoral and economy-wide) have coverage that is greater than union density. This is because even firms with few union members participate in sectoral bargaining and statutory procedures extend the terms of the agreement to all employers in the sector. Selected examples from EU countries are shown in Case study. In the US the wages of highly unionized occupations in the hotel, gaming and restaurant industry in Las Vegas are significantly higher than the wages of identical non-union occupations in Reno.

In the US the Fair Labour Standards Act 1938 created two classes of employees - those paid for the hire of their labour and those undertaking administrative, professional or executive duties that are paid a salary. The latter are exempted from minimum wage laws. Incorrect classification of employees can be costly.

The Role of Managers in Pay Determination

The nature of skills (readily available and transferable) and unpredictable demand tend to create a low market rate for jobs. We identify how British managers are able to exercise considerable discretion over pay within the legal and institutional frameworks outlined above.

Which managers are involved in determining pay will depend on whether workplaces are multi- or single-site; in the WERS sample over three-quarters of HI workplaces are multi-site. In just under half the HI workplaces higher-level managers beyond the workplace and the Board of Directors are directly involved in determining the pay rise, although workplace management is involved in 37 per cent of cases. Where the decision about pay change was made at the establishment (one in eight HI cases), higher-level managers are not consulted in two-thirds of cases. While hotel managers are most likely to be involved, a majority consulted their higher-level colleagues. While pay is largely management-determined in AIS and the PSS, HI workplaces, unsurprisingly, are significantly less likely to involve union representatives in this process. Pay setting arrangements for different occupational groups differ within AIS, the PSS and the HI, and by size of workplace and sub-sector. One must be careful about drawing too many inferences from these because the limited presence of some occupational groups means that numbers of cases can be very small. Even so, higher management clearly takes a leading role in setting pay in the HI, suggesting strong emphasis is placed on organizational cost control.

Case Study: Pay Determination in the European Hospitality Industry

Spain

In 1996 a binding four-year sectoral agreement replaced a labour ordinance which contained a cumbersome pay structure. The new agreement lays down basic conditions regarding grading systems, disciplinary procedures and training, which is monitored by a joint committee of the signatory partners. Pay is determined by an extensive network of collective agreements. Some 555,083 workers (71 per cent of the total HI workforce) were covered by 104 company and 47 provincial agreements.

India

Indian Hotels Company Ltd (IHCL), better known as the Taj group, has set a global benchmark by registering an 80 per cent loyalty with its staff, at a time when turnover in hospitality staff is at a high due to international hotel chains setting up shop in India, says a Gallup survey. The company's employee turnover rates are amongst the lowest in the industry and IHCL senior vice-president (HR) Bernard Martyris attributes it to the high loyalty factor amongst the employees. According to him, the accessibility of senior staff, quick responses to employees' grievances and needs keep the company's employee rolls firm.

Mr Martyris also said despite the group not offering the previously available job security, turnover is still low because it has, in turn, increased pay by 30-35 per cent. Till recently, the Taj was not a good paymaster. And the poor pay structure for the operation staff is the main reason for turnover in our industry. In a year or so, we will be the best paymasters in the country. The company was to conduct a wage revision during the last fiscal, but due to the September 11 terror attacks and its fallout, was unable to do so. Along with pay, IHCL is also targeting not only fast-trackers but also its solid citizens. This, according to Mr Martyris, is the only way to retain employees.

He also attributed the strong affinity of employees to the company, to an internal union. "The very fact that we don't have external influences in our unions is pointer enough. Our unions are powerful and fight for employee rights, but they always take into consideration the interests of the company," he points out.

Along with programmes of tracking employee satisfaction, the Taj group has also put into place systems such as STAR (special thanks and recognition system), wherein employees are encouraged to contribute ideas and are recognised for any special service they render. The patented programme recently won the international Hermes award.

Italy

In 1999 four new collective agreements set minimum pay and conditions for three years, including increases to the number of atypical working arrangements, new options for managing working time and measures to improve training. Some 800,000 employees are covered by the agreements, but in some areas half of employment is in the black economy. The right to bargain locally has been recognized since 1993. In practice company bargaining has continued for organizations employing more than 15 employees.

There is a new option for smaller companies and companies where it has not been customary to bargain regionally. To encourage firms to enter the formal economy special clauses may be negotiated at this level, allowing agreed pay increases to be implemented in an alternative way.

Sweden

Sectoral agreements are combined with local agreements. Employers who are not members of the main employers' organization may be bound by the terms of the sectoral agreement through signing an auxiliary agreement. This is common among small companies who are not members of an employers' organization, and for around half of those workplaces with union members who have no company agreement. Although collective agreements set minimum pay, most employees earn above these amounts.

Germany

Collective agreements have the force of law, acting as a minimum wage, and cover 80 to 90 per cent of the German workforce, although trade union membership is low. McDonald's and other fast food establishments broke away from the HI collective agreement by establishing a new employers' federation Bundersverband der System-gastronomie (BdS) and negotiating separately with the Gewerkschaft Nahrung Genuss Gaststatten (NGG).

The fast food collective agreement on pay and conditions includes pay in lieu, overtime, sick pay and the washing of uniforms. The lack of works councils in stores means there is no guarantee that the agreement will be adhered to.

Netherlands

Employees are covered by a three-part national collective agreement. Part A contains conditions that are binding on the whole sector. Parts B and C give individual establishments the option to negotiate at local level with a works council or other representative body provided the agreement is superior to the sectoral agreement. There is one pay scale covering eleven grades, and 120 job categories have their own job descriptions.

A two-year agreement reached in 1998 provided for pay increases in 1998 and 1999, new early retirement provisions in 2000, greater scope for local level negotiations and changes to working time arrangements.

UK

There is no state-sponsored collective bargaining, so most employers are guided by the NMW introduced in 1999. Two of the largest hotel companies, Jarvis and Thistle Hotels, have entered into company collective agreements. The Jarvis agreement includes a probationary hourly rate (first three months) set at the same rate as the NMW, and a minimum rate that is 18p above the NMW, both applicable at age 18. Premiums apply for designated night work (63p per hour) and unsocial hours (59p per hour). Higher rates apply in London and within the M25 orbital.

Although two-thirds of HI workplaces in WERS have an annual pay review, workers in the LOG in these workplaces are significantly less likely to benefit from an annual pay review than their counterparts in AIS and the PSS where nine in ten workplaces operate an annual review. However, workers in the LOG in one-fifth of HI workplaces are significantly more likely to benefit from more frequent pay reviews. Pay is reviewed less than once a year in 10 per cent of HI workplaces, especially in restaurants (over one-quarter). One in 12 HI workplaces had not actually changed pay at the last review. Workers were most likely to have received an increase of between 3 and 4 per cent, although settlements in hotels were more typically at 4 per cent and above. The HI had slightly more cases of the lowest and highest increases at the last pay review.

In the interim six-year period between the abolition of wages councils and the introduction of the NMW, the lack of a reference point for reviewing pay created pay inertia among small HI firms, widening the pay gap between them and larger companies. Some two years after abolition pay had stayed the same or decreased in nearly one-third of the companies surveyed. In the absence of the review date specified in the wages order, almost half the firms had no fixed review date. Personnel directors stressed that the single major change since abolition was a new flexibility in their company's approach to pay-setting, largely in relation to skills pay, thus widening pay differentials above the minimum rate.

As there was nothing to prevent the paying of higher rates under the wages councils, this may be a reflection of a relative decline in pay for those on minimum rates. The main determinants of pay reviews were the local labour market and competitors' pay rates, followed by company economic performance and cost of living/inflation. Wages councils clearly had a significant impact upon pay determination procedures, pay levels and pay structures in the HI.

Even in the two-year period leading up to the introduction of the NMW, many HI firms did not adjust pay in advance, waiting until 1 April 1999 when it became a legal necessity. In the early stages of the NMW only 50 per cent of small HI firms increased pay annually. Pay increases were highly variable and unstructured. Nevertheless, the NMW, as noted above, has been an important influence on HI workers' pay in conjunction with tight labour market conditions. Many firms across the HI, particularly pubs and restaurants, have moved their anniversary dates to October and now review pay to coincide with increases in the NMW.

The major hotel companies have more highly variable review dates. Adverse business conditions in the hotel sector following the foot-and-mouth epidemic and the slump in international tourism and business travel post-11 September caused a number of the major companies to cancel or delay their pay review. Others froze recruitment, allowing turnover and natural wastage to reduce staff numbers.

However, skill shortages in a tight labour market created recruitment and retention problems in key jobs, with pay rises for those affected. However, in many of the large chains, including De Vere, Hilton International, Jarvis Hotels, Thistle Hotels and Whitbread starter rates were at or very close to the NMW rate of £4.10. The median pay of waiting and bar staff, room attendants and commis chefs was 30-40p an hour above the NMW.

Table: Pay-setting Arrangements for Different Occupational Groups in Context and by Size of Workplace (%)

	AIS	**PSS**	**HI**	**<25**	**25-49**	**50-99**	**100+**
Managers/ administrative	HM (43)	HM (50)	HM (60)**	HM (57)	HM (71)	HM (60)	HM (50)
Professional	WM (27)	WM (39)	WM (30)	IN/SOW (45)	WM (46)	WM (55)	HM/WM (48)
Technical/ scientific	WM (36)	WM (38)(51)	HM (50)	OCB/HM (100)	HM (50)	HM/WM (58)	WM
Clerical and secretarial	WM (34)	WM (42)	WM (36)	SOW (41)	HM (68)	WM (61)	WM (49)
Craft and skilled manual	WM (37)	WM (37)	HM (38)	IN (59)	HM (72)	WM (65)	WM (56)
Personal service	HM (32)	HM/ WM (39)	HM (37)	HM (30)	HM (67)	WM (58)	WM (47)
Sales	HM (45)	HM (50)	HM (61)	HM (65)	HM (66)	HM (50)	WM (56)

Operative and assembly manuals	WM (41)	WM (42)	HM (83)*	HM (100)	HM (100)	HM (34)	HM/WM (50)
Routine unskilled manual	WM (33)	WM (42)	HM (38)	HM (33)	HM (55)	WM (60)	WM (50)

Notes: All establishments where any employees in occupational category. The most common method used where any employees in particular occupational groups. HM = higher management, WM = workplace management, CB = collective bargaining with more than one employer, OCB = collective bargaining at organizational level, WCB = workplace collective bargaining, IN = negotiation with individual employees, SOW = some other way. In cases where two arrangements rank first equal, both are shown. *Significantly different at the 5% level from AIS and PSS. **Significantly different at the 5% level from AIS.

Table. Pay-setting Arrangements for Different Occupational Groups by Sub-sector (%)

	Hotels	Campsites	Restaurants	Bars	Canteens
Managers/ administrative	HM (55)	OCB (72)	HM (57)	HM (75)	CB (45)
Professional	WM (69)	HM (100)	SOW (93)	IN (70)	IN (75)
Technical/ scientific	HM (51)	OCB (95)	WM (100)	HM (100)	—
Clerical and secretarial	WM (53)	OCB (72)	SOW (44)	SOW (61)	CB (55)
Craft and skilled manual	WM (52)	OCB (78)	HM (56)	HM (54)	WCB (40)
Personal service	IN (42)	HM (78)	SOW (39)	HM (85)	CB (78)
Sales	WM (63)	HM (100)	WM (51)	HM (80)	CB (71)
Operative and assembly manuals	HM (60)	HM (100)	HM (85)	HM (100)	WM (100)
Routine unskilled manual	WM (50)	WM (72)	HM (43)	HM (52)	CB (65)

Notes: All establishments where any employees in occupational category. The most common method used where any employees in particular occupational groups. HM = higher management, WM = workplace management, CB = collective bargaining with more than one employer, OCB = collective bargaining at organizational level, WCB = workplace collective bargaining, IN = negotiation with individual employees, SOW = some other way. In cases where two arrangements rank first equal, both are shown.

Case Study: The Cost of Misclassifying Restaurant Managers under the Fair Labour Standards Act

Employee misclassification cost Waffle House more than $3,000,000. Restaurant managers working an average of 89 hours per week were classified as exempt executives. Factors that counted against the company were:

- Unit managers served as grill cooks on the busiest shift.
- The primary training objective was to become a proficient grill operator, with exposure to management duties and responsibilities coming second.
- Managers often substituted for other employees.
- Other employees regularly stood in for absent managers.

Under the Fair Labour Standards Act the managers were entitled to be paid overtime for all hours worked in excess of 40 per week.

Much of the HI is characterized by the absence of grading schemes, and a lack of well-defined differentials between jobs. This, coupled with the lack of job evaluation, is likely to exacerbate pay discrimination. Loosely defined and variable pay structures can be explained in terms of the interplay between labour and product markets, firms' own choices and shocks such as the NMW.

Managers may structure pay to maximize cost savings by limiting hours and ensuring that employees earn below the threshold for National Insurance Contributions (NICs). An overspend on wages can be compensated by reducing the hours of part-time workers on variable hours contracts and the numbers of casual workers on a daily or weekly basis.

The majority of the major hotel companies have pay progression scales for different departments or employee groups, almost all of which are subject to performance (IDS, 2001). Individual performance reviews are also common in fast food, noted below. Up until 2001 employers were able to increase pay for the lowest paid without any repercussions for those further up the scale. The 40p hike in the NMW in 2001 led to a narrowing of differentials within hotels' pay structures, necessitating increases for junior supervisory staff (IDS, 2002).

The 2001 increase also caused McDonald's to shift from paying adult rates at 16, and to reintroduce age-related pay, with different rates for restaurant crew below 18, aged 18-21 and 22 years and over. While national chains set national rates, a number also have differential location-based pay for the provinces, and London and the South-east, in addition to other tight labour markets such as out-of-town retail parks. In small independent firms largely informal pay determination provides considerable scope for discretion within a framework of either individual employer- employee bargaining or unilateral management determination, in spite of the NMW. In a low-paying region nearly one-third of small employers were making use of the development rate. As noted earlier, they justified lower pay for young workers who were less experienced, had lower skills and were less productive, but age in itself was not a determinant of pay.

Case Study: Pay Structures and the Minimum Wage

The new NMW wage structure did not match the practice of most firms. Firms' initial response was to 'pick and mix' or do the minimum required, which meant increasing some adult workers' pay while leaving others' pay at the same level. Even though young workers were already being paid more than the development rate, their pay was also increased at the same time adult workers' pay was adjusted to comply with the NMW. Notional adult minima might apply at age 18 or age 21, but managers exercised considerable discretion to give accelerated progression, so there was no strict wage-for-age policy. There was informality and flexibility about how managers determined individuals' pay as they saw fit. Many could not adequately explain the basis of their pay structures and how employees progressed to higher pay. Most young workers aged 18-21 and many exempt 16- and 17-year-olds were paid more than the development rate.

Differentials were generally maintained because there was still a sizeable gap of £2.00 per hour or more between most workers and the higher paid. In one case the hourly differential between three supervisors had reduced from 50p to 25p. The manager was prepared to restore the differential if asked to do so because it would not be costly.

The Components of Remuneration

Although relatively few countries provide comparable earnings data, as a general rule hotel and restaurant workers across the world earn less than workers in socially comparable positions, and the differential tends to be higher in developing countries and for occupations requiring more skills and responsibilities. Working conditions in the EU (1996) include potentially problematic areas such as irregular working hours, frequent Sunday work, wages without a fixed element in 25 per cent of cases and widespread absence of overtime premiums; wage levels are generally 20 per cent below the EU average. Similar problems are observed in North America. Even where overtime premiums exist, they may rarely be paid.

We should note major problems with comparative statistics. Tips are not always declared for tax and will not be shown, and differences in the skill and training content of occupations in sub-sectors, such as waiting staff, mean that comparisons may not be made on a like-for-like basis. Weekly earnings show a bigger gap than hourly earnings because men work more overtime.

Women's consistently low pay can be explained by three main sets of factors: occupational segregation by gender, methods of pay determination and the concentration of low pay in certain industries, which makes it especially trenchant in the HI. Broadbridge provides support for arguments, showing that nature of skill and trade union activities have been constructed against women. Rubery warns that trends towards performance-related pay (PRP) pose a potential threat to pay equality as discretion in pay determination increases and there is no clear relationship between earnings and job grade. She also suggests that devolving HRM to line managers who are less aware of gender issues will also impact negatively on pay equality.

The size of the pay difference varies across countries, and there are exceptions. Tourism in North Korea is a low-wage sector but is more advantageous to women in terms of earnings inequality and level of earnings. While women have lower pay expectations at career entry and career peak than men, organizational issues such as a 'glass ceiling' blocking entry into higher paying positions are indicative of discrimination. By placing more emphasis on relationships in the workplace than on status women rule out jobs which might bring higher rewards.

The position in Britain may be even more polarized. A survey of the major hotel companies (2000), which might be expected to be 'market leaders', did find that pay was well ahead of the NMW. Only a minority pay premium rates for night or weekend work, and only two-fifths pay overtime at premium rates. New Earnings Survey (NES) data for the hotel sub-sector consistently show adult full-time earnings at two-thirds of average earnings for the whole economy, with overtime pay, shift pay and bonus payments comprising a very small part of total earnings compared to the rest of the economy. The same is also true for the HI as a whole.

The lowest-paid HI workers (lowest decile) rarely receive overtime or incentives. Low pay is linked to a wide range of factors, many of which are specific to the establishment and its competitive strategy. The incidence of low pay is high in single establishments and low in small establishments that are part of a larger organization. Basic pay is 100 per cent of total earnings in two-thirds of small HI firms. In 2002 the median pay of waiting and bar staff, luggage porters, room and leisure centre attendants and commis chefs was between £4.41 and £4.50. By contrast head chefs and sous chefs enjoyed relatively good pay, with median rates in South-east England exceeding £11 per hour.

Table: Patterns of Pay for all Employees on Adult Rates (2002)

	Average gross annual pay (£)	**Average gross weekly pay (£)**	**Increase April 2001/2 (%)**	**Average hourly pay (excl. O/T) (£)**	**Average total weekly (hours)**	**Average weekly overtime (hours)**
Full-time						
AIS	24,603	465	4.6	11.73	39.6	1.8
HI	15,762	299	3.7	7.28	40.9	1.2

Part-time						
AIS	7,903	148	6.0	8.09	19.6	1.0
HI	5,080	93	13.3	6.11	17.9	0.6

Table. Patterns of Pay for Male Employees on Adult Rates (2002)

	Average gross annual pay (£)	Average gross weekly pay (£)	Increase April 2001/2 (%)	Average hourly pay (excl. O/T) (£)	Average total weekly (hours)	Average weekly overtime (hours)
Full-time						
AIS	27,437	514	4.8	12.59	40.9	2.4
HI	18,051	331	2.2	7.87	41.9	1.3
Part-time						
AIS	9,485	165	7.7	10.08	19.2	1.5
HI	-*	100	17.1	7.56	17.8	0.5

Source: NES (2002); ONS (2002).

Table. Patterns of Pay for Female Employees on Adult Rates (2002)

	Average gross annual pay (£)	Average gross weekly pay (£)	Increase April 2001/2 (%)	Average hourly pay (excl. O/T) (£)	Average total weekly (hours)	Average weekly overtime (hours)
Full-time						
AIS	19,811	383	4.5	10.22	37.5	0.7
HI	12,984	257	4.7	6.48	39.6	1.0
Part-time						
AIS	7,593	144	5.8	7.72	19.7	1.0
HI	4,822	89	10.5	5.57	17.9	0.7

Table. Full-time Annual Male Earnings in Context and by Size of Workplace (%)

	AIS	PSS	HI	<25	25-49	50-99	100+
<£9,000	7	11	47*	34	42	56	47
£9,000 to <£12,000	15	18	23	26	31	17	23
£12,000 to <£16,000	24	24	12*	9	16	12	13
£16,000 to <£22,000	28	19	9*	12	5	8	9
£22,000 to <£29,000	15	12	5*	12	4	4	4
> £29,000	12	16	4*	7	3	3	5

Notes: Aggregate percentage of all weighted cases. *Significantly different at the 5% level from AIS and PSS.

Table: Full-time Annual Female Earnings in Context and by Size of Workplace (%)

	AIS	PSS	HI	<25	25-49	50-99	100+
<£9,000	18	24	57*	57	58	62	50
£9,000 to <£12,000	25	25	19	14	18	19	24

£12,000 to <£16,000	23	21	13**	13	12	12	14
£16,000 to <£22,000	20	16	8**	14	6	5	7
£22,000 to <£29,000	10	8	2*	3	2	1	2
> £29,000	4	5	1*	1	2	0	2

*Notes: Aggregate percentage of all weighted cases. *Significantly different at the 5% level from AIS and PSS. **Significantly different at the 5% level from AIS.*

Table: Full-time Annual Male Earnings by Sub-sector (%)

	Hotels	Campsites	Restaurants	Bars	Canteens
<£9,000	48	69	50	37	34
£9,000 to <£12,000	20	10	28	32	26
£12,000 to <£16,000	14	6	7	17	4
£16,000 to <£22,000	9	7	10	10	3
£22,000 to <£29,000	6	1	1	4	15
> £29,000	4	1	4	1	18

Table: Full-time Annual Female Earnings by Sub-sector (%)

	Hotels	Campsites	Restaurants	Bars	Canteens
<£9,000	54	76	54	51	64
£9,000 to <£12,000	21	7	20	27	12
£12,000 to <£16,000	14	6	10	17	10
£16,000 to <£22,000	8	11	12	0	10
£22,000 to <£29,000	1	0	2	2	4
> £29,000	1	0	2	2	2

Notes: *Aggregate percentage of all weighted cases.*

Table: Employees Earning less than £3.50 per hour in Context, by Size of Workplace and Sub-sector (%)

	AIS	PSS	HI	<25	25-49	50-99	100+
None	67	57	40*	47	19	34	40
50%+	8	12	33*	34	49	15	8
	Hotels	*Campsites*	*Restaurants*	*Bars*	*Canteens*		
None	41	4	35	35	80		
50%+	18	0	31	48	12		

Notes: *All weighted cases. *Significantly different at the 5% level from AIS and PSS.*

WERS data indicate a similar disparity across all sub-sectors. Differences in the actual pay levels of full-time employees differ between the AIS, the PSS and the HI, between men and women. The main reason (from a multi-response question) for significant differences in pay levels is hours worked in over two-thirds of HI workplaces. Job grade/classification (59 per cent) and skills/core competences (47 per cent) are of second- and third-order importance.

In AIS and the PSS the two most important factors are job grade/classification and hours worked, with overtime and skills/core competences being the second and third most important factors respectively. Earnings patterns by size of workplace and sub-sector are not clear-cut. The reasons given for these differences are also similarly diverse. In terms of low pay HI workplaces are significantly more likely to have workers earning less than £3.50 per hour and to have half or more workers that are low-paid.

Tips

Tipping is culturally specific and more prevalent in countries characterized by strong needs for achievement and power, where intolerance of uncertainty, anxiety and neuroticism are greater, and where citizens place greater value on status and prestige. In Egypt, the US and Argentina, where people are extroverted and status-seeking, it is customary to tip many service workers. Very few service workers receive tips in Japan, Iceland and Scandinavia, where there is greater emphasis on social than on economic relations.

While one view of tipping is that it is the most efficient way of monitoring and rewarding the efforts of service workers, and may motivate workers to perform well, workers set a price for service that is personalized and difficult for managers to monitor. The relationship between tipping and service quality is weak, even though managers and employees perceive such a relationship.

A range of behavioural variables are thought to affect tips, including good appearance, being on first name terms, particular dress codes and touching and smiling. Uncertainty of pay may be detrimental to job satisfaction and commitment, and even lead to dysfunctional behaviour, e.g. cheating and pilfering. For customers tipping functions in part as a status display, to gain social approval or to compensate poorly paid workers.

The extent to which tips increase gross pay or total reward is highly variable, and appears to be higher where the employee has more control, i.e. takes tips individually. Purcell et al. (1999) found that workers in pubs and bars could enhance their hourly pay by up to £2.00 per hour in larger establishments and by up to £1.00 per hour in smaller establishments. Restaurant workers could only achieve up to £1.00 per hour, but only for evening work in busy city centre establishments, and also received very few fringe benefits. In hotels where an employee sharing system or employer distribution of tips is the norm, tips amount to less, but other terms and conditions are generally better.

Case Study: Pay, Income Tax and National Insurance Contributions

Low pay serves the immediate mutual interests of employer and employee as an avoidance strategy for employment taxes, but this may have other longer-term and more damaging consequences. Avoidance maximizes employees' net pay and minimizes employers' labour costs, but employees are not eligible for a range of benefits, including pensions.

In Britain the threshold at which NICs became payable increased to the same level as the income tax threshold in 2000, a year after the NMW was introduced. This combined threshold was £84 per week when the NMW stood at £3.60 per hour. Thus a worker paid the NMW would only become liable for both deductions after working 23 hours, with the employer being subject to NICs only. Two contrasting effects have been observed.

In 1999 when the NMW and the NIC threshold was still below the income tax threshold, some low-paying employers realigned the hours of their part timers to keep their pay below the NIC threshold. One small firm had to increase the number of employees to cover the same workload over the same hours at mutual cost benefit. This was not 'real' job creation. In 2000 the changes increased the wage: hour ratio of 'exempt' employees thus providing employers with an incentive to increase their part-time workforce on longer hours.

Case Study: Tips in Practice across the World

US

Tipping is almost universal. Waiting staff depend on tips for a living wage, where a set percentage of the bill is automatically expected. Tips can exceed basic pay, and credit card tips often get pooled among staff. Hotel bellmen could double the amount of tips by providing a full service, rather than a limited service.

Spain

Tipping is very common but amounts to no more than a few coins, and credit card tips are almost unheard of.

UK

Staff keep cash tips, either individually or on a pooled basis, and do not pay tax on them, unless they are declared. Staff working in pubs, bars and restaurants are more likely to benefit from tips than hotel staff. Staff are not entitled to receive tips or a service charge that are added to a credit card in addition to the NMW, although employers can use these payments to top up pay to the level of the NMW. This situation was finally confirmed by a ruling of the European Court of Human Rights in 2002. Where tips are paid into a tronc, the tronc master shares them among employees who are taxed on them.

Italy

Restaurants may add 10-15 per cent to meals but customers are normally expected to add 10 per cent. Credit card tips are passed on to waiting staff.

New Zealand

Tipping is not widespread in restaurants. Managers consider that tips are a private transaction between server and customer and are not taken into account when setting pay.

Australia

Tipping usually applies only in high-class restaurants. Credit card tips are usually divided among staff.

Case Study: The Tronc and Hierarchical Pay in Designer Restaurants

Each employee is awarded a number of points according to their position. Departments are allocated a set percentage of the tronc, which is divided by the total number of points based on total employees per shift. Chefs view the tronc as a bonus to their salary, whereas it is a supplement to low basic wages for waiting staff.

In City Centre Restaurants, which operates chains such as Caffe Uno and Garfunkels, it is claimed that waiting staff in London make so much in tips they could work without being paid a basic wage. Basic rates, set low, are topped up to the NMW with centrally collected tips. Pizza Express introduced a similar system when the NMW was introduced, but soon abandoned it amid adverse publicity. The company now encourages individual staff to keep their own tips, believing it is morally wrong to use tips or a service charge to subsidize wages.

Incentive- and Performance-related Pay

On a global basis variable pay linked to performance is not yet common, but is emerging in countries such as the US, the UK and Australia, particularly among large hotel groups. Incentive pay falls broadly into two categories: PRP and payment by results (PBR). The former normally measures performance against previously determined criteria expressed as targets or objectives and has particular resonance with both a customer service-focused ethos and an HR philosophy designed to generate motivated and committed employees. A payment system that rewards employees for attaining quality goals is more likely to result in improved SQ.

By comparison PBR schemes, which measure fixed outputs, may be more appropriate to the factory production line. However, it is also important not to lose sight of fact that employee control also underpins both PRP and PBR, with PRP reflecting a tightening of the way in which individual performance is regulated. Hence increased performance may be required for the same or less pay where schemes replace non-performance based systems or provide for a derisory performance-related element.

Another set of circumstances driving incentive pay centres upon improving recruitment and retention, and reducing high turnover. Dermody (2002) reports how US restaurants use incentive programmes to retain employees. Schemes are most often tied to business volume and generally offer servers incentives to sell more items. Independent restaurants use creative incentive practices, such as unique gifts and team incentives more frequently than chain restaurants, which apply daily contests with a cash increase tied to individual performance. Few front office or back-of-house staff benefit from such schemes.

Other schemes as part of performance management may be more selective, targeting managers, e.g. Wolverhampton and Dudley, which runs family-friendly pubs, or key workers, e.g. TGI Fridays, Pret a Manger, KFC, Select Service Partner and Welcome Break, which have all succeeded in reducing turnover markedly. Competency-based pay linked to the completion of training modules is also widely used. McDonald's employees can gain an extra 15p increase per hour every four months if they achieve 93.5 per cent performance. In practice only a small minority benefit because performance review sheets are not completed on time or even at all.

Profit-related and sales-related schemes are the most common basis for incentive pay among major hotel companies, 70 per cent of which operate some form of bonus scheme. The criterion of good customer service is less common, with a few instances of chefs being rewarded according to gross profit on food or by minimizing food costs. Profit sharing and share ownership may be segregated by gender as more benefits accrue to full-time workers who are more likely to be male. The criteria for PRP for Flightpath Telephone Sales staff were based on hard skills (e.g. individual sales targets) and soft skills (e.g. handling calls). Supervisors could listen to and tape employees' performance, hence employees' ability to 'deep act' directly shaped their pay.

From WERS variable pay schemes, including dividend-based schemes, are slightly more common in the HI and the PSS (just over 60 per cent) than in AIS (53 per cent). Above average proportions of large workplaces and bars have such schemes. In all groupings profit-related payments or bonuses are the most common type of variable pay. While just over half of HI workplaces have profit-related payments or bonuses and deferred profit-sharing schemes, the proportion rises to over three-quarters in large workplaces and bars. Conversely most restaurant workers do not benefit from these schemes. Employee share ownership schemes are also more common in the HI than in AIS and the PSS. Individual or group performance-related schemes are less likely to be found in the HI than in AIS and the PSS.

PRP on its own is not widespread, as it applies in only one in nine HI workplaces, affecting managers and administrative staff in three-quarters of these workplaces. The pattern of usage among other occupational groups is different from in AIS and the PSS. In the HI professional staff and manual workers (craft, skilled and unskilled) are more likely to benefit from such schemes than their equivalents in AIS and the PSS. Conversely clerical and secretarial and sales staffs in AIS and the PSS are more likely to have PRP than their counterparts in the HI. Some of these variations are likely to arise because of the different occupational characteristics of each group. The application of PRP to occupational groups also varies by size of workplace and sub-sector because of their different occupational make-up.

Where PRP applies to non-managerial employees in the HI (N= 15) a greater proportion of them are included in the scheme than in AIS and the PSS. Where PRP has been paid to non-managerial employees in the last 12 months, all have been included in the scheme in just over half of these HI workplaces. Individual performance/output is significantly less likely to be used as the basis for PRP in the HI, where schemes are most likely to be group- or team-based. Individual performance/output is usually measured or assessed by a supervisor, whereas other measures of output are more likely to be used in AIS and the PSS.

Case Study: Contemporary Incentive, Performance and Competency-based Pay in Britain

The Marriott Hanbury Hall Hotel has profit share for managers and team leaders. Waiting staff can earn extra pay for selling additional coffees and desserts. A variety of non-cash recognition awards are available to reward very good performance. Accor Hotels provides in-house skill-based programmes that link pay increases to the achievement of new skills.

McDonald's moved to a single performance review for merit-based pay in 2002. Staff are assessed between July and September, with the corresponding increase awarded at the end of September. Individual performance pay ranged from 0 per cent (needs improvement) to 6 per cent (excellent). Most received 3 per cent (satisfactory), and others 4.5 per cent (good).

Select Service Partner (UK Rail Division) introduced a new pay structure in 2002 based on completion of relevant training modules. Each stage takes around three months, and the company has applied for recognition under the NVQ scheme. Pub retailers commonly link pay progression to training. The BII estimates one in four pub workers is studying for an NVQ/SVQ. Pizza Express pays a discretionary bonus to back-of-house staff who are not in a position to earn tips, linked to the profitability of the restaurant.

Pret a Manger pays a weekly bonus worth 75p per hour on top of basic rates for every hour worked. Mystery shoppers visit all shops and award points for efficiency, quality and speed of service. The shop has to score 90 per cent or over to qualify. A card for outstanding service worth £50 in cash can also be awarded.

A contract catering company paid £100 to a supervisor whose idea of filling confectionery machines with home-made or branded cookies increased gross profit from 18 per cent to 40 per cent. Staff could also earn £100 for leads to new business, plus a further £250 if the contract was successful. One-quarter of new business came from such suggestions.

Other Terms and Conditions of Employment

Although details of global practices are rarely reported, workers within the EU are entitled to four weeks' paid holiday, while pensions are highly variable among member states. In Spain employees retiring at 65 usually receive three months' salary (subject to a minimum of 15 years' service). Provincial and company agreements also provide incentives to retire early for longer-serving employees, e.g. an extra eight months' pay at 60.

Evidence suggests that some hospitality businesses, mainly small firms, had to increase workers' basic holiday entitlement and introduce holiday pay to meet the requirements of the WTR. Some of the larger hotel companies now give between 21 and 30 days per annum related to service. Meals, drinks and uniforms, which may be free or subject to a small charge, and discounts are among the most commonly provided fringe benefits.

Table: Non-pay Terms and Conditions in Context and by Size of Workplace (%)

	AIS	PSS	HI	<25	25-49	50-99	100+
Employer pension scheme	65	55	36*	43	20	30	34
Company car/ allowance	15	15	0*	0	0	1	5
Private health insurance	15	20	9***	3	19	17	18
4 weeks+ paid leave (excl. public holidays)	83	78	67**	71	53	69	72
Sick pay in excess of statutory requirements	64	61	43*	43	36	51	48
None of these	11	14	30*	29	43	18	26

Notes: *All weighted cases. *Significantly different at the 5% level from AIS and the PSS. **Significantly different at the 5% level from AIS. ***Significantly different at the 5% level from PSS.*

Table: Non-pay Terms and Conditions by Sub-sector (%)

	Hotels	Campsites	Restaurants	Bars	Canteens
Employer pension scheme	35	78	37	27	81
Company car/ allowance	2	0	0	0	0

Private health insurance	19	0	10	0	19
4 weeks+ paid leave (excl. public holidays)	84	78	70	50	93
Sick pay in excess of statutory requirements	49	78	40	32	89
None of these	12	22	27	48	7

***Note:** All weighted cases*

These indicate just how badly HI employers fare compared to counterparts in AIS and the PSS, especially in bars.

Performance Appraisal

Performance appraisal, one facet of performance management, has a number of different purposes beyond providing the basis for reviewing pay.

Case Study: Performance Appraisal in US Hotels

Performance appraisal is conducted annually for all staff. Most managers use more than one type of appraisal, and appraisals have more than one purpose. Half the managers use a management-by-objectives approach. However not all managers use follow-up sessions to feedback the results. The most frequent application of performance appraisals is for compensation decisions, followed by assessing whether objectives have been met, establishing training needs and determining promotions. A majority considered that appraisals were important to their business.

Annual or six-monthly appraisal in Australia and Singapore forms part of employee development, with management by objectives being almost universal. While systems distinguish between managerial and operative staff in both countries, appraisal is more commonly used to determine pay in Singapore than in Australia where award rates of payment, rather than individual contracts, govern pay rates. Managers have more scope to vary pay in Singapore because of workplace collective agreements.

Within Britain appraisals are regarded as an essential business tool by HR managers to improve company and individual performance. Performance appraisal goals focusing on quality goals, behaviour critical to achieving those goals and use of customer-driven data are more compatible with improving SQ. The identification of training and development needs and evaluating individual performance are the main reasons performance appraisals are used in the private sector in Britain, with most large organizations appraising all employees.

From WERS the four main purposes of appraisal in the HI, which also apply in AIS and the PSS, are to give feedback on an employee's performance, to set/evaluate training and development needs, to give employees a chance to discuss future career moves, and to review and set objectives. Performance appraisal is more likely to be used to determine a pay increase in the HI (half the sub-sample) than in AIS and the PSS. However, performance appraisal is not directly linked to reviews or changes in individual employees' pay in almost all of those cases, the exceptions being found only in large workplaces.

WERS shows that in Britain managers and administrative staffs in the HI are significantly more likely to be appraised formally than their counterparts in AIS and the PSS. Conversely professional, technical and scientific, and clerical and secretarial staff are significantly less likely to be have formal appraisals. A minority of workplaces in AIS and the PSS (one-quarter) and 18 per cent of HI workplaces do not formally appraise any of the specified occupational groups. Further details about appraisals from WERS are given for non-managerial employees only.

Formal performance appraisal schemes covering all or almost all staff have been observed in a large hotels and designer restaurants. WERS shows that performance appraisal of non-managerial employees is less likely to occur in the HI (56 per cent of all cases), and where it applies coverage is slightly less comprehensive. Most private sector schemes operate a formalized process with an annual interview between manager and subordinate, typically of between one and two hours' duration. Within hospitality and leisure Sodexho and David Lloyd Leisure carry out regular reviews outside the appraisal process, in the latter case informally as a precursor that could lead to formal disciplinary action.

WERS shows that where appraisal is used, all employees are included in the scheme in half of HI workplaces compared to 65 per cent in AIS and 73 per cent in PSS. The HI is significantly less likely to operate annual appraisals and significantly more likely to have appraisals that do not conform to a fixed pattern. In all groupings appraisal is most likely to be conducted by the employee's immediate superior, with the wider involvement of another manager occurring in a large minority of cases, especially in restaurants.

Employees are often suspicious of appraisals which, when conducted badly, can side-step crucial issues and lead to one party unleashing pent-up frustrations, leading ultimately to a deterioration in the employment relationship. Dickens (1998) argues that impression management rather than good performance may count for more in obtaining a good rating. Appraisers are usually men who may use proxy measures for measuring commitment, such as visible hours at work and working beyond contract which penalize women.

10

Tracking Transaction at Hotels

TRACKING TRANSACTION

An advanced computer-based electronic security management system is instrumental in making the Mirage Resort Hotel a progressive facility. Security has assumed an increasingly important role in the hotel business. The larger the facility and the more diverse the features, services, and amenities, the more demanding the need for comprehensive security management. Nowhere is this more evident than at a 100-acre entertainment complex like the Mirage Resort Hotel in Las Vegas, where security concerns are heightened by the cash-intensive casino operation.

The creation of a fully integrated security environment at the Mirage represents an exciting new dimension in security management. Opened in 1989, the desert resort is among the most progressive facilities of its type. The Mirage has three 30-story towers and more than 3,000 rooms, including suites, villas, and bungalows with private pools. Two ballrooms, at 20,000- and 40,000-square feet, are available for special events, and meeting rooms can handle groups up to 5,000 people. The complex includes waterfalls, an erupting volcano, a tropical plant atrium, and an artificial coral reef aquarium with sharks and tropical fish. Also available for the enjoyment of guests and visitors are natural animal habitats: one for a pair of rare Royal White tigers, the other for six Atlantic Bottlenose dolphins.

An array of entertainment, recreational, and shopping opportunities are featured, including a 1,500-seat theater and around-the-clock casino operations. Guests can find restaurants, health and fitness centres, interconnected lagoon-shaped swimming pools, boutiques, and lounges. Special events such as prize fights and boat and auto shows compound the importance of security.

Security control in a gaming resort as large and complex as the Mirage is a demanding and never-ending challenge. Sophisticated security controls are in force in the casino, where millions of dollars are transacted every hour in games, including slot machines, video poker, keno, craps, blackjack, baccarat, and poker. Strict compliance with gaming laws and established casino procedures is controlled by close supervision, surveillance, and carefully monitored audits.

An advanced computer-based electronic security management system, the Polaroid ID-2000 Plus, plays a central role in supporting the Mirage's integrated security environment. The system has proven to be a formidable management tool. Designed for expansion, the modular system is a core component in the recording and payroll programme.

The system combines advanced data base, computer, and electronic imaging technologies. It provides, for example, a streamlined ID card and badge production capability and a responsive, economical way to manage employee-related security information.

The system also serves as an auditing aid to track activities, such as the number of meals served to employees in the cafeteria each day. Swipe readers at cash registers in the cafeteria make the process fast and efficient.

Specific information about the resort's 7,000 employees is input, stored, and retrieved by the digital electronic security management system. It captures image data, including colour portraits and signatures; generates photo ID cards and management reports; and communicates with other data bases. Report-generating capabilities simplify the tracking of ID cards that have been issued for active and former employees. The system also facilitates the monitoring of staff levels.

The electronic production and data base system is connected to a file server in the computer centre. Several sites are now on-line by means of a local area network (LAN) using standard Ethernet connections and Novell network software. Additional terminals or systems can be added for expansion. One of the locations integrated by the LAN is the ID card and badge production centre in the human resources department. New employees are processed and badged at this location; other areas on the network use the system to validate employee security information.

Verification terminals are installed in the security and finance departments, casino surveillance, and the casino cash cage. Authorized individuals can validate, on-screen, employee photos, signatures, and related data. Although verification information is easily obtained by entering an employee number, access to the complete data base is limited to supervisory personnel. Information available for access includes the employee's full name, signature sample, colour portrait, ID number, job title, work location, and date of hire or termination. The individual's affiliation as a Mirage employee or corporate employee is shown.

Powering the system is a high-speed 386 CPU using special workstation software, which incorporates password authorization and an internal audit trail to prevent system abuse. Using an optional 180 megabyte magnetic disk, the Mirage system can store approximately 14,000 full-colour portraits or 11,500 portraits and signatures. Optional storage modules, including larger capacity magnetic disk drives and optical disk drives, are available. Active files, including signatures, colour portraits, and related textual information, are safely stored in digital format on the hard disk. Safety backups of the complete system are made on magnetic tape by the computer centre at least three times a week. If an employee is terminated or quits, the photo and signature files are deleted to save storage space. Text files, however, are stored indefinitely.

Information systems helped define the requirements and objectives of the departments involved. The system has improved productivity on several operating levels. Working closely with Polaroid engineers, information systems developed a maintenance strategy with flexible service levels and contingency provisions for priority service in designated areas. If emergency maintenance service is required, downtime in critical operations will be minimized.

Producing more than 6,000 ID CARDS a year could be an expensive, time-consuming operation. For the Mirage's human resources department, however, it is merely routine.

Human resources is responsible for processing new employees, issuing new ID cards and badges, replacing damaged or lost badges, and responding to the continuing need for special events badges. To handle the challenges of ID card production the company relies on the production speed and efficiency of the computer-based security management system.

"Compared to the marathon effort involved in producing new ID cards when the Mirage first opened," reflects Monalee Stockner, human resources supervisor, "normal day-to-day activities are calm." ID cards were produced for more than 7,000 employees by the human resources team, with assistance from several temporary employees and a few of the management system devices on loan from Polaroid.

Employee processing and imaging activities were completed during a five-day whirlwind operation involving 10- to 12-hour shifts. Cards were assembled at night. According to Stockner, "Without the speed and automated features of the computerized production system, the job could not have been done as quickly, economically, or efficiently."

The electronic production workstation includes an operator console consisting of a colour video camera, electronic flash lighting, portrait and text monitors, keyboard, and a signature capture device. A colour film recorder, film cutter, laminator, and print development timers are included in the output unit. Information acquisition for an ID card, including text entries and video imaging of the subject's portrait and signature, takes less than five minutes per person. The badge is given to the employee the same day. Temporary special event IDs are produced for employees assigned to such activities as large parties, banquets, conventions, and prize fights. Since the Mirage was opened, more than 50,000 employee ID cards have been produced.

An operator can enter employee information and capture, digitally store, and retrieve high-fidelity colour portraits and signatures or access data from existing computer data bases. A freeze-frame feature allows the operator to preview and freeze the subject's video portrait before the card is made.

A built-in signature capture camera stores signatures from a signed signature card. At the touch of a button the system electronically merges the digitized video portrait, signature, text, and multicolour Mirage logo contained in the software package. Information entered is contained on a new-hire document prepared by the employee's department. It includes pertinent information about the employee, his or her job title, and where he or she works.

ID cards can be produced in many of visual formats. More than a dozen variations are used by the Mirage to distinguish between different personnel classifications and affiliations. These include Mirage employees, corporate staff, and contractors. Special formats have also been developed for restricted areas or for temporary use at special events.

Although the electronic security management system can automatically assign sequential employee numbers, human resources prefers to control this function. In this way, blocks of numbers can be reserved for special applications in the system. When the employee number is entered, a bar code representing the number is automatically generated and printed on an adhesive-back label by a printer. Inexpensive, hard-copy, black-and-white thermal reference images can also be produced in seconds by a printer at the production station.

With a single keystroke, electronically assembled images for two separate employee badges are exposed on a sheet of instant colour print film. Development takes about a minute. Prints are then die-cut and inserted into a special laminate sandwich with a printed insert containing card use guidelines and the bar code label. The envelope is then permanently sealed. The finished card is attractive, durable, and virtually tamperproof. After lamination the bar code is verified with a test device, which displays the employee number.

Remotely Located Verification

Terminals integrated through the LAN facilitate employee recognition, signature validation, and confirmation of employment status. In addition to the information verification capabilities of the production workstation, data verification terminals on the network provide valuable information for security and management-related functions. Security staff. Responsible for the safety of patrons and protection of the Mirage's physical assets, the security staff also plays an active role in maintaining guest relations and providing emergency services.

The 275-person security staff, larger than the police departments of many small cities, operates around the clock. Security's responsibilities include controlling access in restricted areas, knowing the location of employees in emergencies, and monitoring property removal.

"The ability to access an employee's security records in seconds, to determine where they can be located, saves valuable time in an emergency," says Jennifer Keeney, security coordinator. "We can locate an employee quickly, for example, should there be an emergency at home, without having to make lots of phone calls and be faced with unnecessary delays. We can see what the person looks like and even get fast thermal prints to help our staff recognize the person. In emergencies, visual recognition is extremely important, especially with a work force involving thousands of people."

Photo ID badges need not be worn in most areas. Employees can carry the ID card in a wallet or purse. In instances where individuals are not recognized by security personnel at employee entrances or in restricted areas, they will be asked to show their ID card. ID information for new hires or terminated employees is available at all verification terminals on a same-day basis.

In yet another important function, the ability to compare signatures with samples stored in the security management system's digital memory has streamlined the Mirage's property removal procedures. Because signatures of people authorized to approve property passes can be easily validated, it is now easier to control the removal of property. Thermal prints of authorized signatures for property removal forms are kept on file and current at various security stations.

Casino surveillance. Rapid information verification is critical for the casino surveillance group. Operating around the clock, 365 days a year, a team of trained observers keeps a watchful eye on cash transactions, operational procedures, and dealer interactions with patrons.

Patricia Cipolla, director of surveillance, is emphatic about the importance of security control. "Our job," she states, "is to protect the Mirage's assets and its patrons. We watch the money and the way the games are run. Any deviation in established procedures signals that something may be wrong."

Ceiling-mounted video cameras can record the activities at any game in the casino. Videotapes of randomly selected games or those being monitored are available for review on video monitors located in the surveillance area.

Should a transaction involving markers, redemption slips, bills, and credits, or a dealer's performance deviate from established guidelines, information about the dealer can be accessed instantly. Since the videotape can be seen in normal or close-up modes, surveillance specialists start the process by zooming in on the dealer's name badge. By entering the name at the verification terminal, employee information is instantly displayed, including a colour portrait and signature sample.

If irregularities are observed, other than what appears to be an honest mistake, the surveillance team may continue monitoring the dealer. A random check of a particular table could, for example, reveal a disparity between the dealer's photo and the name shown on the badge. This disparity would be checked out immediately with a casino supervisor.

In other instances, the dealer's name may not appear on the casino schedule for the shift. The disparity could be attributed to a last-minute schedule change, which can be easily verified by calling the floor supervisor. Occasionally, casino accounting is advised that an audit of documents pertaining to a particular game may be warranted.

"Instant access to employee information, especially ID pictures, makes our job a lot easier," says Cipolla. "It often took hours or days to scour through computer printouts to pinpoint the person involved in a specific transaction. The task can now be done in minutes. The search process, which also involved phone calls to casino supervisors, wasted valuable time, was cumbersome, and expensive." Casino accounting. Casino accounting operates two shifts a day and is responsible for important audit functions for the Mirage's gaming activities. The department is responsible for maintaining the casino's operational integrity and for strict compliance with established procedures.

Timely information about gaming activities and people who authorize transactions is necessary for effective management. "The most important piece of information available," comments Robert Galvin, casino accounting manager, "is an employee's ID number. For us, it provides the means to access a key piece of data, employee signature samples."

The accounting department's data verification terminal provides instant access to information needed for transaction audits. Matching photos to names or comparing signature samples with those appearing on documents is extremely helpful.

Cash cage. Because of the large amounts of money involved, the casino cash cage may require complete ID verification, including signatures and photos of unfamiliar people. In the past, matching signatures on cash disbursement forms or receipts to signature cards took hours or even days to accomplish. It now takes minutes. Performing rapid searches of information with specific parameters, such as name, employee number, title, department, and job description, has resulted in significant productivity improvement.

"Immediate access to essential information," says Galvin, "has resulted in better control, increased audit speed, and reduced labour hours. Since we've been linked to the security management system, productivity has improved dramatically." The verification terminal, also used by internal auditing and gaming control board personnel, allows greater audit frequency and improved monitoring of money flow.

An innovative time and attendance system, to be fully implemented by early 1993, is being phased into the Mirage's operations on a controlled schedule. The ambitious undertaking is expected to produce enormous cost savings and efficiency improvements while providing significant benefits for both employees and management. As an integral part of a comprehensive management control system, badges provide the media for time clock entries.

According to Ernie Pearce, director of information systems, "The new time and attendance system, now in use by several departments, is one of the most progressive programmes to be introduced at the Mirage. The sophisticated, computerized time-keeping and payroll system improves the interaction between supervisors and the work force. It also eliminates many of the payroll-related transaction errors that inconvenienced employees and wasted valuable company time.

"The ability to use the benefits of the security management system's large data base, along with the photo ID badge as a clock entry system," continues Pearce, "provides important functional and economic advantages."

Using sophisticated computer-based time clocks with bar code readers, the new system integrates employee work-time and payroll information with the security management data base. In this way, a long-standing information gap has been bridged. The new, high-tech computer-based clocks—to be located at every work location—will allow employees to use their ID cards to log in and out in a virtually error-free system.

The "smart" clocks are programmed with all the necessary operating parameters. These include authorized clock locations for different departments, employees' normal start and stop times, and overtime pay scales, including holidays, IRS regulations, and applicable union rules.

The new system will improve efficiency and minimize transaction discrepancies, such as illegible manual entries. It will also eliminate time-keeping problems for people working at remote locations or whose work locations vary.

In the past, bar codes have been used only to track the number of meals served in the cafeteria. With the new time-keeping system, however, they will play a more significant role in overall efficiency.

An opaque strip covering the bar code prevents tampering and reduces the likelihood that copies could be used to fool the clocks. Appearing opaque to the eye and to copy machines, the protected bar code is scanned without difficulty by bar code readers. Applied to the inside of the laminate envelope, the strip is considered tamperproof. The Mirage's electronic security management system, which has been in operation for more than two years, has provided cost-effective solutions for a variety of problems. Software-driven and modular, important upgrades can be achieved simply by replacing a disk or a module.

The combined data base, management, and electronic imaging system is easy to use, requires minimal training, and is inexpensive to operate. During its first 18 months of operation the system was on-line 24 hours a day, seven days a week, with virtually trouble-free performance. An international company was preparing to evacuate 15 expatriate employees and dependents from a country that had suffered an earthquake. When it came time to meet at the departure point, 25 people showed up. Those arranging for the evacuation had not known that two technical teams were in the country supporting clients at the time. The additional evacuees, who had heard of the evacuation informally from individuals at the local office, disrupted the company's plan.

There were not enough vehicles to get everyone to the airport in one trip, and there were not enough seats on the airplane that had been reserved. The other employees had made their way to the departure point hoping to get a seat because the local office employee did not tell them of the limited transportation or inform them that it would be safer to wait in the hotel until other transportation could be arranged.

The company evacuated the 15 people originally expected at that time, and the additional 10 employees were flown out two days later. This meant that an evacuation that should have been completed in approximately 12 hours— from when the employees and dependents arrived at the rendezvous point until they actually departed—ended up lasting 60 hours. Fortunately, everyone was able to get out safely, but the delay could have been disastrous.

As companies seek new business in far-flung markets, their employees increasingly need to travel and work around the globe. Companies must be prepared to help these employees through any contingencies, including earthquakes, civil unrest, and other crises.

While some risks are greater in developing countries, emergency situations requiring evacuation can arise anywhere. For instance, Singapore, a relatively safe and natural-disaster-free city, suffered from severe smog in 1999 as the result of forest fires that were raging in nearby Indonesia. The conditions made the city unbearable and forced many foreign personnel to evacuate. Other examples of such incidents include an earthquake in Taiwan, civil unrest in Indonesia, a coup in Fiji, and the invasion of Kuwait—all of which necessitated the evacuation of international personnel.

Most companies with international operations have detailed plans in place for evacuating their expatriate personnel should the local security situation deteriorate or in case of a natural disaster. But as the case highlighted at the beginning of this article illustrates, these plans often fail to address the evacuation of another category of employees; Those who are visiting on a business trip when a disaster strikes.

The evacuation of international travelers often falls between the travel advisory service, which provides employees with information on areas where it might be dangerous to travel, and evacuation planning efforts, which focus on expatriate personnel based in the country. Many companies do not even know how many employees are visiting a particular international location. In the event of an emergency, they might spend hours, if not days, trying to determine which employees are there.

This problem especially affects companies that are organized along functional lines rather than geographically. It is not uncommon for an in-country office to report to a certain department, such as marketing. Personnel from other departments might travel in and out of the country without ever contacting the local office.

To avoid confusion, companies must coordinate their travel security and international evacuation programmes. Corporate security should serve as a central point for activity and information related to evacuation planning, coordinating the role of other players in the travel process, such as internal departments, travel service providers, employees, host country offices, and hotels.

How travel information is collected, maintained, and distributed will vary among companies. Generally, however, security should not bother with routine tracking of employee travel plans. Instead, the security department can enlist the help of various internal departments to ensure that it is able to locate employees on travel in an emergency. For example, security should ask human resources or travel service providers to collect the data on employee travel. In an emergency, security will know that it can turn to this resource for the information.

Security may want to ask the company's public relations department to communicate the details of the travel and evacuation plan to staff as part of the internal communications programme.

Travel Service Provider

A company's travel service provider, whether a company employee or outside firm, can play an important role in gathering information about employees traveling abroad. Generally, these firms keep detailed records for billing purposes, and those records can help the security department to determine the location of employees when needed. The travel service company could also provide weekly or daily reports of which employees are traveling and to where.

In addition to regular reports, the travel service provider should be able to give the company access to its staffs travel records 24 hours a day in case of an emergency. Many companies have erroneously assumed that they could get the necessary staff location information from travel service providers in an emergency.

The provider can also be required to book only designated hotels, perhaps ones where corporate security has verified the safety and security of the facility. In addition, because travel itineraries often change while employees are on the road, if the travel service provider has an office in a host country, employees can contact it to change hotel and flight reservations rather than going directly to the hotel or airline. This means that the changes will immediately be keyed into the system, and the information can be distributed to the corporate security department or another internal point of contact, such as human resources. In addition, the provider can be asked to include emergency telephone numbers and procedures with each airline ticket issued to employees.

The security department should periodically audit the programme for tracking employee travel to make sure that the records are being kept and that the contact telephone numbers and other information are all up to date. It also might be useful to test the programme under simulated conditions.

At the same time, security needs to keep the travel agent advised of any high-risk areas so that he or she can caution current or future travelers or, in serious cases, refer them back to security. In companies where there is an approval system for travel, those responsible for approving travel requests must be brought into the system so that they don't approve travel to "no-go" areas.

Employees

In many cases, employees make their own travel changes by contacting the airline or hotel directly, or they use the hotel concierge or business centre. Employees should be required to advise a designated corporate contact or the travel service provider of these changes.

Some companies now require employees to submit weekly movement sheets listing travel destinations and contact details for the week to come. It is generally advisable to include these schedules with some other form of business report, such as the employees' weekly progress or sales reports, to increase the level of compliance.

One multinational telecommunications company, which has employees traveling to more than 20 countries every day of the year, implemented a Web-based itinerary tracking system to allow employees to update their travel schedules online. Employees can use any computer with Internet access to enter the password-protected site and update their information.

Host Country Offices

The company's offices abroad are also important players in the security process. Though it would be difficult for international offices to report all of the internal travel movements of visiting employees, they should at least be required to track which employees are visiting their countries and where they are staying. This task can be made easier by requiring the traveling employees to check in with the local office or to go there to connect to the computer network or access their corporate e-mail account.

If the local offices will be responsible for making in-country travel and accommodation arrangements for visiting employees, they should be required to use only designated hotels and they should be asked to provide contact information for hotels and transportation providers as well as other reservation details to headquarters. One company with several international offices encouraged travelers to check in with the local offices by setting up workstations specifically for travelers and providing technical support to help them connect to the corporate mail system. This approach worked well, especially in the countries where local communications were unreliable.

However, the company neglected to put in place a system for the local office to report to headquarters about the travelers in the country. When an earthquake struck, the main office did not know how many employees were in the vicinity of the earthquake or how to locate them. The information was available at the local office, but it was unreachable.

At a minimum, international offices should be required to monitor the internal travel of visitors if a situation shows signs of deteriorating, even if they do not track which employees are visiting their country during normal times. They should also be able to locate and provide assistance, including evacuation, for visiting employees.

Similarly, headquarters or travel vice providers should notify the host country office when employees plan to travel there, though in practice this depends on the company. For instance, if another division of the company runs the host country office, the traveler's division might not even have the contact details for the host country office. Also intra-office politics plays a role.

Host Country Hotels

The hotels that employees use while traveling play an important part in the security process. A strong business relationship between a company and the hotel can be key. The more nights per year that the company contracts for, the more willing a hotel will be to comply with additional security demands. For instance, contracts with hotels can require them to report to a designated corporate contact when employees are staying there and to provide assistance to the employees in case of an emergency. Also, hotels can be expected to provide basic medical care through a contracted doctor as well as emergency cash.

Larger hotels that employ a full-time security manager are preferable. The hotel security manager can be given procedures to follow for corporate employees if an evacuation is necessary. These procedures should provide detailed instructions on how and to where employees should be evacuated.

Any reporting procedures and phone numbers for relevant contacts should also be given to the hotel's security manager. Obviously, there will be costs associated with services such as evacuating employees, and arrangements for payment must be made with the hotel.

Nonresident Situations

An international nonprofit organization was holding a conference with

150 delegates in a country where it did not have a representative office. The organization had been meticulous with its evacuation planning for all the countries where it had offices, but it failed to draw up a plan for the conference locale. As a result, when civil unrest suddenly erupted, the organization struggled to get everyone out of the area safely.

All the delegates had come from different parts of the world on many different airlines, and they were staying at hotels scattered around the city. When the company tried to get the delegates out, gathering them together and trying to book 150 people on about 20 different airlines initially proved to be an impossible task. Later, the organization decided to prioritize the flights to four airlines, choosing the most available and reliable and issuing new tickets for the delegates who were not originally scheduled to depart on those flights.

The delegates should have been required to travel on certain airlines (this would also have been cheaper because they would have received a preferential rate), and they should have been booked into fewer hotels that were closer together. Also, arrangements could have been made with the airlines to assist with an evacuation.

If security had done a risk assessment, the organization would have known that the potential for civil unrest was high. In such a case, even if the group did not change the venue, it could have required that delegates fly into a neighbouring country so that everyone could then take the same charter flight to the conference city, which would have made evacuation much easier.

As this case illustrates, special plans are needed for countries where the company does not have a permanent presence but to which company employees travel regularly or in large numbers. When problems occur in such areas, employees will have no support from a local office that, even without prior notice, typically has some vehicles, houses, cash, and local employees who know their way around.

A traveller to a country without a company office would have to rely on the embassy, if there is one, the hotel, and in some cases, the client he or she was visiting. But the company can smooth the way by providing contact information to authorities, such as the embassy, and by making prior arrangements with hotels and other resources.

Plan preparation. Though it is nearly impossible to draw up separate plans for every country to which company employees travel, a basic threat assessment will determine which of these countries are a high risk. Plans should be created for these countries first. Then, more generic plans should be written and distributed.

The plans should provide instructions for what to do in case of an emergency, factors to consider when trying to leave the country, and resources where employees can seek assistance. Appropriate actions might include traveling in groups, keeping small denominations of cash to give away at roadblocks for the purpose of extortion, traveling in two vehicles in case one breaks down, getting to the airport early, and repeatedly checking that an airplane seat has not been "mistakenly" given to someone else. In addition, evacuees should carry only limited luggage, keeping documents and valuables in a hand-carried bag in case they lose or have to abandon their luggage. Telephone numbers for the police, embassies, airlines, the travel service provider, and other sources of assistance should also be included.

Local Contacts

Corporate security might consider contracting with local security companies in international locations to provide assistance in an emergency. An agreement can be made with a local security company whereby it will locate, secure, and, if necessary, evacuate the company's employees in the host country for a set fee or agreed upon hourly rate. These companies can also provide assistance to the traveling employee for minor emergencies, such as a lost passport or traffic accident. While this might also he done in locations where the company has a permanent facility, it is especially useful if the company does not maintain an office in the country.

Communications

Some local security companies with strong emergency response capabilities may also have satellite communications, which means they might be among the few groups reachable immediately following a disaster. Being able to speak with someone in the country to get firsthand information about local conditions and the well-being of employees is key.

Not being able to reach traveling staff or a local office after receiving news of a disaster can often result in the company activating its crisis management team and spending hours working on numerous scenarios and outcomes, only to find out that employees have escaped unscathed.

Travel Claims

Back at company headquarters or the employee's home office, the department responsible for reimbursing travel expenses is in the position to assist with the enforcement of travel security policies. One obvious option is for the company to refuse to reimburse employees for accommodations other than those approved by security. The department can also ensure that employees use the company's travel service provider and not their own travel agent by paying the travel service provider directly.

One U.S.-based multinational firm was able to increase employee use of designated international hotels by contracting with the hotel chain to pay the employees their per diem allowances. The company did not reimburse general travel expenses for accommodation, meals, and incidentals but instead paid a daily allowance via the hotels. The choice was simple. If employees wanted the money, they would have to use the designated hotel. The system achieved almost 100 percent compliance.

It will often be necessary, however, for traveling employees to pay for a number of expenses themselves. Typically, the best approach is to issue the employee a corporate credit card with sufficient limits to pay for several air tickets, rent vehicles, and so forth. But in countries with deteriorating security situations, cash is king.

After an earthquake or other natural disaster, there may not be electrical power to run ATM machines or the point-of-sales machines required to process credit card transactions. Telephone lines may be down or congested, making telephone authorization for a credit card transaction impossible. During civil unrest, merchants may be reluctant to accept credit cards for fear of not being reimbursed by local banks for the transactions.

Traveling employees should, therefore, be required to carry enough cash with them at all times to pay for meals, taxis, and "exit taxes," which are often collected by groups that set up roadblocks on the roads leading to international airports.

The best approach is for the traveller to keep a small "mugger's toll" where it can be quickly accessed and to hide the rest on one's person. Cash should be both in local currency and U.s. dollars and should be in small denominations.

Corporate travel is unavoidable. And in a world where both natural and man-made disasters are increasing in number, close encounters with crises are also inevitable. But security can ensure that those situations do not result in loss of life by coordinating the company's travel and emergency response plans and getting all parties to understand the importance of compliance.

In 1998, governments and international organizations continued their active efforts to increase regulatory and criminal enforcement of various laws to stem the tide of transnational crime. These efforts were reflected in the criminalization of various business and financial transactions, the imposition of new due diligence measures on the private sector and the concomitant weakening of privacy and confidentiality laws, strengthened penalties for non-compliance with regulatory efforts, and new law enforcement techniques, such as undercover sting operations, wiretapping, expanded powers to search homes and businesses, and controlled deliveries. So obtrusive are many of the law enforcement techniques and the privatization of law enforcement, whereby governments transfer their responsibilities to the private sector, that many professionals engaged in international transfer of wealth counseling analogized the trends to those in Aldous Huxley's A Brave New World (or perhaps the Steve Miller Band's rendition).

This discussion outlines the trends in six areas and draws some practice pointers from the trends. Section II will discuss the activities of international organizations that are driving much of the strategy, framework, and minimum standards for the development of an international anti-money laundering regime. Increasingly, international organizations, both of a universal and a more regional level, are consciously trying to build alliances and networks with each other and the private sector.

In Section III, selective elements of the substantive law of anti-money laundering are considered in the context of recent developments, such as the continued erosion of secrecy and the imposition of increased due diligence requirements. Section IV discusses major case and miscellaneous developments, such as the failure of Russian offshore banks in Antigua.

Section V highlights the growth of international tax enforcement, the increased reporting requirements and unilateral extraterritorial application of the law, the increasing bilateral and multilateral cooperation, and the new traps for the wary due to tax enforcement developments.

In Section VI, international asset forfeiture trends are highlighted. These activities pose a much graver threat to the ability of clients to do business internationally than ten years ago. The goal of immobilizing the assets of transnational criminals has become increasingly the watchword. While the rights of innocent third parties are protected in principle, it sometimes takes a lot of money and professional acumen for such persons to obtain due process.

Section VII focuses on criminal cooperation mechanisms. Section VIII discusses the use of international human rights provisions as a shield for defendants, fiduciaries, and intermediaries in the context of international anti-money laundering and financial crime cases.

As an introductory matter, the life cycle of money laundering is important to grasp. It has three cycles:

1. Placement, whereby the criminal has enormous amounts of dirty money in the form usually of cash that he needs to place or initiate in a way that neither law enforcement nor the private sector will identify as the proceeds of crime;
2. Layering, which involves the creation of many layers between the dirty money and the ultimately cleaned money through the use of offshore vehicles, such as trusts in secrecy jurisdictions, in tandem with multiple, entitles, such as companies, and secrecy mechanisms, such as nominees, stamen, bearer shares, and sophisticated structuring; and
3. Integration is achieved when the criminal has transformed the dirty money through enough layers of the laundering cycle that a legitimate banker, lawyer, or fiduciary, even one with cutting edge due diligence, would never suspect the criminal source of the money.

   Integration means that, in 1999, the money of the many heirs of Joseph Kennedy, the famous former bootlegger during the prohibition days, now is not questioned. Indeed, the money even finances federal elections (e.g., of the U.S. President, Senate, and House). In Colombia, the money of the Cali cartel has been integrated for two or three decades into the leading pharmaceutical companies, soccer teams, and also the financing of political elections (e.g., the United States imposed sanctions due to the financing of Samper's election).

Much of the emphasis of the politics of international anti-money laundering is to try to deprive criminals—especially transnational criminals—and organized crime of the fruits of the crimes and the means of their committing more crimes. Another goal is to allocate the seized proceeds to governments and law enforcement. Hence, the economics and politics of anti-money laundering are to redistribute economics and power of crime. To help with the fight, governments and international organizations have solicited the collaboration of the private sector to prevent money laundering through know-your-customer and identifying and reporting to law enforcement suspicious transactions.

11

Foreign Exchange

Authorised dealers may remit foreign exchange upto a reasonable limit, at the request of a traveller towards his hotel accommodation, tour arrangements, etc., in the countries proposed to be visited by him, provided it is out of the foreign exchange purchased by the traveller from an authorised person (including exchange drawn for private travel abroad) in accordance with the Rules, Regulations and Directions in force.

Authorised dealers may effect remittances at the request of agents in India who have tie up arrangements with hotels/agents, etc., abroad for providing hotel accommodations or making other tour arrangements for travellers from India provided the authorised dealer is satisfied that the remittance is being made out of the foreign exchange purchased by the concerned traveller from an authorised person (including exchange drawn for private travel abroad) in accordance with the Rules, Regulations and Directions in force. Authorised dealer may open foreign currency accounts in the name of agents in India who have tie up arrangements with hotels/agents, etc., abroad for providing hotel accommodations or making other tour arrangements for travellers from India provided:

- The credits to the account are by way of depositing
- Collections made in foreign exchange from travellers, and
- Refunds received from outside India on account of cancellation of bookings/tour arrangements, etc., and
- the debits in foreign exchange are for making payments towards hotel accommodation, tour arrangements, etc., outside India, in accordance with (ii) above.

An Act to consolidate and amend the law relating to foreign exchange with the objective of facilitating external trade and payments and for promoting the orderly development and maintenance of foreign exchange market in India.

BE it enacted by Parliament in the Fiftieth Year of the Republic of India as follows:—

SHORT TITLE, EXTENT, APPLICATION AND COMMENCEMENT

1. This Act may be called the Foreign Exchange Management Act, 1999.
2. It extends to the whole of India.
3. It shall also apply to all branches, offices and agencies outside India owned or controlled by a person resident in India and also to any contravention thereunder committed outside India by any person to whom this Act applies.
4. It shall come into force on such date as the Central Government may, by notification in the Official Gazette, appoint:

Provided that different dates may be appointed for different provisions of this Act and any reference in any such provision to the commencement of this Act shall be construed as a reference to the coming into force of that provision.

In this Act, unless the context otherwise requires—

- "Adjudicating Authority" means an officer authorised under sub-section (1) of section 16;
- "Appellate Tribunal" means the Appellate Tribunal for Foreign Exchange established under section 18;
- "authorised person" means an authorised dealer, money changer, off-shore banking unit or any other person for the time being authorised under sub-section (1) of section 10 to deal in foreign exchange or foreign securities;
- "Bench" means a Bench of the Appellate Tribunal;
- "capital account transaction" means a transaction which alters the assets or liabilities, including contingent liabilities, outside India of persons resident in India or assets or liabilities in India of persons resident outside India, and includes transactions referred to in sub-section (3) of section 6;
- "Chairperson" means the Chairperson of the Appellate Tribunal;
- "chartered accountant" shall have the meaning assigned to it in clause (b) of sub-section (1) of section 2 of the Chartered Accountants Act, 1949 (38 of 1949);
- "currency" includes all currency notes, postal notes, postal orders, money orders, cheques, drafts, travellers cheques, letters of credit, bills of exchange and promissory notes, credit cards or such other similar instruments, as may be notified by the Reserve Bank;
- "currency notes" means and includes cash in the form of coins and bank notes;

- "current account transaction" means a transaction other than a capital account transaction and without prejudice to the generality of the foregoing such transaction includes:—
  - Payments due in connection with foreign trade, other current business, services, and short-term banking and credit facilities in the ordinary course of business,
  - Payments due as interest on loans and as net income from investments,
  - Remittances for living expenses of parents, spouse and children residing abroad, and
  - Expenses in connection with foreign travel, education and medical care of parents, spouse and children;
- "Director of Enforcement" means the Director of Enforcement appointed under sub-section (1) of section 36;
- "Export", with its grammatical variations and cognate expressions, means—
  - The taking out of India to a place outside India any goods,
  - Provision of services from India to any person outside India;
- "Foreign currency" means any currency other than Indian currency;
- "Foreign exchange" means foreign currency and includes—
  - Deposits, credits and balances payable in any foreign currency,
  - Drafts, travellers cheques, letters of credit or bills of exchange, expressed or drawn in Indian currency but payable in any foreign currency,
  - Drafts, travellers cheques, letters of credit or bills of exchange drawn by banks, institutions or persons outside India, but payable in Indian currency;
- "Foreign security" means any security, in the form of shares, stocks, bonds, debentures or any other instrument denominated or expressed in foreign currency and includes securities expressed in foreign currency, but where redemption or any form of return such as interest or dividends is payable in Indian currency;
- "Import", with its grammatical variations and cognate expressions, means bringing into India any goods or services;
- "Indian currency" means currency which is expressed or drawn in Indian rupees but does not include special bank notes and special one rupee notes issued under section 28A of the Reserve Bank of India Act, 1934 (2 of 1934);
- "Legal practitioner" shall have the meaning assigned to it in clause (i) of sub-section (1) of section 2 of the Advocates Act, 1961 (25 of 1961);

- "Member" means a Member of the Appellate Tribunal and includes the Chairperson thereof;
- "Notify" means to notify in the Official Gazette and the expression "notification" shall be construed accordingly;
- "Person" includes—
  - An individual,
  - A Hindu undivided family,
  - A company,
  - A firm,
  - An association of persons or a body of individuals, whether incorporated or not,
  - Every artificial juridical person, not falling within any of the preceding sub-clauses, and
  - Any agency, office or branch owned or controlled by such person;
- "Person resident in India" means—
  - A person residing in India for more than one hundred and eighty-two days during the course of the preceding financial year but does not include—
    a. A person who has gone out of India or who stays outside India, in either case—
    b. For or on taking up employment outside India, or
    c. For carrying on outside India a business or vocation outside India, or
    d. For any other purpose, in such circumstances as would indicate his intention to stay outside India for an uncertain period;
    e. A person who has come to or stays in India, in either case, otherwise than—
    f. For or on taking up employment in India, or
    g. For carrying on in India a business or vocation in India, or
    h. For any other purpose, in such circumstances as would indicate his intention to stay in India for an uncertain period;
  - Any person or body corporate registered or incorporated in India,
  - An office, branch or agency in India owned or controlled by a person resident outside India,
  - An office, branch or agency outside India owned or controlled by a person resident in India;
- "Person resident outside India" means a person who is not resident in India;

- "Prescribed" means prescribed by rules made under this Act;
- "Repatriate to India" means bringing into India the realised foreign exchange and—
  - The selling of such foreign exchange to an authorised person in India in exchange for rupees, or
  - The holding of realised amount in an account with an authorised person in India to the extent notified by the Reserve Bank, and includes use of the realised amount for discharge of a debt or liability denominated in foreign exchange and the expression "repatriation" shall be construed accordingly;
- "Reserve Bank" means the Reserve Bank of India constituted under sub-section (1) of section 3 of the Reserve Bank of India Act, 1934 (2 of 1934);
- "Security" means shares, stocks, bonds and debentures, Government securities as defined in the Public Debt Act, 1944 (18 of 1944), savings certificates to which the Government Savings Certificates Act, 1959 (46 of 1959) applies, deposit receipts in respect of deposits of securities and units of the Unit Trust of India established under sub-section (1) of section 3 of the Unit Trust of India Act, 1963 (52 of 1963) or of any mutual fund and includes certificates of title to securities, but does not include bills of exchange or promissory notes other than Government promissory notes or any other instruments which may be notified by the Reserve Bank as security for the purposes of this Act; (zb) "service" means service of any description which is made available to potential users and includes the provision of facilities in connection with banking, financing, insurance, medical assistance, legal assistance, chit fund, real estate, transport, processing, supply of electrical or other energy, boarding or lodging or both, entertainment, amusement or the purveying of news or other information, but does not include the rendering of any service free of charge or under a contract of personal service; (zc) "Special Director (Appeals)" means an officer appointed under section 18; (zd) "specify" means to specify by regulations made under this Act and the expression "specified" shall be construed accordingly; (ze) "transfer" includes sale, purchase, exchange, mortgage, pledge, gift, loan or any other form of transfer of right, title, possession or lien.

Regulation and Management of Foreign Exchange

Save as otherwise provided in this Act, rules or regulations made thereunder, or with the general or special permission of the Reserve Bank, no person shall—

(a) Deal in or transfer any foreign exchange or foreign security to any person not being an authorised person;

(b) Make any payment to or for the credit of any person resident outside India in any manner;

(c) Receive otherwise through an authorised person, any payment by order or on behalf of any person resident outside India in any manner;

Explanation—For the purpose of this clause, where any person in, or resident in, India receives any payment by order or on behalf of any person resident outside India through any other person (including an authorised person) without a corresponding inward remittance from any place outside India, then, such person shall be deemed to have received such payment otherwise than through an authorised person;

(d) Enter into any financial transaction in India as consideration for or in association with acquisition or creation or transfer of a right to acquire, any asset outside India by any person.

Explanation—For the purpose of this clause, "financial transaction" means making any payment to, or for the credit of any person, or receiving any payment for, by order or on behalf of any person, or drawing, issuing or negotiating any bill of exchange or promissory note, or transferring any security or acknowledging any debt.

Holding of Foreign Exchange

Save as otherwise provided in this Act, no person resident in India shall acquire, hold, own, possess or transfer any foreign exchange, foreign security or any immovable property situated outside India.

Current Account Transactions

Any person may sell or draw foreign exchange to or from an authorised person if such sale or drawal is a current account transaction:

Provided that the Central Government may, in public interest and in consultation with the Reserve Bank, impose such reasonable restrictions for current account transactions as may be prescribed.

Capital Account Transactions

1. Subject to the provisions of sub-section (2), any person may sell or draw foreign exchange to or from an authorised person for a capital account transaction.
2. The Reserve Bank may, in consultation with the Central Government, specify—

(a) Any class or classes of capital account transactions which are permissible;

(b) The limit up to which foreign exchange shall be admissible for such transactions:
Provided that the Reserve Bank shall not impose any restriction on the drawal of foreign exchange for payments due on account of amortization of loans or for depreciation of direct investments in the ordinary course of business.

3. Without prejudice to the generality of the provisions of sub-section (2), the Reserve Bank may, by regulations, prohibit, restrict or regulate the following—
   (a) Transfer or issue of any foreign security by a person resident in India;
   (b) Transfer or issue of any security by a person resident outside India;
   (c) Transfer or issue of any security or foreign security by any branch, office or agency in India of a person resident outside India;
   (d) Any borrowing or lending in foreign exchange in whatever form or by whatever name called;
   (e) Any borrowing or lending in rupees in whatever form or by whatever name called between a person resident in India and a person resident outside India;
   (f) Deposits between persons resident in India and persons resident outside India;
   (g) Export, import or holding of currency or currency notes;
   (h) Transfer of immovable property outside India, other than a lease not exceeding five years, by a person resident in India;
   (i) Acquisition or transfer of immovable property in India, other than a lease not exceeding five years, by a person resident outside India;
   (j) Giving of a guarantee or surety in respect of any debt, obligation or other liability incurred—
      (i) By a person resident in India and owed to a person resident outside India; or
      (ii) By a person resident outside India.
4. A person resident in India may hold, own, transfer or invest in foreign currency, foreign security or any immovable property situated outside India if such currency, security or property was acquired, held or owned by such person when he was resident outside India or inherited from a person who was resident outside India.
5. A person resident outside India may hold, own, transfer or invest in Indian currency, security or any immovable property situated in

India if such currency, security or property was acquired, held or owned by such person when he was resident in India or inherited from a person who was resident in India.

6. Without prejudice to the provisions of this section, the Reserve Bank may, by regulation, prohibit, restrict, or regulate establishment in India of a branch, office or other place of business by a person resident outside India, for carrying on any activity relating to such branch, office or other place of business.

Export of Goods and Services

1. Every exporter of goods shall—
   (a) Furnish to the Reserve Bank or to such other authority a declaration in such form and in such manner as may be specified, containing true and correct material particulars, including the amount representing the full export value or, if the full export value of the goods is not ascertainable at the time of export, the value which the exporter, having regard to the prevailing market conditions, expects to receive on the sale of the goods in a market outside India;
   (b) Furnish to the Reserve Bank such other information as may be required by the Reserve Bank for the purpose of ensuring the realisation of the export proceeds by such exporter.
2. The Reserve Bank may, for the purpose of ensuring that the full export value of the goods or such reduced value of the goods as the Reserve Bank determines, having regard to the prevailing market conditions, is received without any delay, direct any exporter to comply with such requirements as it deems fit.
3. Every exporter of services shall furnish to the Reserve Bank or to such other authorities a declaration in such form and in such manner as may be specified, containing the true and correct material particulars in relation to payment for such services.

Realisation and Repatriation of Foreign Exchange

8. Save as otherwise provided in this Act, where any amount of foreign exchange is due or has accrued to any person resident in India, such person shall take all reasonable steps to realise and repatriate to India such foreign exchange within such period and in such manner as may be specified by the Reserve Bank.

Exemption from Realisation and Repatriation in Certain Cases

The provisions of sections 4 and 8 shall not apply to the following, namely:—

(a) Possession of foreign currency or foreign coins by any person up to such limit as the Reserve Bank may specify;

(b) Foreign currency account held or operated by such person or class of persons and the limit up to which the Reserve Bank may specify;

(c) Foreign exchange acquired or received before the 8th day of July, 1947 or any income arising or accruing thereon which is held outside India by any person in pursuance of a general or special permission granted by the Reserve Bank;

(d) Foreign exchange held by a person resident in India up to such limit as the Reserve Bank may specify, if such foreign exchange was acquired by way of gift or inheritance from a person referred to in clause *(c)*, including any income arising therefrom;

(e) Foreign exchange acquired from employment, business, trade, vocation, services, honorarium, gifts, inheritance or any other legitimate means up to such limit as the Reserve Bank may specify; and

(f) Such other receipts in foreign exchange as the Reserve Bank may specify.

Authorised Person

1. The Reserve Bank may, on an application made to it in this behalf, authorise any person to be known as authorised person to deal in foreign exchange or in foreign securities, as an authorised dealer, money changer or off-shore banking unit or in any other manner as it deems fit.
2. An authorisation under this section shall be in writing and shall be subject to the conditions laid down therein.
3. An authorisation granted under sub-section (1) may be revoked by the Reserve Bank at any time if the Reserve Bank is satisfied that—
   (a) It is in public interest so to do; or
   (b) The authorised person has failed to comply with the condition subject to which the authorisation was granted or has contravened any of the provisions of the Act or any rule, regulation, notification, direction or order made thereunder:
   Provided that no such authorisation shall be revoked on any ground referred to in clause (b) unless the authorised person has been given a reasonable opportunity of making a representation in the matter.
4. An authorised person shall, in all his dealings in foreign exchange or foreign security, comply with such general or special directions

or orders as the Reserve Bank may, from time to time, think fit to give, and, except with the previous permission of the Reserve Bank, an authorised person shall not engage in any transaction involving any foreign exchange or foreign security which is not in conformity with the terms of his authorisation under this section.

5. An authorised person shall, before undertaking any transaction in foreign exchange on behalf of any person, require that person to make such declaration and to give such information as will reasonably satisfy him that the transaction will not involve, and is not designed for the purpose of any contravention or evasion of the provisions of this Act or of any rule, regulation, notification, direction or order made thereunder, and where the said person refuses to comply with any such requirement or makes only unsatisfactory compliance therewith, the authorised person shall refuse in writing to undertake the transaction and shall, if he has reason to believe that any such contravention or evasion as aforesaid is contemplated by the person, report the matter to the Reserve Bank.
6. Any person, other than an authorised person, who has acquired or purchased foreign exchange for any purpose mentioned in the declaration made by him to authorised person under sub-section (5) does not use it for such purpose or does not surrender it to authorised person within the specified period or uses the foreign exchange so acquired or purchased for any other purpose for which purchase or acquisition of foreign exchange is not permissible under the provisions of the Act or the rules or regulations or direction or order made thereunder shall be deemed to have committed contravention of the provisions of the Act for the purpose of this section.

Reserve Bank's Powers to Issue Directions to Authorised Person

1. The Reserve Bank may, for the purpose of securing compliance with the provisions of this Act and of any rules, regulations, notifications or directions made thereunder, give to the authorised persons any direction in regard to making of payment or the doing or desist from doing any act relating to foreign exchange or foreign security.
2. The Reserve Bank may, for the purpose of ensuring the compliance with the provisions of this Act or of any rule, regulation, notification, direction or order made thereunder, direct any authorised person to furnish such information, in such manner, as it deems fit.
3. Where any authorised person contravenes any direction given by the Reserve Bank under this Act or fails to file any return as directed

by the Reserve Bank, the Reserve Bank may, after giving reasonable opportunity of being heard, impose on the authorised person a penalty which may extend to ten thousand rupees and in the case of continuing contravention with an additional penalty which may extend to two thousand rupees for every day during which such contravention continues.

Power of Reserve Bank to Inspect Authorised Person

1. The Reserve Bank may, at any time, cause an inspection to be made, by any officer of the Reserve Bank specially authorised in writing by the Reserve Bank in this behalf, of the business of any authorised person as may appear to it to be necessary or expedient for the purpose of—
   (a) Verifying the correctness of any statement, information or particulars furnished to the Reserve Bank;
   (b) Obtaining any information or particulars which such authorised person has failed to furnish on being called upon to do so;
   (c) Securing compliance with the provisions of this Act or of any rules, regulations, directions or orders made thereunder.
2. It shall be the duty of every authorised person, and where such person is a company or a firm, every director, partner or other officer of such company or firm, as the case may be, to produce to any officer making an inspection under sub-section (1), such books, accounts and other documents in his custody or power and to furnish any statement or information relating to the affairs of such person, company or firm as the said officer may require within such time and in such manner as the said officer may direct.

Contravention and Penalties

1. If any person contravenes any provision of this Act, or contravenes any rule, regulation, notification, direction or order issued in exercise of the powers under this Act, or contravenes any condition subject to which an authorisation is issued by the Reserve Bank, he shall, upon adjudication, be liable to a penalty up to thrice the sum involved in such contravention where such amount is quantifiable, or up to two lakh rupees where the amount is not quantifiable, and where such contravention is a continuing one, further penalty which may extend to five thousand rupees for every day after the first day during which the contravention continues.
2. Any Adjudicating Authority adjudging any contravention under sub-section (1), may, if he thinks fit in addition to any penalty which he may impose for such contravention direct that any

currency, security or any other money or property in respect of which the contravention has taken place shall be confiscated to the Central Government and further direct that the foreign exchange holdings, if any of the persons committing the contraventions or any part thereof, shall be brought back into India or shall be retained outside India in accordance with the directions made in this behalf.

Explanation—For the purposes of this sub-section, "property" in respect of which contravention has taken place, shall include—

(a) Deposits in a bank, where the said property is converted into such deposits;

(b) Indian currency, where the said property is converted into that currency; and

(c) Any other property which has resulted out of the conversion of that property.

Enforcement of the orders of Adjudicating Authority.

1. Subject to the provisions of sub-section (2) of section 19, if any person fails to make full payment of the penalty imposed on him under section 13 within a period of ninety days from the date on which the notice for payment of such penalty is served on him, he shall be liable to civil imprisonment under this section.

2. No order for the arrest and detention in civil prison of a defaulter shall be made unless the Adjudicating Authority has issued and served a notice upon the defaulter calling upon him to appear before him on the date specified in the notice and to show cause why he should not be committed to the civil prison, and unless the Adjudicating Authority, for reasons in writing, is satisfied—

   (a) That the defaulter, with the object or effect of obstructing the recovery of penalty, has after the issue of notice by the Adjudicating Authority, dishonestly transferred concealed, or removed any part of his property, or

   (b) That the defaulter has, or has had since the issuing of notice by the Adjudicating Authority, the means to pay the arrears or some substantial part thereof and refuses or neglects or has refused or neglected to pay the same.

3. Notwithstanding anything contained in sub-section (1), a warrant for the arrest of the defaulter may be issued by the Adjudicating Authority if the Adjudicating Authority is satisfied, by affidavit or otherwise, that with the object or effect of delaying the execution of the certificate the defaulter is likely to abscond or leave the local limits of the jurisdiction of the Adjudicating Authority.

4. Where appearance is not made pursuant to a notice issued and served under sub-section (1), the Adjudicating Authority may issue a warrant for the arrest of the defaulter.
5. A warrant of arrest issued by the Adjudicating Authority under sub-section (3) or sub-section
6. May also be executed by any other Adjudicating Authority within whose jurisdiction the defaulter may for the time being be found.
7. Every person arrested in pursuance of a warrant of arrest under this section shall be brought before the Adjudicating Authority issuing the warrant as soon as practicable and in any event within twenty-four hours of his arrest (exclusive of the time required for the journey):

   Provided that, if the defaulter pays the amount entered in the warrant of arrest as due and the costs of the arrest to the officer arresting him, such officer shall at once release him.

   Explanation—For the purposes of this sub-section, where the defaulter is a Hindu undivided family, the *karta* thereof shall be deemed to be the defaulter.
8. When a defaulter appears before the Adjudicating Authority pursuant to a notice to show cause or is brought before the Adjudicating Authority under this section, the Adjudicating Authority shall give the defaulter an opportunity showing cause why he should not be committed to the civil prison.
9. Pending the conclusion of the inquiry, the Adjudicating Authority may, in his discretion, order the defaulter to be detained in the custody of such officer as the Adjudicating Authority may think fit or release him on his furnishing the security to the satisfaction of the Adjudicating Authority for his appearance as and when required.
10. Upon the conclusion of the inquiry, the Adjudicating Authority may make an order for the detention of the defaulter in the civil prison and shall in that event cause him to be arrested if he is not already under arrest:

    Provided that in order to give a defaulter an opportunity of satisfying the arrears, the Adjudicating Authority may, before making the order of detention, leave the defaulter in the custody of the officer arresting him or of any other officer for a specified period not exceeding fifteen days, or release him on his furnishing security to the satisfaction of the Adjudicating Authority for his appearance at the expiration of the specified period if the arrears are not satisfied.
11. When the Adjudicating Authority does not make an order of detention under sub-section (9), he shall, if the defaulter is under arrest, direct his release.

12. Every person detained in the civil prison in execution of the certificate may be so detained,—
    a. Where the certificate is for a demand of an amount exceeding rupees one crore, up to three years, and
    b. In any other case, up to six months:

       Provided that he shall be released from such detention on the amount mentioned in the warrant for his detention being paid to the officer-in-charge of the civil prison.
13. A defaulter released from detention under this section shall not, merely by reason of his release, be discharged from his liability for the arrears, but he shall not be liable to be arrested under the certificate in execution of which he was detained in the civil prison.
14. A detention order may be executed at any place in India in the manner provided for the execution of warrant of arrest under the Code of Criminal Procedure, 1973 (2 of 1974).

Power to Compound Contravention

1. Any contravention under section 13 may, on an application made by theperson committing such contravention, be compounded within one hundred and eighty days from the date of receipt of application by the Director of Enforcement or such other officers of the Directorate of Enforcement and Officers of the Reserve Bank as may be authorised in this behalf by the Central Government in such manner as may be prescribed.
2. Where a contravention has been compounded under sub-section (1), no proceeding or further proceeding, as the case may be, shall be initiated or continued, as the case may be, against the person committing such contravention under that section, in respect of the contravention so compounded.

Appointment of Adjudicating Authority

1. For the purpose of adjudication under section 13, the Central Government may, by an order published in the Official Gazette, appoint as many officers of the Central Government as it may think fit, as the Adjudicating Authorities for holding an inquiry in the manner prescribed after giving the person alleged to have committed contravention under section 13, against whom a complaint has been made under sub-section
2. (hereinafter in this section referred to as the said person) a reasonable opportunity of being heard for the purpose of imposing any penalty:

Provided that where the Adjudicating Authority is of opinion that the said person is likely to abscond or is likely to evade in any manner, the payment of penalty, if levied, it may direct the said person to furnish a bond or guarantee for such amount and subject to such conditions as it may deem fit.

3. The Central Government shall, while appointing the Adjudicating Authorities under sub-section (1), also specify in the order published in the Official Gazette, their respective jurisdictions.
4. No Adjudicating Authority shall hold an enquiry under sub-section (1) except upon a complaint in writing made by any officer authorised by a general or special order by the Central Government.
5. The said person may appear either in person or take the assistance of a legal practitioner or a chartered accountant of his choice for presenting his case before the Adjudicating Authority.
6. Every Adjudicating Authority shall have the same powers of a civil court which are conferred on the Appellate Tribunal under sub-section (2) of section 28 and—
   (a) All proceedings before it shall be deemed to be judicial proceedings within the meaning of sections 193 and 228 of the Indian Penal Code (45 of 1860);
   (b) Shall be deemed to be a civil court for the purposes of sections 345 and 346 of the Code of Criminal Procedure, 1973 (2 of 1974).
7. Every Adjudicating Authority shall deal with the complaint under sub-section (2) as expeditiously as possible and endeavour shall be made to dispose of the complaint finally within one year from the date of receipt of the complaint:

Provided that where the complaint cannot be disposed off within the said period, the Adjudicating Authority shall record periodically the reasons in writing for not disposing off the complaint within the said period.

Appeal to Special Director (Appeals)

1. The Central Government shall, by notification, appoint one or more Special Directors (Appeals) to hear appeals against the orders of the Adjudicating Authorities under this section and shall also specify in the said notification the matter and places in relation to which the Special Director (Appeals) may exercise jurisdiction.
2. Any person aggrieved by an order made by the Adjudicating Authority, being an Assistant Director of Enforcement or a Deputy Director of Enforcement, may prefer an appeal to the Special Director (Appeals).
3. Every appeal under sub-section (1) shall be filed within forty-five days from the date on which the copy of the order made by the

Adjudicating Authority is received by the aggrieved person and it shall be in such form, verified in such manner and be accompanied by such fee as may be prescribed:

Provided that the Special Director (Appeals) may entertain an appeal after the expiry of the said period of forty-five days, if he is satisfied that there was sufficient cause for not filing it within that period.

4. On receipt of an appeal under sub-section (1), the Special Director (Appeals) may after giving the parties to the appeal an opportunity of being heard, pass such order thereon as he thinks fit confirming, modifying or setting aside the order appealed against.
5. The Special Director (Appeals) shall send a copy of every order made by him to the parties to appeal and to the concerned Adjudicating Authority.
6. The Special Director (Appeals) shall have the same powers of a civil court which are conferred on the Appellate Tribunal under sub-section (2) of section 28 and—
   (a) All proceedings before him shall be deemed to be judicial proceedings within the meaning of sections 193 and 228 of the Indian Penal Code (45 of 1860);
   (b) Shall be deemed to be a civil court for the purposes of sections 345 and 346 of the Code of Criminal Procedure, 1973 (2 of 1974).

Establishment of Appellate Tribunal

The Central Government shall, by notification, establish an Appellate Tribunal to be known as the Appellate Tribunal for Foreign Exchange to hear appeals against the orders of the Adjudicating Authorities and the Special Director (Appeals) under this Act.

Appeal to Appellate Tribunal

1. Save as provided in sub-section (2), the Central Government or any person aggrieved by an order made by an Adjudicating Authority, other than those referred to sub-section (1) of section 17, or the Special Director (Appeals), may prefer an appeal to the Appellate Tribunal:

   Provided that any person appealing against the order of the Adjudicating Authority or the Special Director (Appeals) levying any penalty, shall while filing the appeal, deposit the amount of such penalty with such authority as may be notified by the Central Government:

   Provided further that where in any particular case, the Appellate Tribunal is of the opinion that the deposit of such penalty would cause undue hardship to such person, the Appellate Tribunal may dispense with such deposit subject to such conditions as it may deem fit to impose so as to safeguard the realisation of penalty.

2. Every appeal under sub-section (1) shall be filed within a period of forty-five days from the date on which a copy of the order made by the Adjudicating Authority or the Special Director (Appeals) is received by the aggrieved person or by the Central Government and it shall be in such form, verified in such manner and be accompanied by such fee as may be prescribed:

   Provided that the Appellate Tribunal may entertain an appeal after the expiry of the said period of forty-five days if it is satisfied that there was sufficient cause for not filing it within that period.

3. On receipt of an appeal under sub-section (1), the Appellate Tribunal may, after giving the parties to the appeal an opportunity of being heard, pass such orders thereon as it thinks fit, confirming, modifying or setting aside the order appealed against.

4. The Appellate Tribunal shall send a copy of every order made by it to the parties to the appeal and to the concerned Adjudicating Authority or the Special Director (Appeals), as the case may be.

5. The appeal filed before the Appellate Tribunal under sub-section (1) shall be dealt with by it as expeditiously as possible and endeavour shall be made by it to dispose of the appeal finally within one hundred and eighty days from the date of receipt of the appeal:

   Provided that where any appeal could not be disposed of within the said period of one hundred and eighty days, the Appellate Tribunal shall record its reasons in writing for not disposing of the appeal within the said period.

6. The Appellate Tribunal may, for the purpose of examining the legality, propriety or correctness of any order made by the Adjudicating Authority under section 16 in relation to any proceeding, on its own motion or otherwise, call for the records of such proceedings and make such order in the case as it thinks fit.

Composition of Appellate Tribunal

1. The Appellate Tribunal shall consist of a Chairperson and such number of Members as the Central Government may deem fit.

2. Subject to the provisions of this Act,—

   (a) The jurisdiction of the Appellate Tribunal may be exercised by Benches thereof;

   (b) A Bench may be constituted by the Chairperson with one or more Members as the Chairperson may deem fit;

   (c) The Benches of the Appellate Tribunal shall ordinarily sit at New

Delhi and at such other places as the Central Government may, in consultation with the Chairperson, notify;

(d) The Central Government shall notify the areas in relation to which each Bench of the Appellate Tribunal may exercise jurisdiction.

3. Notwithstanding anything contained in sub-section (2), the Chairperson may transfer a Member from one Bench to another Bench.
4. If at any stage of the hearing of any case or matter it appears to the Chairperson or a Member that the case or matter is of such a nature that it ought to be heard by a Bench consisting of two Members, the case or matter may be transferred by the Chairperson or, as the case may be, referred to him for transfer, to such Bench as the Chairperson may deem fit.

Qualifications for Appointment

1. A person shall not be qualified for appointment as the Chairperson or a Member unless he—
   (a) In the case of Chairperson, is or has been, or is qualified to be, a Judge of a High Court; and
   (b) In the case of a Member, is or has been, or is qualified to be, a District Judge.
2. A person shall not be qualified for appointment as a Special Director (Appeals) unless he—
   (a) Has been a member of the Indian Legal Service and has held a post in Grade I of that Service; or
   (b) Has been a member of the Indian Revenue Service and has held a post equivalent to a Joint Secretary to the Government of India.

Term of Office

The Chairperson and every other Member shall hold office as such for a term of five years from the date on which he enters upon his office:

Provided that no Chairperson or other Member shall hold office as such after he has attained,—

(a) In the case of the Chairperson, the age of sixty-five years;

(b) In the case of any other Member, the age of sixty-two years.

Terms and Conditions of Service

The salary and allowances payable to and the other terms and conditions of service of the Chairperson, other Members and the Special Director

(Appeals) shall be such as may be prescribed: Provided that neither the salary and allowances nor the other terms and conditions of service of the Chairperson or a Member shall be varied to his disadvantage after appointment.

Vacancies

If, for reason other than temporary absence, any vacancy occurs in the office of the Chairperson or a Member, the Central Government shall appoint another person in accordance with the provisions of this Act to fill the vacancy and the proceedings may be continued before the Appellate Tribunal from the stage at which the vacancy is filled.

Resignation and Removal

1. The Chairperson or a Member may, by notice in writing under his hand addressed to the Central Government, resign his office:

   Provided that the Chairperson or a Member shall, unless he is permitted by the Central Government to relinquish his office sooner, continue to hold office until the expiry of three months from the date of receipt of such notice or until a person duly appointed as his successor enters upon his office or until the expiry of term of office, whichever is the earliest.

2. The Chairperson or a Member shall not be removed from his office except by an order by the Central Government on the ground of proved misbehaviour or incapacity after an inquiry made by such person as the President may appoint for this purpose in which the Chairperson or a Member concerned has been informed of the charges against him and given a reasonable opportunity of being heard in respect of such charges.

Member to act as Chairperson in Certain Circumstances

1. In the event of the occurrence of any vacancy in the office of the Chairperson by reason of his death, resignation or otherwise, the senior-most Member shall act as the Chairperson until the date on which a new Chairperson, appointed in accordance with the provisions of this Act to fill such vacancy, enters upon his office.
2. When the Chairperson is unable to discharge his functions owing to absence, illness or any other cause, the senior most Member shall discharge the functions of the Chairperson until the date on which the Chairperson resumes his duties.

Staff of Appellate Tribunal and Special Director (Appeals)

1. The Central Government shall provide the Appellate Tribunal and

the Special Director (Appeals) with such officers and employees as it may deem fit.

2. The officers and employees of the Appellate Tribunal and office of the Special Director (Appeals) shall discharge their functions under the general superintendence of the Chairperson and the Special Director (Appeals), as the case may be.

3. The salaries and allowances and other conditions of service of the officers and employees of the Appellate Tribunal and office of the Special Director (Appeals) shall be such as may be prescribed.

Procedure and powers of Appellate Tribunal and Special Director

1. The Appellate Tribunal and the Special Director (Appeals) shall not be bound by the procedure laid down by the Code of Civil Procedure, 1908 (5 of 1908) but shall be guided by the principles of natural justice and, subject to the other provisions of this Act, the Appellate Tribunal and the Special Director (Appeals) shall have powers to regulate its own procedure.
2. The Appellate Tribunal and the Special Director (Appeals) shall have, for the purposes of discharging its functions under this Act, the same powers as are vested in a civil court under the Code of Civil Procedure, 1908 (5 of 1908); while trying a suit, in respect of the following matters, namely:—
   (a) Summoning and enforcing the attendance of any person and examining him on oath;
   (b) Requiring the discovery and production of documents;
   (c) Receiving evidence on affidavits;
   (d) Subject to the provisions of sections 123 and 124 of the Indian Evidence Act, 1872 (1 of 1872) requisitioning any public record or document or copy of such record or document from any office;
   (e) Issuing commissions for the examination of witnesses or documents;
   (f) Reviewing its decisions;
   (g) Dismissing a representation of default or deciding it *ex parte;*
   (h) Setting aside any order of dismissal of any representation for default or any order passed by it *ex parte;* and
   (i) Any other matter which may be prescribed by the Central Government.
3. An order made by the Appellate Tribunal or the Special Director (Appeals) under this Act shall be executable by the Appellate

Tribunal or the Special Director (Appeals) as a decree of civil court and, for this purpose, the Appellate Tribunal and the Special Director (Appeals) shall have all the powers of a civil court.

4. Notwithstanding anything contained in sub-section (3), the Appellate Tribunal or the Special Director (Appeals) may transmit any order made by it to a civil court having local jurisdiction and such civil court shall execute the order as if it were a decree made by that court.
5. All proceedings before the Appellate Tribunal and the Special Director (Appeals) shall be deemed to be judicial proceedings within the meaning of sections 193 and 228 of the Indian Penal Code (45 of 1860) and the Appellate Tribunal shall be deemed to be a civil court for the purposes of sections 345 and 346 of the Code of Criminal Procedure, 1973 (2 of 1974)

Distribution of Business Amongst Benches

Where Benches are constituted, the Chairperson may, from time to time, by notification, make provisions as to the distribution of the business of the Appellate Tribunal amongst the Benches and also provide for the matters which may be dealt with by each Bench.

Power of Chairperson to Transfer Cases

On the application of any of the parties and after notice to the parties, and after hearing such of them as he may desire to be heard, or on his own motion without such notice, the Chairperson may transfer any case pending before one Bench, for disposal, to any other Bench.

Decision to be by Majority

If the Members of a Bench consisting of two Members differ in opinion on any point, they shall state the point or points on which they differ, and make a reference to the Chairperson who shall either hear the point or points himself or refer the case for hearing on such point or points by one or more of the other Members of the Appellate Tribunal and such point or points shall be decided according to the opinion of the majority of the Members of the Appellate Tribunal who have heard the case, including those who first heard it.

Right of appellant to take assistance of legal practitioner or chartered accountant and of Government, to appoint presenting officers.

1. A person preferring an appeal to the Appellate Tribunal or the Special Director (Appeals) under this Act may either appear in person or take the assistance of a legal practitioner or a chartered accountant of his choice to present his case before the Appellate Tribunal or the Special Director (Appeals), as the case may be.

2. The Central Government may authorise one or more legal practitioners or chartered accountants or any of its officers to act as presenting officers and every person so authorised may present the case with respect to any appeal before the Appellate Tribunal or the Special Director (Appeals), as the case may be.

Members, etc. to be Public Servants

The Chairperson, Members and other officers and employees of the Appellate Tribunal, the Special Director (Appeals) and the Adjudicating Authority shall be deemed to be public servants within the meaning of section 21 of the Indian Penal Code (45 of 1860).

Civil court not to have Jurisdiction

No civil court shall have jurisdiction to entertain any suit or proceeding in respect of any matter which an Adjudicating Authority or the Appellate Tribunal or the Special Director (Appeals) is empowered by or under this Act to determine and no injunction shall be granted by any court or other authority in respect of any action taken or to be taken in pursuance of any power conferred by or under this Act.

Appeal to High Court

Any person aggrieved by any decision or order of the Appellate Tribunal may file an appeal to the High Court within sixty days from the date of communication of the decision or order of the Appellate Tribunal on any question of law arising out of such order:

Provided that the High Court may, if it is satisfied that the appellant was prevented by sufficient cause from filing the appeal within the said period, allow it to be filed within a further period not exceeding sixty days.

Explanation—In this section "High Court" means—

(a) The High Court within the jurisdiction of which the aggrieved party ordinarily resides or carries on business or personally works for gain; and

(b) Where the Central Government is the aggrieved party, the High Court within the jurisdiction of which the respondent, or in a case where there are more than one respondent, any of the respondents, ordinarily resides or carries on business or personally works for gain.

Directorate Of Enforcement

1. The Central Government shall establish a Directorate of Enforcement with a Director and such other officers or class of officers as it thinks fit, who shall be called officers of Enforcement, for the purposes of this Act.

2. Without prejudice to provisions of sub-section (1), the Central Government may authorise the Director of Enforcement or an Additional Director of Enforcement or a Special Director of Enforcement or a Deputy Director of Enforcement to appoint officers of Enforcement below the rank of an Assistant Director of Enforcement.
3. Subject to such conditions and limitations as the Central Government may impose, an officer of Enforcement may exercise the powers and discharge the duties conferred or imposed on him under this Act.

Power of Search, Seizure, etc

1. The Director of Enforcement and other officers of Enforcement, not below the rank of an Assistant Director, shall take up for investigation the contravention referred to in section 13.
2. Without prejudice to the provisions of sub-section (1), the Central Government may also, by notification, authorise any officer or class of officers in the Central Government, State Government or the Reserve Bank, not below the rank of an Under Secretary to the Government of India to investigate any contravention referred to in section 13.
3. The officers referred to in sub-section (1) shall exercise the like powers which are conferred on income-tax authorities under the Income-tax Act, 1961 (43 of 1961) and shall exercise such powers, subject to such limitations laid down under that Act.

Empowering other Officers

1. The Central Government may, by order and subject to such conditions and limitations as it thinks fit to impose, authorise any officer of customs or any central excise officer or any police officer or any other officer of the Central Government or a State Government to exercise such of the powers and discharge such of the duties of the Director of Enforcement or any other officer of Enforcement under this Act as may be stated in the order.
2. The officers referred to in sub-section (1) shall exercise the like powers which are conferred on the income-tax authorities under the Income-tax Act, 1961 (43 of 1961), subject to such conditions and limitations as the Central Government may impose.

Presumption as to Documents in Certain Cases

Where any document—

(i) Is produced or furnished by any person or has been seized from the custody or control of any person, in either case, under this Act or under any other law; or

(ii) Has been received from any place outside India (duly authenticated by such authority or person and in such manner as may be prescribed) in the course of investigation of any contravention under this Act alleged to have been committed by any person, and such document is tendered in any proceeding under this Act in evidence against him, or against him and any other person who is proceeded against jointly with him, the court or the Adjudicating Authority, as the case may be, shall—

(a) Presume, unless the contrary is proved, that the signature and every other part of such document which purports to be in the handwriting of any particular person or which the court may reasonably assume to have been signed by, or to be in the handwriting of, any particular person, is in that person's handwriting, and in the case of a document executed or attested, that it was executed or attested by the person by whom it purports to have been so executed or attested;

(b) Admit the document in evidence notwithstanding that it is not duly stamped, if such document is otherwise admissible in evidence;

(c) In a case falling under clause *(i)*, also presume, unless the contrary is proved, the truth of the contents of such document.

Suspension of Operation of this Act

1. If the Central Government is satisfied that circumstances have arisen rendering it necessary that any permission granted or restriction imposed by this Act should cease to be granted or imposed, or if it considers necessary or expedient so to do in public interest, the Central Government may, by notification, suspend or relax to such extent either indefinitely or for such period as may be notified, the operation of all or any of the provisions of this Act.
2. Where the operation of any provision of this Act has under sub-section (1) been suspended or relaxed indefinitely, such suspension or relaxation may, at any time while this Act remains in force, be removed by the Central Government by notification.
3. Every notification issued under this section shall be laid, as soon as may be after it is issued, before each House of Parliament, while it is in session, for a total period of thirty days which may be comprised in one session or in two or more successive sessions, and if, before the expiry of the session immediately following the session or the successive sessions aforesaid, both Houses agree in making any modification in the notification or both Houses agree that the notification should not be issued, the notification shall thereafter

have effect only in such modified form or be of no effect, as the case may be; so, however, that any such modification or annulment shall be without prejudice to the validity of anything previously done under that notification.

Power of Central Government to Give Directions

For the purposes of this Act, the Central Government may, from time to time, give to the Reserve Bank such general or special directions as it thinks fit, and the Reserve Bank shall, in the discharge of its functions under this Act, comply with any such directions.

Contravention by Companies

1. Where a person committing a contravention of any of the provisions of this Act or of any rule, direction or order made thereunder is a company, every person who, at the time the contravention was committed, was in charge of, and was responsible to, the company for the conduct of the business of the company as well as the company, shall be deemed to be guilty of the contravention and shall be liable to be proceeded against and punished accordingly:

   Provided that nothing contained in this sub-section shall render any such person liable to punishment if he proves that the contravention took place without his knowledge or that he exercised due diligence to prevent such contravention.

2. Notwithstanding anything contained in sub-section (1), where a contravention of any of the provisions of this Act or of any rule, direction or order made thereunder has been committed by a company and it is proved that the contravention has taken place with the consent or connivance of, or is attributable to any neglect on the part of, any director, manager, secretary or other officer of the company, such director, manager, secretary or other officer shall also be deemed to be guilty of the contravention and shall be liable to be proceeded against and punished accordingly.

   Explanation—For the purposes of this section—

   (i) "Company" means any body corporate and includes a firm or other association of individuals; and

   (ii) "Director", in relation to a firm, means a partner in the firm.

Death or Insolvency in Certain Cases

Any right, obligation, liability, proceeding or appeal arising in relation to the provisions of section 13 shall not abate by reason of death or insolvency of the person liable under that section and upon such death or insolvency such rights and obligations shall devolve on the legal representative of such person or the official receiver or the official assignee, as the case may be: Provided that a legal representative of the deceased shall be liable only to the extent of the inheritance or estate of the deceased.

Bar of Legal Proceedings

No suit, prosecution or other legal proceeding shall lie against the Central Government or the Reserve Bank or any officer of that Government or of the Reserve Bank or any other person exercising any power or discharging any functions or performing any duties under this Act, for anything in good faith done or intended to be done under this Act or any rule, regulation, notification, direction or order made thereunder.

Removal of Difficulties

1. If any difficulty arises in giving effect to the provisions of this Act, the Central Government may, by order, do anything not inconsistent with the provisions of this Act for the purpose of removing the difficulty:

   Provided that no such order shall be made under this section after the expiry of two years from the commencement of this Act.
2. Every order made under this section shall be laid, as soon as may be after it is made, before each House of Parliament.

Power to Make Rules

1. The Central Government may, by notification, make rules to carry out the provisions of this Act.
2. Without prejudice to the generality of the foregoing power, such rules may provide for,—
   (a) The imposition of reasonable restrictions on current account transactions under section 5;
   (b) The manner in which the contravention may be compounded under sub-section (1) of section 15;
   (c) The manner of holding an inquiry by the Adjudicating Authority under sub-section (1) of section 16;
   (d) The form of appeal and fee for filing such appeal under sections 17 and 19;
   (e) The salary and allowances payable to and the other terms and conditions of service of the Chairperson and other Members of the Appellate Tribunal and the Special Director (Appeals) under section 23;
   (f) The salaries and allowances and other conditions of service of the officers and employees of the Appellate Tribunal and the office of the Special Director (Appeals) under sub-section (3) of section 27;

(g) the additional matters in respect of which the Appellate Tribunal and the Special Director (Appeals) may exercise the powers of civil court under clause *(i)* of sub-section (2) of section 28;

(h) the authority or person and the manner in which any document may be authenticated under clause *(ii)* of section 39; and

(i) any other matter which is required to be, or may be, prescribed.

Power to Make Regulations

1. The Reserve Bank may, by notification, make regulations to carry out the provisions of this Act and the rules made thereunder.
2. Without prejudice to the generality of the foregoing power, such regulations may provide for,—
   (a) The permissible classes of capital account transactions, the limits of admissibility of foreign exchange for such transactions, and the prohibition, restriction or regulation of certain capital account transactions under section 6;
   (b) The manner and the form in which the declaration is to be furnished under clause *(a)* of sub-section (1) of section 7;
   (c) The period within which and the manner of repatriation of foreign exchange under section 8;
   (d) The limit up to which any person may possess foreign currency or foreign coins under clause (a) of section 9;
   (e) The class of persons and the limit up to which foreign currency account may be held or operated under clause *(b)* of section 9;
   (f) The limit up to which foreign exchange acquired may be exempted under clause (d) of section 9;
   (g) The limit up to which foreign exchange acquired may be retained under clause (e) of section 9;
   (h) Any other matter which is required to be, or may be, specified.

Rules and Regulations to be Laid before Parliament

Every rule and regulation made under this Act shall be laid, as soon as may be after it is made, before each House of Parliament, while it is in session for a total period of thirty days which may be comprised in one session or in two or more successive sessions, and if, before the expiry of the session immediately following the session or the successive sessions aforesaid, both Houses agree in making any modification in the rule or regulation, or both Houses agree that the rule or regulation should not be made, the rule or regulation shall thereafter have effect only in such modified form or be of no effect, as the case may be; so, however, that any such modification or annulment shall be without prejudice to the validity of anything previously done under that rule or regulation.

Repeal and Saving

1. The Foreign Exchange Regulation Act, 1973 (46 of 1973) is hereby repealed and the Appellate Board constituted under sub-section (1) of section 52 of the said Act (hereinafter referred to as the repealed Act) shall stand dissolved.
2. On the dissolution of the said Appellate Board, the person appointed as Chairman of the Appellate Board and every other person appointed as Member and holding office as such immediately before such date shall vacate their respective offices and no such Chairman or other person shall be entitled to claim any compensation for the premature termination of the term of his office or of any contract of service.
3. Notwithstanding anything contained in any other law for the time being in force, no court shall take cognizance of an offence under the repealed Act and no adjudicating officer shall take notice of any contravention under section 51 of the repealed Act after the expiry of a period of two years from the date of the commencement of this Act.
4. Subject to the provisions of sub-section (3) all offences committed under the repealed Act shall continue to be governed by the provisions of the repealed Act as if that Act had not been repealed.
5. Notwithstanding such repeal,—
   (a) Anything done or any action taken or purported to have been done or taken including any rule, notification, inspection, order or notice made or issued or any appointment, confirmation or declaration made or any licence, permission, authorization or exemption granted or any document or instrument executed or any direction given under the Act hereby repealed shall, in so far as it is not inconsistent with the provisions of this Act, be deemed to have been done or taken under the corresponding provisions of this Act;
   (b) Any appeal preferred to the Appellate Board under sub-section (2) of section 52 of the repealed Act but not disposed of before the commencement of this Act shall stand transferred to and shall be disposed of by the Appellate Tribunal constituted under this Act;
   (c) Every appeal from any decision or order of the Appellate Board under sub-section (3) or sub-section (4) of section 52 of the repealed Act shall, if not filed before the commencement of this Act, be filed before the High Court within a period of sixty days of such commencement:

   Provided that the High Court may entertain such appeal after the expiry of the said period of sixty days if it is satisfied that the appellant was prevented by sufficient cause from filing the appeal within the said period.

6. Save as otherwise provided in sub-section (3), the mention of particular matters in sub-sections (2), (4) and (5) shall not be held to prejudice or affect the general application of section 6 of the General Clauses Act, 1897 (10 of 1897) with regard to the effect of repeal.

The Conservation of Foreign Exchange

1. Short title, extent and commencement — (1) This Act may be called the Conservation of Foreign Exchange and Prevention of Smuggling Activities Act, 1974.
   (a) It extends to the whole of India.
   (b) It shall come into force on such date as the Central Government may, by notification in the Official Gazette, appoint.
2. Definitions- In this Act, unless the context otherwise requires,—
   (a) "Appropriate Government" means, as respects a detention order made by the Central Government or by an officer of the Central Government or a person detained under such order, the Central Government, and as respects a detention order made by a State Government or by an officer of a State Government or a person detained under such order, the State Government;
   (b) "Detention order" means an order made under section 3;
   (c) "Foreigner" has the same meaning as in the Foreigners Act, 1946 (31 of 1946);
   (d) "Indian customs waters" has the same meaning as in clause (28) of the Customs Act, 1962 (52 of 1962);
   (e) "Smuggling" has the same meanings as in clause (39) of section 2 of the Customs Act, 1962, and all its grammatical variations and cognate expressions shall be construed accordingly;
   (f) "State Government", in relation to a Union territory, means the Administrator thereof;
   (g) Any reference in this Act to a law which is not in force in the State of Jammu and Kashmir shall, in relation to that State, be construed as a reference to the corresponding law, if any, in force in that State.
3. Power to make orders detaining certain persons —
   (1) The Central Government or the State Government or any officer of the Central Government, not below the rank of a Joint Secretary to that Government, specially empowered for the purposes of this section by that Government, or any officer of the State Government, not below the rank of a Secretary to that Government, specially empowered for the purposes of this

section by that Government, may, if satisfied, with respect to any person (including a foreigner), that, with a view to preventing him from acting in any manner prejudicial to the conservation or augmentation of foreign exchange or with a view to preventing him from

i. Smuggling goods, or
ii. Abetting the smuggling of goods, or
iii. Engaging in transporting or concealing or keeping smuggled goods, or
iv. Dealing in smuggled goods otherwise than by engaging in transporting or concealing or keeping smuggled goods, or
v. Harbouring persons engaged in smuggling goods or in abetting the smuggling of goods, it is necessary so to do, make an order directing that such person be detained:

[Provided that no order of detention shall be made on any of the grounds specified in this sub-section on which an order of detention may be made under section 3 of the Prevention of Illicit Traffic in Narcotic Drugs and Psychotropic Substances Act, 1988 or under section 3 of the Jammu and Kashmir Prevention of Illicit Traffic in Narcotic Drugs and Psychotropic Substances ordinance, 1988.].

(2) When any order of detention is made by a State Government or by an officer empowered by a State Government, the State Government shall, within ten days, forward to the Central Government a report in respect of the order.

(3) For the purposes of clause (5) of article 22 of the Constitution, the communication to a person detained in pursuance of a detention order of the grounds on which the order has been made shall be made as soon as may be after the detention, but ordinarily not later than five days, and in exceptional circumstances and for reasons to be recorded in writing, not later than fifteen days, from the date of detention.

4. Execution of detention orders - A detention order may be executed at any place in India in the manner provided for the execution of warrants of arrest under the Code of Criminal Procedure, 1973 (2 of 1974).

5. Power to regulate place and conditions of detention - Every person in respect of whom a detention order has been made shall be liable -

(a) To be detained in such place and under such conditions including conditions as to maintenance, interviews or communication with others, discipline and punishment for breaches of discipline, as the appropriate Government may, by general or special order, specify; and

(b) To be removed from one place of detention to another place of detention, whether within the same State or in another State by order of the appropriate Government;

Provided that no order shall be made by a State Government under clause (b) for the removal of a person from one State to another State except with the consent of the Government of that other State.

5A. Grounds of detention severable — Where a person has been detained in pursuance of an order of detention under sub-section(1) which has been made on two or more grounds, such order of detention shall be deemed to have been made separately on each of such grounds and accordingly -

(a) Such order shall not be deemed to be invalid or inoperative merely because one or some of the grounds is or are -

i. Vague,

ii. Non-existent,

iii. not relevant,

iv. Not connected or not proximately connected with such person, or

v. Invalid for any other reason whatsoever, and it is not, therefore, possible to hold that the Government or officer making such order would have been satisfied as provided in sub-section (1) of section 3 with reference to the remaining ground or grounds and made the order of detention;

(b) The Government or officer making the order of detention shall be deemed to have made the order of detention under the said sub-section (1) after being satisfied as provided in that sub-section with reference to the remaining ground or grounds.]

6. Detention order not to be invalid or inoperative on certain grounds - No detention order shall be invalid or inoperative merely by reason -

a. That the person to be detained thereunder is outside the limited of the territorial jurisdiction of the Government or the officer making the order of detention, or

b. That the place of detention of such person is outside the said limits.

7. Powers in relation to absconding persons(1) If the appropriate Government has reason to believe that a person in respect of whom a detention order has been made has absconded or is concealing himself so that the order cannot be executed, the Government may -

(a) Make a report in writing of the fact to a Metropolitan Magistrate or a Magistrate of the first class having jurisdiction in the place where the said person ordinarily resides; and thereupon the provisions of sections 82, 83, 84 and 85 of the Code of Criminal Procedure, 1973 (2 of 1974), shall apply in respect of the said person and his property as if the order directing that he be detained were a warrant issued by the Magistrate;

(b) By order notified in the Official Gazette direct the said person to appear before such officer, at such place and within such period as may be specified in the order; and if the said person fails to comply with such direction, he shall, unless he proves that it was not possible for him to comply therewith and that he had, within the period specified in the order, informed the officer mentioned in the order of the reason which rendered compliance therewith impossible and of his whereabouts, be punishable therewith impossible and of his whereabouts, be punishable with imprisonment for a term which may extend to one year or with fine or with both.

(2) Nothwithstanding anything contained in the Code of Criminal Procedure, 1973 (2 of 1974), every offence under clause(b) of sub-section (1) shall be cognizable.

8. Advisory Board- For the purposes of sub-clause (a) of clause (c) of clause (7) of article 22 of the Constitution,—

(a) the Central Government and each State Government shall, wherever necessary, constitute one or more Advisory Boards each of which shall consist of a Chairman and two other persons possessing the qualifications specified in sub-clause (a) of clause (4) of article 22 of the Constitution;

(b) Save as otherwise provided in section 9, the appropriate Government shall, within five weeks from the date of detention of a person under a detention order make a reference in respect thereof to the Advisory Board constituted under clause (a) to enable the Advisory Board to make the report under sub-clause (a) of clause (4) of article 22 of the Constitution;

(c) The Advisory Board to which a reference is made under clause (b) shall after considering the reference and the materials placed before it and after calling for such further information as it may deed necessary from the appropriate Government or from any person called for the purpose through the appropriate Government, from the person concerned, and if, in any particular case, it considers it essential so to do or if the person concerned desires to be heard in person, after hearing him person, prepare its report specifying in a separate paragraph thereof its opinion as to whether or not there is sufficient cause for the detention of the person concerned and submit the same within eleven weeks from the date of detention of the person concerned;

(d) When there is a difference of opinion among the members forming the Advisory Board the opinion of the majority of such members shall be deemed to be the opinion of the Board;

(e) A person against whom an order of detention has been made under this Act shall not be entitled to appear by any legal practitioner in any matter connected with the reference to the Advisory Board, and the proceedings of the Advisory Board and its report, excepting that part of the report in which the opinion of the Advisory Board is specified, shall be confidential;

(f) In every case where the Advisory Board has reported that there is in its opinion sufficient cause for the detention of a person, the appropriate Government may confirm the detention order and continue the detention of the person concerned for such period as it thinks fit and in every case where the Advisory Board has reported that there is in its opinion no sufficient cause for the detention of the person concerned, the appropriate Government shall revoke the detention order and cause the person to be released forthwith.

9. Cases in which and circumstances under which persons may be detained for period longer than three months without obtaining the opinion of Advisory Board- (1)Notwithstanding anything contained in this Act, any person (including a foreigner) in respect of whom an order of detention is made under this Act at any time before the 31st July, 1996, may be detained without obtaining, in accordance with the provisions of sub-clause (a) of clause (4) of article 22 of the Constitution, the opinion of an Advisory Board for a period longer than three months but not exceeding six months from the date of his detention, where the order of detention has been made against such person with a view to preventing him from smuggling goods or abetting the smuggling of goods or engaging in transporting or concealing or keeping smuggled goods and the Central Government or any Officer of the Central Government, not below the rank of an Additional Secretary to that Government, specially empowered for the purpose of this section by that Government, is satisfied that such person—

(a) Smuggles or is likely to smuggle goods into, out of or through any area highly vulnerable to smuggling; or

(b) Abets or is likely to abet the smuggling of goods into, out of or through any area highly vulnerable to smuggling; or

(c) Engages or is likely to engage in transporting or concealing or keeping smuggled goods in any area highly vulnerable to smuggling, and makes a declaration to that effect within five weeks of the detention of such person.

Explanation 1 - In this sub-section, "area highly vulnerable to smuggling" means, -

i. The Indian customs waters, contiguous to the State of Goa, Gujarat,Karnataka, Kerala, Maharashtra, Tamil Nadu and the Union territories of Daman and Diu and Pondicherry;
ii. The Inland area fifty kilometres in width from the coast of India falling within the territories of the States of Goa, Gujarat,Karnataka, Kerala, Maharashtra,Tamil Nadu and the Union territories of Daman and Diu and Pondicherry;
iii. The inland area fifty kilometres in width from the India-Pakistan border in the State of Gujarat, Jammu and Kashmir, Punjab and Rajasthan;
iv. The customs air port of Delhi; and
v. Such further or other Indian customs waters, or inland area not exceeding one hundred kilometres in width from any other coast or border of India, or such other customs station, as the Central Government may, having regard to the vulnerability of such waters, area or customs station, as the case may be, to smuggling, by notification in the Official Gazette, specify in this behalf.

Explanation 2 - (1) For the purposes of Explanation 1, "customs airport" and "customs station" shall have the same meaning as in clauses (10) and (13) of section 2 of the Customs Act, 1962 (52 of 1962), respectively.

(2) In the case of any person detained under a detention order to which the provisions of sub-section (1) apply, section 8 shall have effect subject to the following modifications, namely:

(i) In clause (b), for the words "shall, within five weeks", the words "shall, within four months and two weeks" shall be substituted;

(ii) In clause (c), -

(1) For the words "the detention of the person concerned", the words "the continued detention of the person concerned" shall be substituted;

(2) For the words "eleven weeks", the words "five months and three weeks" shall be substituted;

(iii) In clause (f), for the words "for the detention", at both the places where they occur, the words "for the continued detention" shall be substituted.

10. Maximum period of detention - The maximum period for which any person may be detained in pursuance of any detention order to which the provisions of section 9 do not apply and which has been confirmed under clause (f) of section 8 shall be a period of one year from the date of detention or the specified period, whichever period

expires late and the maximum period for which any person may be detained in pursuance of any detention order to which the provisions of section 9 apply and which has been confirmed under clause (f) of section 8 read with sub- section (2) of section 9 shall be a period of two years from the date of detention or the specified period, whichever period expires later;

Provided that nothing contained in this section shall affect the power of the appropriate Government in neither case to revoke or modify the detention order at any earlier time.

Explanation In this section and section 10A - "specified period" means the period during which the Proclamation of Emergency issued under clause (1) of article 352 of the Constitution on the 3rd day of December, 1971 and the Proclamation of Emergency issued under that clause on the 25th day of June, 1975, are both in operation.

10A. Extension of period of detention—

1. Notwithstanding anything contained in any other provision of this Act, the detention of every person detained under a detention order which has been confirmed under clause (f) of section 8 before the commencement of the Conservation of Foreign Exchange and Prevention of Smuggling Activities (Amendment) Act, 1976, and which is in force immediately before such commencement shall, unless his detention has been continued by the appropriate Government under the said clause for a period shorter than one year from the date of his detention, continue until the expiry of a period of one year from the date of his detention under such order or until the expiry of the specified period, whichever period expires later:
   Provided that nothing contained in this sub-section shall affect the power of the appropriate Government to revoke or modify such detention order at any earlier time.
2. Notwithstanding anything contained in any other provision of this Act, the detention of every person detained under a detention order which has been confirmed under clause (f) of section 8 read with sub-section (2) of section 9 before the commencement of the Conservation of Foreign Exchange and Prevention of Smuggling Activities (Amendment) Act, 1976, and which is in force immediately before such commencement, shall, unless his detention has been continued by the appropriate Government under the said clause (f) read with the said sub-section (2) for a period shorter than two years from the date of his detention, continue until the expiry of a period of two years from the date of his detention under such

order or until the expiry of the specified period, whichever period expires later:

Provided that nothing contained in this sub-section shall affect the power of the appropriate Government to revoke or modify such detention order at any earlier time.

11. Revocation of detention orders –

(1) Without prejudice to provisions of section 21 of the General Clauses Act, 1897 (10 of 1897), a detention order may, at any time, be revoked or modified -

a. Notwithstanding that the order has been made by an officer of a State Government, by that State Government or by the Central Government;

b. Notwithstanding that the order has been made by an officer of the Central Government or by a State Government, by the Central Government.

(2) The revocation of a detention order shall not bar the making of another detention order under section (3) against the same person.

12. Temporary release of persons detained –

1. The Central Government may, at any time, direct that any person detained in pursuance of a detention order made by that Government or an officer subordinate to that Government or by a State Government or by an officer subordinate to a State Government, may be released for any specified period either without conditions or upon such conditions specified in the directions as that person accepts, and may, at any time, cancel his release.
2. A State Government may, at any time, direct that any person detained in pursuance of a detention order made by that Government or by an officer subordinate to that Government may be released for any specified period either without conditions or upon such conditions specified in the direction as that person accepts, and may, at any time, cancel his release.
3. In directing the release of any person under sub-section (1) or sub-section (1A) the Government directing the release may require him to enter into a bond with sureties for the due observance of the conditions specified in the direction.
4. Any person released under sub-section(1) or sub-section(1A) shall surrender himself at the time and place, and to the authority, specified in the order directing his release or cancelling his release, as the case may be.

5. If any person fails without sufficient cause to surrender himself in the manner specified in sub-section(3) he shall be punishable with imprisonment for a term which may extend to two years, or with fine, or with both.
6. If any person released under sub-section(1) or sub-section(1A) fails to fulfill any of the conditions imposed upon him under the said sub-section or in the bond entered into by him, the bond shall be declared to be forfeited and any person bound thereby shall be liable to pay the penalty thereof.
7. Notwithstanding anything contained in any other law and save as otherwise provided in this section, no person against whom a detention order made under this Act is in force shall be released whether on bail or bail bond or otherwise.

12A. Special provisions for dealing with emergency -

1. Notwithstanding anything contained in this Act or any rules of natural justice, the provisions of this section shall have effect during the period of operation of the Proclamation of Emergency issued under clause (1) of article 352 of the Constitution on the 3rd day of December, 1971, or the Proclamation of Emergency issued under that clause on the 25th day of June, 1975, or a period of twenty four months from the 25th day of June, 1975, whichever period is the shortest.-
2. When making an order of detention under this Act against any person after the commencement of the Conservation of Foreign and Prevention of Smuggling Activities (Amendment) Act, 1975, the Central Government or the State Government or, as the case may be, the officer making the order of detention shall consider whether the detention of such person under this Act is necessary for dealing effectively with the emergency in respect of which the Proclamations referred to in sub-section (1) have been issued (hereafter in this section referred to as the emergency) and if, on such consideration, the Central Government or the State Government or, as the case may be, the officer is satisfied that it is necessary to detain such person for effectively dealing with the emergency, that Government or officer may make a declaration to that effect and communicate a copy of the declaration to the person concerned:

   Provided that where such declaration is made by an officer, it shall be reviewed by the appropriate Government within fifteen days from the date of making of the declaration and such declaration shall cease to have effect unless it is confirmed by that Government, after such review, within the said period of fifteen days.

3. The question whether the detention of any person in respect of whom a declaration has been made under sub-section (2) continues to be necessary for effectively dealing with the emergency shall be reconsidered by the appropriate Government within four months from the date of such declaration and thereafter at intervals not exceeding four months, and if, one such reconsideration, it appears to the appropriate Government that the detention of the person is no longer necessary for effectively dealing with the emergency, the Government may revoke the declaration.
4. In making any consideration, review or reconsideration under sub-section (2) or (3) the appropriate Government or officer may, if such Government or officer considers it to be against the public interest to do otherwise, act on the basis of the information and materials in its or his possession without disclosing the facts or giving an opportunity of making a representation to the person concerned.
5. It shall not be necessary to disclose to any person detained under a detention order to which the provisions of sub-section (2) apply, the grounds on which the order has been made during the period the declaration made in respect of such person under that sub-section is in force, and, accordingly, such period shall not be taken into account for the purpose of sub-section (3) of section 3
6. In the case of every person detained under a detention order to which the provisions of sub-section (2) apply, being a person in respect of whom a declaration has been made thereunder, the period during which such declaration is in force shall not be taken into account for the purpose of computing -
   - The periods specified in clauses (b) and (c) of section 8
   - The periods of "one year" and "five weeks" specified in sub-section (1), the period of "one year" specified in sub-section (2)(i), and the period of "six months" specified in sub-section (3), of section 9.

13. Protection of action taken in good faith- No suit or other legal proceeding shall lie against the Central Government or a State Government, and no suit, prosecution or other legal proceedings shall lie against any person, for anything in good faith done or intended to be done in pursuance of this Act.
14. Repeal—The Maintenance of Internal Security (Amendment) Ordinance, 1974 (11 of 1974), shall, on the commencement of this Act, stand repealed and accordingly the amendments made in the Maintenance of Internal Security Act, 1971 (26 of 1971), by

the said Ordinance shall, on such commencement, cease to have effect.

Customs Valuation

In exercise of the powers conferred by Section 156 of the Customs Act, 1962 (52 of 1962), read with Section 22 of the General Clauses Act, 1897 (10 of 1897), and in supersession of the Customs Valuation Rules, 1963 except as respect things done or omitted to be done before such super session, the Central Government hereby makes the following rules, namely:—

1. Short title, commencement and application—
   - (These rules may be called the Customs Valuation (Determination of Price of Imported Goods) Rules, 1988.
   - They shall come into force on the 16th August, 1988.
   - They shall apply imported goods where a duty of customs is chargeable by reference to their value.

2. Definitions— (1) In these rules, unless the context otherwise requires,-

   1[(a) "Computed value" means the value of imported goods determined in accordance with rule 7A of these rules; (aa) " deductive value" means the value determined in accordance with rule 7 of these rules;]

   (b) "Goods of the same class or kind", means imported goods that are within a group of range of imported goods produced by a particular industry of industrial sector and includes identical goods of similar goods;

   (c) "Identical goods" means imported goods -
   - Which are same in all respects, including physical characteristics, quality and reputation as the goods being valued except for minor differences in appearance that do not affect the value of the goods;
   - Produced in the country in which the goods being valued were produced; and
   - produced by the same person who produced the goods, or where no such goods are available, goods produced by a different person, but shall not include imported goods where engineering, development work, art work, design work, plan or sketch undertaken in India were completed directly or indirectly by the buyer on these imported goods free of charge or at a reduced cost for use in connection with the production and sale for export of these imported goods;

   (d) "Produced" includes grown, manufactured and mined;

   (e) "Similar goods" means imported goods –

- Which although not alike in all respects, have like characteristics and like component materials which enable them to perform the same functions and to be commercially interchangeable with the goods being valued having regard to the quality, reputation and the existence of trade mark;
- Produced in the country in which the goods being valued were produced; and
- Produced by the same person who produced the goods being valued, or where no such goods are available, goods produced by a different person, but shall not include imported goods where engineering, development work, art work, design work, plan or sketch undertaken in India were completed directly or indirectly by the buyer on these imported goods free of charge or at a reduced cost for use in connection with production and sale for export of these imported goods;

(f) "Transaction value" means the value determined in accordance with Rule 4 of these rules.

2. For the purpose of these rules, persons shall be deemed to be " related " only if –
   - They are officers or directors of one another's businesses;
   - They are legally recognized partners in business;
   - They are employer and exployee;
   - Any person directly or indirectly owns, controls or holds 5 percent or more of the outstanding voting stock or shares of both of them;
   - One of them directly or indirectly controls the other;
   - Both of them are directly or indirectly controlled by a third person;
   - Together they directly or indirectly control a third person; or
   - They are members of the same family.

Explanation I– The term " person" also includes legal persons.

Explanation II—Persons who are associated in the business of one another in that one is the sole agent or sole distributor or sole concessionaire, however described, of the other shall be deemed to be related for the purpose of these rules, if they fall within the criteria of this sub-rule.

3. Determination of the method of valuation—For the purpose of these rules—
   - The value of imported goods shall be the transaction value;
   - If the value cannot be determined under the provisions of clause (i) above, the value shall be determined by proceeding sequentially through Rules 5 to 8 of these rules.

1. Transaction value— (1) The transaction value of imported goods shall be the price actually paid or payable for the goods when sold for export to India, adjusted in accordance with the provisions of Rule 9 of these rules.
2. The transaction value of imported goods under sub-rule (1) above shall be accepted provided that—
   - There are no restrictions as to the disposition or use of the goods by the buyer other than restrictions which are imposed or required by law or by the public authorities in India;
     or
   - Limit the geographical area in which the goods may be resold;
     or
   - Do not substantially affect the value of the goods;
   - The sale or price is not subject to same condition or consideration for which a value cannot be determined in respect of the goods being valued;
   - no part of the proceeds of any subsequent resale, disposal or use of the goods by the buyer will accrue directly or indirectly to the seller unless an appropriate adjustment can be made in accordance with the provisions of Rule 9 of these rules; and
   - the buyer and seller are not related, or where the buyer and seller are related, that transaction value is acceptable for customs purposes under the provisions of sub-rule below.
3. (a) Where the buyer and seller are related, the transaction value shall be accepted provided that the examination of the circumstances of the sale of the imported goods indicate that the relationship did not influence the price.

   (b) In a sale between related persons, the transaction value shall be accepted, whenever the importer demonstrates that the declared value of the goods being valued, closely approximates to one of the following values ascertained at or about the same time-
   - The transaction value of identical goods, or of similar goods, in sales to unrelated buyers in India;
   - The deductive value for identical goods or similar goods;
   - The computed value for identical goods or similar goods.]

Provided that in applying the values used for comparison, due account shall be taken of demonstrated difference in commercial levels, quantity levels, adjustments in accordance with the provisions of Rule 9 of these rules and cost incurred by the seller in sales in which he and the buyer are not related;

   (c) Substitute values shall not be established under the provisions of clause (b) of this sub-rule.

1. Transaction of value of identical goods. - (1) (a) Subject to. the provisions of Rule 3 of these rules, the value of imported goods shall be the transaction value of identical goods sold for export to India and imported at or about the same time as the goods being valued.

   (b) In applying this rule, the transaction value of identical goods in a sale at the same commercial level and in substantially the same quantity as the goods being valued shall be used to determine the value of imported goods.

   (c) Where no sale referred to in clause (b) of sub-rule (1) of this rule, is found, the transaction value of identical goods sold at a different commercial level or in different quantities or both, adjusted to take account of the difference attributable to commercial level or to the quantity or both, shall be used, provided that such adjustments shall be made on the basis of the demonstrated evidence which clearly establishes the reasonableness and accuracy of the adjustments, whether such adjustment leads to an increase or decrease in the value. (2) Where the cost and charges referred to in sub-rule (2) of Rule 9 of these rules are included in the transaction value of identical goods, an adjustment shall be made, if there are significant differences in such costs and charges between the goods being valued and the identical goods in question arising from differences in distances and means of transport. (3) In applying this rule, if more than one transaction value of identical goods is found; the lowest such value shall be used to determine the value of imported goods.

2. Transaction value of similar goods—

   - Subject to the provisions of Rule 3 of these rules, the value of imported goods shall be the transaction value of similar goods sold for export to India and imported at or about the same time as the goods being valued.
   - The provisions of clauses (b) and (c) of sub-rule (1), sub-rule (2) and sub-rule(3),of Rule 5 of these rules shall, mutatis mutandis, also apply in respect of similar goods.

Determination of value when transaction values is not available—If the value of imported goods cannot be determined under the provisions of rules 4, 5and 6, the value shall be determined under the provisions of rule 7 or, when the value cannot be determined under that rule, under rule 7A: Provided that at the request of the importer, and with the approval of the proper officer, the order of application of rules 7 and 7A shall be reversed.]

3. Deductive value—
   - Subject to the provisions of Rule 3 of these rules, if the goods being valued or identical or similar imported goods are sold in India, in the condition as imported at or about the time at which the declaration for determination of value is presented, the value of imported goods shall be based on the unit price at which the imported goods or identical or similar imported goods are sold in the greatest aggregate quantity to persons who are not related to the sellers in India, subject to the following deductions:—
     i. Either the commission usually paid or agreed to be paid or the additions usually made for profits and general expenses in connection with sales in India of imported goods of the same class or kind;
     ii. The usual costs of transport and insurance and associated costs incurred within India;
     iii. The customs duties and other taxes payable in India by reason of importation or sale of the goods.
   - If neither the imported goods nor identical nor similar imported goods are sold at or about the same time of importation of the goods being valued, the value of imported goods shall, subject otherwise to the provisions of sub-rule (1) of this rule, be based on the unit price at which the imported goods or identical or similar imported goods are sold in India, at the earliest date after importation but before the expiry of ninety days after such importation.
   - (a) If neither the imported goods not identical nor similar imported goods are sold in India in the conditions as imported, then, the value shall be based on the unit price at which the imported goods, after further processing, are sold in the greatest aggregate quantity to persons who are not related to the seller in India (b) In such determination, due allowance shall be made for the value added by processing and the deductions, provided for in items (i) to (iii) of sub-rule (1) of this rule.

Computed value—Subject to the provisions of rule 3, the value of imported goods shall be based on a computed value, which shall consist of the sum of:

a. The cost of value of materials and fabrication or other processing employed in producing the imported goods;
b. An amount for profit and general expenses equal to that usually reflected in sales of goods of the same class or kind as the goods being valued which are made by producers in the country of exportation for export to India;

c. Rhe cost or value of all other expenses under sub-rule (2) of rule 9 of these rules.]

- Residual method—(1) Subject to the provisions of Rule 3 of these rules, where the value of imported goods cannot be determined under the provisions of any of the preceding rules, the value shall be determined using reasonable means consistent with the principles and general provisions of these rules and sub-section (1) of Section 14 of the Customs Act, 1962 (52 of 1962) and on the basis of data available in India. (2) No value shall be determined under the provisions of (5) this rule on the basis of-
  - The selling price in India of the goods produced in India;
  - A system which provides for the acceptance for customs purposes \ of the highest of the two alternative values;
  - The price of the goods on the domestic market of country of exportation; [(iii a) the cost of production other than computed values which have been determined for identical or similar goods in accordance with the provisions of rule 7A.]
  - The price of the goods for the export to a country other than India;
  - Minimum customs values; or
  - Arbitrary or fictitious values.

d. Cost and services— (1) In determining the transaction value, there shall be added to the price actually paid or payable for the imported goods,-

- The following cost and services, to the extent they are incurred by the buyer but are not included in the price actually paid or payable for the imported goods, namely:
  - Commissions and brokerage, except buying commissions;
  - the cost of containers which are treated as being one for customs purposes with the goods in question;
  - the cost of packing whether for labour or materials;
- The value, apportioned as appropriate, of the following goods and services where supplied directly or indirectly by the buyer free of charge or at reduced cost for use in connection with the production and sale for export of imported goods, to the extent that such value has not been included in the price actually paid of payable, namely:
  - Materials, components, parts and similar items incorporated in the imported goods;
  - Tools, dies, moulds and similar items used in the production of the imported goods;

  - Materials consumed in the production of the imported goods;
  - Engineering, development, art work, design work, and and plans and sketches undertaken elsewhere than in India and necessary for the production of the imported goods;
- Royalties and license fees related to the imported goods that the buyer is required to pay, directly or indirectly, as a condition of the sale of the goods being valued, to the extent that such royalties and fees are not included in the price actually paid or payable.
- The value of any part of the proceeds of any subsequent resale, disposal or use of the imported goods that accrues, directly or indirectly, to the seller;
- All other payments actually made or to be made as a condition of sale of the imported goods, by the buyer to the seller, or by the buyer to a third party to satisfy an obligation of the seller to the extent that such payments are not included in the price actually paid of payable.

f. For the purposes of sub-section (1) and sub section (1A) of section14 of the Customs Act, 1962 (52 of 1962) and these rules, the value of the imported goods shall be the value of such goods, for delivery at the time and place of importation and shall include—
   - The cost of transport of the imported goods to the place of importation;
   - Loading, unloading and handling charges associated with the delivery of the imported goods at the place of importation; and
   - The cost of insurance:
     - Where the coast of transport referred to in clause (a) is not ascertainable, such cost shall be twenty percent of the free on board value of the goods;
     - The charges referred to in clause (b) shall be one per cent of the free on board value of the goods plus the coast of transport referred to in clause (a) plus the coast of insurance referred to in clause (c);
     - Where the coast referred to in clause (c) is not ascertainable, such cost shall be 1.125% of free on board value of the goods;

Provided further that in the case of goods imported by air, where the cost referred to in clause (a) is ascertainable, such cost shall not exceed twenty per cent of free on board value of the goods:

Provided also that where the free on board value of the goods is not ascertainable, the coasts referred to in clause (a) shall be twenty per cent of the free on board value of the goods plus cost of insurance for clause (i) above and the cost referred to in clause (c) shall be 1.125 % of the free on board value of the goods plus cost of transport for clause (iii) above].

- Additions to the price actually paid or payable shall be made under this rule on the bases of objective and quantifiable data.
- No addition shall be made to the price actually paid or payable in determining the value of the imported goods except as provided for in this rule.

1. Declaration by the importer—
2. The importer or his agent shall furnish —
   - A declaration disclosing full and accurate details relating to the value of imported goods; and
   - Any other statement, information or document including an invoice of the manufacturer or producer of the imported goods where the oops are imorted from or through a person other than the manufacturer or producer, as considered necessary by the proper officer for determination of the value of imported goods under these rule.]
3. Nothing contained in these rules shall be construed as restricting or calling into question the right of the proper officer of customs to satisfy himself as to the truth or accuracy of any statement, information, document or declaration presented for valuation purposes.

(3) The provisions of the Customs Act, 1962 (52 of 1962) relating to confiscation, penalty and prosecution shall apply to cases where wrong declaration, information, statement or documents are furnished under these rules.

10A. Rejection of declared value – (1) When the proper officer has reason to doubt the truth or accuracy of the value declared in relation to any imported goods, he may ask the importer of such goods to furnish further information including documents or other evidence and if, after receiving such further information, or in the absence of a response of such importer, the proper officer still has reasonable doubt about the truth or accuracy of the value so declared, it shall be deemed that the value of such imported goods cannot be determined under the provisions of sub-rule (1) of rule 4.(2) At the request of and importer, the proper officer, shall intimate the importer in writing the grounds for doubting the truth or accuracy of the value declared in relation to goods imported by such importer and provide a reasonable opportunity of being heard, before taking a final decision under sub-rule (1).]

11. Settlement of dispute— In case of dispute between the importer and the proper officer of customs valuing the goods, the same shall be resolved consistent with the provisions contained in sub-section (1) of Section 14 of the Customs Act, 1962 (52 of 1962).

12. Interpretative Notes— The interpretative notes specified in the Schedule to these rules shall apply for the interpretation of these rules.

1. Substituted by M.F. (D.R) Notification No.26/95-Cus.(N.T.),dated 24-4-1995.
2. Inserted by M.F.(D.R.) Notification No.26/95-Cus,(N.T.), dated 24-4-1995.
3. Inserted by M.F.(D.R.) Notification No.26/95-Cus.(N.T.), dated 24-4-1995.
4. Inserted by M.F.(D.R.) Notification No.26/95-Cus.(N.T.),dated 24-4-1995
5. Substituted by M.F.(D.R.)F.No.528/167/88-Cus.,(TV)/ICD, dated 6-9-1988.
6. Inserted by M.F.(D.R.)Notification No.26/95-Cus.(N.T.),dated 24-4-95
7. Substituted by M.F.(D.R.)Notification No.39/90(N.T.)-Cus., dated 5-7-1990
8. Substituted (w.e.f.1-10-1991) by M.F.(D.R.) Notification No.67/91 Cus. (N.T.), dated 1-10-1991.
9. Inserted by M.F.(D.R.)Notification No.10/98-Cus.(N.T.),dated 19-2-1998.

Index

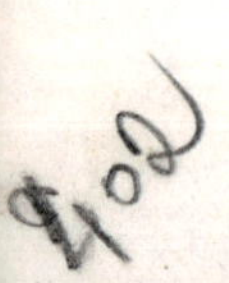